A SIMPLER, HEALTHIER WAY TO COOK

EatingWell®
IN SEASON

The Farmers' Market Cookbook

Introduction by **Dr. Preston Maring** and **Peter Jaret**

Foreword by **Nell Newman**

By Jessie Price and the Editors of EatingWell

Principal Photography by Ken Burris

Join us at
www.eatingwell.com
for more delicious recipes and the inspiration
and information you need
to make healthy eating a way of life.

© Copyright 2009 by Eating Well, Inc.,
publisher of EATINGWELL®, Where Good Taste
Meets Good Health | 823A Ferry Road,
P.O. Box 1010, Charlotte, VT 05445
www.eatingwell.com

Library of Congress Cataloging-in-Publication
Data has been applied for.

ISBN 978-0-88150-856-7

Front cover photograph by Ken Burris: Bean &
Tomato Salad with Honey Vinaigrette (*page 86*)

Authors: Preston Maring, M.D., Peter Jaret & the Editors
of EATINGWELL | **Food Editor:** Jessie Price | **Principal
Photography:** Ken Burris | **Additional credits:** page 254

EATINGWELL MEDIA GROUP
CEO: Tom Witschi | **Editorial Director:** Lisa Gosselin

Published by
The Countryman Press
P.O. Box 748, Woodstock, VT 05091

Distributed by
W.W. Norton & Company, Inc.
500 Fifth Avenue, New York, NY 10110

Printed in China by R.R. Donnelley

10 9 8 7 6 5 4

Waltham, Vermont

CONTENTS

I can remember my first farmers' market. It was 1989 and as I rode my bike through Santa Cruz, California, near where I live, I came upon a display of fruits and vegetables piled high and wide on card tables and the tailgates of pickup trucks—all jammed in an abandoned parking lot. There was a weathered-looking gentleman with a crumpled straw hat belting out folk songs on an old guitar and dozens of earthy-looking farmers, beaming and proud to speak of their work and their land, who encouraged me to sample a snap pea, a radish.

The farmers' market in Santa Cruz hasn't changed that much in 20-plus years—but it has gotten bigger and it is no longer a rarity. Over the past decade the number of farmers' markets across the United States has almost doubled.

These markets are flourishing because they honor the basic premise that our land, food, health and happiness are inextricably linked. As you will learn in the following pages, the simple act of shopping at local farmers' markets is profound and one of the best things we can do for our own health and that of the planet. For me it's my weekly (sometimes twice a week) way to get grounded, reconnect with great friends and, with the help of this book, get inspired to cook what is local and fresh that particular day.

Take one of my favorite market discoveries, tomatillos. I've taken to roasting them on a baking sheet or firing them on a grill: split into halves then blended with jalapeño peppers, a little vinegar and a touch of salt, it's a great salsa (try Tomatillo Sauce on page 115). Or, I make the tomatillo gazpacho on page 83.

I've since started growing tomatillos in my garden; the job of picking, roasting and blending has become a seasonal ritual. The result is dozens of jars of salsa for friends and enough in the freezer to last throughout the year. Come to think of it, that's sort of how my dad, Paul Newman, started

bottling and selling his salad dressing, the one that launched Newman's Own.

I also try to keep a rotation of salad greens growing in my garden as well as tomatoes, basil, peaches and more. The chickens that run around my yard keep the bugs under control and help elevate the basic omelet to godly status. Between my garden and my farmers' market, upwards of 70 percent of my diet is local.

As our world has gotten more focused on quick, cheap and easy ways to feed ourselves—and we've started packaging and shipping food great distances—our connection to the land has been lost, and a certain social fragmentation has occurred. To me the farmers' market is about closing the distance between people and places, a way to remember traditions and crafts. It's a way to put down, quite literally, good roots.

In much the way a seed is the beginning of something wonderful—of, say, a tree that will produce apples—so too is this book a seed to stir your imagination and passion for cooking with the fruits of the land. It's also about connecting you to the place where you live, helping you to learn more about your neighboring farmers—their long days working the soil, and the choices they have to make to provide for not only their families but also their communities.

EatingWell in Season: The Farmers' Market Cookbook can be your guide to rebuilding your connection to food and the earth. After flipping through these pages and making these recipes, you will want to seek out the local markets wherever you are, visit the farms and perhaps even plant your own seeds.

—*Nell Newman, founder of Newman's Own Organics*

> ❝ Though I do not believe a plant will spring up where no seed has been, I have great faith in a seed. Convince me that you have a seed there, and I am prepared to expect wonders. ❞
>
> — HENRY DAVID THOREAU

Charlotte Berry Farm, Vermont

Garden-fresh summer vegetables

A Recipe for Life

Seven reasons why farmers' markets will help you find healthier, simpler ways to shop, cook and live

BY DR. PRESTON MARING & PETER JARET

Stop by my farmers' market on a Friday morning at the peak of summer and you might hear Lone Oak Ranch's Marlene Gonzalez, a fourth-generation organic farmer, describe what a pluot is (a cross between a plum and an apricot). Or Roberto Rodriguez, who grows some of the sweetest strawberries you'll ever taste, reveal why he decided to switch nearly half of his 37 acres of fields to organic agriculture so his 6-year-old would not be exposed to pesticides. Nearby, at Nunez Farm's stall, you might well overhear shoppers exchanging recipes for Japanese eggplant. If it's late fall or winter, you might see a kid tasting a pomegranate or persimmon for the first time, looking wary at first, and then breaking into a broad grin. Everywhere you wander, you'll catch the yeasty smell of fresh bread from Vital Vittles (a bakery in Berkeley, which mills its own flour) and the sweet perfume of fresh-cut flowers grown by Abel Fernandes. But what's different about this market is that you'll also see doctors and nurses racing out on their breaks to grab a bag of tender salad greens or a basket of colorful squash to take home. You may also see visiting family members pick up bunches of cut flowers for a patient's room and armloads of fresh fruit and vegetables for the coming week.

If I sound like a proud father when I talk about "my" market, that's how I feel. Six years ago, I was walking across the lobby of the Kaiser Permanente Medical Center in Oakland, California, where I work as a primary-care physician, when I noticed some vendors selling jewelry and purses. I remember thinking what a clever idea it was to set up shop where thousands of people come and go every day, even if hawking fashion accessories seemed a little incongruous at a major metropolitan hospital. And then I had another thought: if someone can make a go of selling purses and jewelry, why not use the space to promote something that really reflects the values of our health-care program?

Why not a farmers' market? There seemed to be no reason not to and at least seven good reasons why everyone—patients, doctors and even you—should shop, cook and eat from a farmers' market.

1. Get Inspired

The truth is I've always loved farmers' markets. I love to cook, and farmers' markets are the best place to find the freshest vegetables and fruits of the season. The farmers' market offers all the inspiration my wife and I need to make something special for dinner, whether it's a homemade pizza with leeks, tomatoes, feta and prawns or an asparagus-potato frittata like you'll find on page 36. Thanks to farmers' markets, we've been introduced to fruits and vegetables we didn't know much about before, such as kohlrabi (a Sputnik-looking relative of cabbage with a mild, sweet taste, perfect raw or baked into a gratin like you will find on page 159).

Farmers' markets keep us in touch with the seasons in a way I have come to cherish—the arrival of asparagus and the first luscious strawberries in the spring, sun-ripened heirloom tomatoes and succulent fresh corn at the height of summer, a rainbow

> ❝ The surest way to escape the Western diet is simply to depart the realms it rules: the supermarket, the convenience store, and the fast-food outlet. It is hard to eat badly from the farmers' market, from a CSA box… or from your garden. ❞
>
> — MICHAEL POLLAN,
> *In Defense of Food*

cornucopia of peppers and squash come fall, and winter's citrus crop and savory root vegetables, which we love to roast with chunks of fennel, a recipe we discovered by hanging out at farmers' markets.

As a physician, I know that a diet built around fresh, seasonal fruits and vegetables like these is the cornerstone of preventive medicine. I also know that like most people, my colleagues—doctors, nurses, staff members—as well as our patients, are so busy they don't always have time to go to a farmers' market.

Why not, I found myself thinking, bring the market to them? I didn't know the first thing about running a farmers' market. But it didn't take me long to find the director of a local farmers' market association who enthusiastically agreed to help. After months of planning, on May 16, 2003, a bright and breezy spring day, our first farmers' market opened for business. It was like a block party. People poured out of the hospital. There was a palpable sense of excitement. I think everyone there understood right away the connection between good food and good health. People really caught the spirit of it. It was a day I'll never forget.

As far as I know, ours was one of the first farmers' markets ever established at a major medical center. To be honest, when it first started, I didn't know whether or not it would survive. Five and a half years later, it's still open for business and drawing enthusiastic crowds every Friday. As a primary-care physician, I take pride in having helped many people focus on the basics for good health. I'm also proud to have helped create our thriving farmers' market—and not just because people love shopping here. I love what it says about our health-care program. And I love what it says about our community.

2. Follow a Better Diet

Too often people think of hospitals as places that just care for the sick. That's part of what we do, of course. But another crucial part is keeping people healthy. And there's no better way to inspire healthy eating than a market packed with local, farm-fresh fruits and

America's Best Farmers' Markets

We asked the readers of EATINGWELL Magazine and *eatingwell.com* to tell us about their favorite markets. Here and on the following pages are the top five picks:

DANE COUNTY FARMERS' MARKET
Madison, Wisconsin | dcfm.org

With its location in one of the country's richest agricultural regions and its all-out community feel, the Dane County Farmers' Market leads the EATINGWELL list of America's top farmers' markets. You'll find a bounty of greens, roots and fruits from the glaciated, gently rolling land. Build lunch or dinner around sorrel, black radishes and sunchokes from Harmony Valley Farm. Set in a peaceful, secluded valley by the Mississippi River, the farm is not only all-organic but manages its land to have minimal impact on local birds and wildlife. Cold and damp Wisconsin farmland has also proven ideal for potatoes. The perfect side to dinner on the grill are the varietal spuds from Butter Mountain Potatoes. Finish off your meal with cheese from wind- and solar-powered Bleu Mont Dairy. Swiss artisan Willi Lehner taught his son to age cheeses on cedar planks in a straw-bale cave and their bandaged Cheddar is worth waiting in line for. —*Bruce Weinstein & Mark Scarbrough*

"You can get just about anything... organic and sustainably raised meat, including bison and venison, and eggs... locally grown and milled flour, locally grown oats.... I literally do not need to go to the grocery store during peak months."

—Leslie Linser, Madison, WI

vegetables. I'm convinced that our farmers' market has helped make the people who work here and those who visit a little healthier.

For 30 years I've watched one patient of mine struggle with a weight problem. But once she began to do most of her shopping at the farmers' market, she changed her diet to include more fruits and vegetables and lost close to 30 pounds. And on the elevator recently, I chatted with a man who works as an engineer at the hospital who told me he'd lost so much weight that his work clothes were too loose. When I congratulated him, he said, "Hey, this is really thanks to you and thanks to the market." I'm so convinced of the health benefits of basing your diet around seasonal farm-fresh produce that I've even written prescriptions for patients for arugula salad with lemon vinaigrette.

Of course it's hardly news that fruits, vegetables, nuts and legumes are good for you—they provide fiber, vitamins and minerals. Still, the evidence for just *how* good they are continues to amaze me. Study after study shows that eating foods from the garden helps keep blood pressure and cholesterol from climbing and lowers the danger of developing diabetes. A nationwide study published a few years ago and coordinated by Kaiser Permanente in Oregon showed unequivocally that reducing salt intake and eating a healthy diet rich in fruits, vegetables and low-fat dairy products significantly reduced blood pressure.

In one of the latest and most persuasive studies, researchers from Harvard gathered data from more than 72,000 women over two decades, as part of the well-known Nurses' Health Study. Women who followed the so-called "prudent diet," made up of many of the foods on display at farmers' markets—fruits and vegetables, legumes, nuts and whole grains—had a 28 percent lower risk of dying of heart disease. In contrast, those who ate a "Western diet" rich in high-fat, sugary and processed foods had a 22 percent higher risk of dying of heart disease and a 16 percent higher cancer risk. For some of these women, the difference between these two ways of eating was literally a matter of life and death. I'm convinced it is for most of the rest of us as well.

The Mediterranean diet—abounding in fruits, vegetables, beans, lentils, whole grains and healthy plant oils, such as olive and peanut oil—has become almost synonymous with optimal health. With good reason, as studies from around the world continue to

continued on page 14

UNION SQUARE GREENMARKET
New York, New York | cenyc.org

It's hard to believe that it was once difficult to get a decent tomato in Manhattan. In 1985, restaurateur Danny Meyer opened his signature Union Square Cafe near the Greenmarket so his chefs would have access to the best of the season. The market has since become the perfect mix of midtown professionalism and downtown shabby chic. Stop by early and watch top chefs cart away wheelbarrows full of chanterelles, heirloom eggplants and apricots. Producers come from a roughly 200-mile radius, bringing the best from farms in rural Connecticut and New Jersey as well as more in New York. Start out with raspberry apple cider from

Red Jacket Orchards of Geneva, New York. The orchard has been in the same family for almost 50 years and delivers picture-perfect apples, stone fruits and berries. For a great lunch, check out the slightly sour, aged cheeses from Cato Corner Farm in Colchester, Connecticut. Pair these with radishes from Stokes Farm in Old Tappan, New Jersey. The Greenmarket literally saved this farm, transforming it from a failing, fifth-generation, wholesale operation to a thriving, direct-to-consumer producer of vegetables, herbs and flowers. —*B.W. & M.S.*

"I found one stall selling puntarelle, a vegetable I've only seen in Rome! There was even a recipe, with the traditional anchovy dressing."

—Tracy Carroll, New York, NY

Eating Well by Color

A simple way to load up on nature's superfoods

In the last couple of decades, scientists have discovered more reasons (beyond vitamins and fiber) to pack your diet with fruits and vegetables: phytochemicals. All plants contain these compounds, which protect them from a variety of dangers—from harmful UV rays to predatory pests. We take in phytochemicals when we eat fruits and vegetables and, as it turns out, they protect us too. Some act as antioxidants, mopping up unstable "free radical" molecules that can damage cells and lead to the development of heart disease, cancer, Alzheimer's and other health issues. Others work by boosting the immune system.

What's fascinating is that nature seems to have a way of highlighting these beneficial nutrients by giving them bright colors that allow you to spot them at a glance. For example, anthocyanins make blueberries blue and may help to keep your mind sharp. Tomatoes get their ruby hue from lycopene, a phytochemical that may help to prevent prostate cancer. To get the maximum disease-fighting power that phytochemicals can provide, choose foods that represent all colors of the rainbow. The USDA suggests paying particular attention to orange (2 cups per week) and dark green (3 cups per week) produce, both good sources of vitamin A and other important nutrients. Use our vibrant color wheel to inspire you.

1 *Red* — Red foods, such as tomatoes and watermelon, contain **lycopene**, a phytochemical that may help protect against prostate and breast cancers.

Guava	Red peppers	Watermelon
Pink grapefruit	Tomatoes	

2 *Orange* — **Alpha** and **beta carotene** make foods like carrots and sweet potatoes so brilliantly orange. The body converts these compounds into the active form of vitamin A, which helps keep your eyes, bones and immune system healthy. These phytochemicals also operate as antioxidants, sweeping up disease-promoting free radicals.

Apricots	Oranges	Tangerines
Cantaloupe	Papaya	Winter squash
Carrots	Pumpkin	
Mango	Sweet potatoes	

3
4 *Yellow & Green, part 1* (leafy greens) — Many yellow and green vegetables are good sources of **lutein** and **zeaxanthin**, phytochemicals that accumulate in the eyes and help prevent age-related macular degeneration, a leading cause of blindness in older people. Leafy greens are also rich in **beta carotene**.

Artichoke	Wax beans	Mustard greens
Corn	Arugula	Turnip greens
Lettuce	Chard	
Summer squash	Collards	

5 *Green, part 2* (cruciferous) — Cruciferous vegetables, such as broccoli and kale, provide compounds called **indoles** and **isothiocyanates**, which may help prevent cancer by amping up the production of enzymes that clear toxins from the body.

Broccoli	Cauliflower	Kale
Brussels sprouts	Green cabbage	

6
7 *Blue & Purple/Deep Red* — Blue, purple and deep-red fruits and vegetables are full of **anthocyanins** and **proanthocyanins**, antioxidants associated with keeping the heart healthy and the brain functioning optimally.

Blackberries	Plums	Radishes (red)
Blueberries	Cranberries	Raspberries
Eggplant	Grapes	Strawberries

show. A study published in the December 2007 *Archives of Internal Medicine* showed that the Mediterranean diet reduces risks of cancer and heart disease and improves the odds of living a long life. A study conducted by researchers at the University of Athens also showed a strong association between a largely plant-based diet and longevity. And when researchers at the University of Las Palmas de Gran Canaria, in Spain, reviewed 35 studies, they found that the Mediterranean eating pattern improved cholesterol levels, boosted antioxidants, protected against insulin resistance (a risk factor for diabetes) and helped keep blood vessels healthy.

Several large studies have shown that people with heart disease can dramatically improve their health by making fruits and vegetables the centerpiece of their diet and replacing saturated fats (such as those you might get from dairy and meat) with unsaturated fats (such as those in avocados and nuts). That's very good news, of course. But our real goal should be to prevent diseases in the first place.

That's why I always find it a joy to see kids at our farmers' market, and not only because they seem to be having such a good time. Starting healthier eating habits early in life is likely to offer the biggest payoff

of all. Along with more physical activity, a healthy diet with nutrient-rich, low-calorie foods is just about the only prescription we have to end the epidemic of weight problems and diabetes among children. In many ways, a healthier diet will also help kids grow into healthy adults. Another study from Kaiser Permanente showed that a diet abundant in fruits and vegetables increased bone density during those critical teen years. I like to think the kids who come through our market and sample a fresh peach or a handful of cherry tomatoes will go on to make healthier choices for the rest of their lives.

3. Cook for Your Health

The list of health benefits associated with a diet centered around plant-based foods goes on and on. If we could put all those together in one pill, we'd have a blockbuster drug. But it wouldn't be as colorful or delicious as the prescription you can fill at a farmers' market. So why do most Americans still fall woefully short on the optimal number of servings of fruits and vegetables—between 5 and 9 a day, depending on how many calories you consume?

There are many reasons, of course. But the leading

continued on page 17

PORTLAND FARMERS MARKET
Portland, Oregon | portlandfarmersmarket.org

In 1992, Portland's market at Albers Hill had only 13 vendors. Today, there are hundreds. With no government funding, the market has grown the old-fashioned way—with fundraisers, auctions and volunteers—and is a true grass-roots success story. The market helped initiate the Eat Local Challenge (*eatlocal.net*). Being a locavore is easy in Portland: the Hood River Valley is one of the world's top pear-growing areas; the Willamette Valley, at over 5,200 square miles, has become a haven not only for pinot noir, but also for organic heirloom tomatoes, leafy greens and delectable berries. The Shadbolts of Cherry Country will be glad to show you the joys of the Royal Ann cherry, usually chemically morphed into maraschinos but best (and rarely) enjoyed for the sweet, juicy sparkplug it is. Gilson Marine Farms sells abalone, clams and oysters from Netarts Bay, briny wonders for the grill any night. And don't miss the festivals the market hosts, like the Tomato Fiesta in September and the Great Pumpkin Event before Halloween. —*B. W. & M.S.*

" I learn about a new thing here each year! First it was cardoons, now pimiento de Padron peppers (sauté quickly in olive oil). Yum!"

—Julia Wood, Lake Oswego, OR

Balance Your Diet

Vegetables and fruits form the foundation of a healthy diet. But you can't live on produce alone. To get all your essential nutrients, you'll also need to eat whole grains, lean protein (fish, lean meat, beans or low-fat dairy foods) and healthy fats, including nuts and olive oil. How much do you need? Balance your diet in three easy steps.

Divide your plate.

Does your plate look more like A or B?

Whatever you answered, you should aim to model (or keep modeling) your plate after B. Low-calorie—yet satisfying—vegetables fill half the plate. The other half is divided into two equal portions (quarters). One is filled with a lean protein, the other with a whole-grain or starchy vegetable.

Calculate your calories.

Eating a balanced diet means not only getting enough of specific nutrients, such as vitamin C and beta carotene, but also eating the right number of calories for your size.

The following equation will help you determine the number of calories you need to maintain your current weight.

Your body weight X 12 = _____

Subtract 500 calories from this number to lose 1 pound per week. To lose 2 pounds per week, subtract 1,000. If you calculate a calorie target that's less than 1,200, set your calorie goal at 1,200. For more help on losing weight healthfully, check out *The EatingWell Diet* book, *eatingwell.com/diet*.

Eat by the Pyramid.

To get even more accurate about ensuring nutritional balance in your diet, eat by the USDA's MyPyramid recommended intakes for all the major food groups. Simply follow the guides in the column below that's closest to the calorie level you calculated in Step 2.

A

B

Recommended daily intakes by Pyramid group for a range of calorie levels:

Calorie level	1,600	1,800	2,000	2,200	2,400	2,600	2,800	3,000
Grains*	5 oz.-eq.	6 oz.-eq.	6 oz.-eq.	7 oz.-eq.	8 oz.-eq.	9 oz.-eq.	10 oz.-eq.	10 oz.-eq.
Vegetables**	2 cups	2.5 cups	2.5 cups	3 cups	3 cups	3.5 cups	3.5 cups	4 cups
Fruits***	1.5 cups	1.5 cups	2 cups	2 cups	2 cups	2 cups	2.5 cups	2.5 cups
Milk (or dairy)	3 cups	3 cups	3 cups	3 cups	3 cups	3 cups	3 cups	3 cups
Meat, Beans†	5 oz.-eq.	5 oz.-eq.	5.5 oz.-eq.	6 oz.-eq.	6.5 oz.-eq.	6.5 oz.-eq.	7 oz.-eq.	7 oz.-eq.
Oils	5 tsp.	5 tsp.	6 tsp.	6 tsp.	7 tsp.	8 tsp.	8 tsp.	10 tsp.
Discretionary calories††	132	195	267	290	362	410	426	512

Note: *These suggested food amounts are calculated to meet USDA recommended nutrient intakes. The contributions from each group are based on the "nutrient-dense" form of the food, without added fats or sugars (for example, lean meats, fat-free dairy products, grains with no added sugars).* **A 1-oz. grain equivalent = 1/2 cup of pasta, rice or oatmeal, 1 cup of whole-grain cold cereal, 1 slice of bread, 1/2 of an English muffin.* ***A 1/2 cup of vegetables or 1 cup of raw leafy greens = 1 vegetable serving.* ****1 cup of cut fruit or 1 medium whole fruit (orange, apple, banana) = 1 fruit serving.* †*A 1-oz. equivalent = 1 oz. lean meat, poultry or fish, 1/4 cup cooked beans or tofu.* ††*"Discretionary calories" are those remaining in the calorie total when all the food-group portions and nutrients are consumed. You can "spend" them on whatever you want, such as a piece of chocolate or a glass of wine.*

Is Organic Produce Healthier?

There are at least two good arguments for eating organic: fewer pesticides and more nutrients. Let's start with pesticides. Pesticides can be absorbed into fruits and vegetables, and leave trace residues. The Environmental Working Group (EWG), a nonprofit, nonpartisan organization, pored over the results of nearly 51,000 USDA and FDA tests for pesticides on 44 popular produce items and identified the types of fruits and vegetables that were most likely to have higher trace amounts. Most people have no problems eating conventionally grown produce but if you feel strongly about pesticide residues, the EWG's list at right should help you shop.

As for nutrients, in 2007 a study out of Newcastle University in the United Kingdom reported that organic produce boasted up to 40 percent higher levels of some nutrients (including vitamin C, zinc and iron) than its conventional counterparts. Additionally, a 2003 study in the *Journal of Agricultural and Food Chemistry* found that organically grown berries and corn contained 58 percent more polyphenols—antioxidants that help prevent cardiovascular disease—and up to 52 percent higher levels of vitamin C than those conventionally grown. Recent research by that study's lead author, Alyson Mitchell, Ph.D., an associate professor of food science and technology at the University of California, Davis, pinpoints a potential mechanism to explain why organic techniques may sometimes yield superior produce.

It's a difference in soil fertility, says Mitchell: "With organic methods, the nitrogen present in composted soil is released slowly and therefore plants grow at a normal rate, with their nutrients in balance. Vegetables fertilized with conventional fertilizers grow very rapidly and allocate less energy to develop nutrients." Buying conventional produce from local farmers also has benefits. Nutrient values in produce peak at prime ripeness, just after harvest. As a general rule, the less produce has to travel, the fresher and more nutrient-rich it remains.

A 2008 review by the Organic Center of almost 100 studies on the nutritional quality of organic produce compared the effects conventional and organic farming methods have on specific nutrients. The report's conclusion: "Yes, organic plant-based foods are, on average, more nutritious."

Bottom line: "Eating more fresh fruits and vegetables in general is the point," says Mitchell. If buying all organic isn't a priority—or a financial reality for you—you might opt to buy organic specifically when you're selecting foods that are most heavily contaminated with pesticide and insecticide residues.

Preferably Organic —Most Commonly Contaminated

Apples	Nectarines
Bell peppers	Peaches
Celery	Pears
Cherries	Potatoes
Grapes *(imported)*	Spinach
Lettuce	Strawberries

If Budget Allows, Buy Organic

Blueberries	Lemons
Cantaloupe	Mushrooms
Carrots	Oranges
Cauliflower	Plums
Cucumbers	Raspberries
Grapefruit	Sweet potatoes
Grapes *(domestic)*	Tangerines
Green beans	Tomatoes
Honeydew	Watermelon
Hot peppers	Winter squash

It's Your Call —Least Commonly Contaminated

Asparagus	Kiwi
Avocado	Mango
Bananas	Onions
Broccoli	Papaya
Cabbage	Peas *(frozen)*
Corn *(frozen)*	Pineapple
Eggplant	

Source: Environmental Working Group. Go to foodnews.org *for updates.*

one, I think, is that the choices closest at hand are those from fast-food outlets. And in some places, those are just about the *only* choices.

That's why bringing the market to the medical center proved to be so powerful. If you make healthy food available and visible, people will try it. It's a little like putting a bowl of fruit front and center in the kitchen so you or your children will grab an apple or a peach for a snack—except in this case we've put an entire farmers' market on the street where people come and go. And we know at least some people are eating more healthy food as a result. In 2005 we conducted a survey and found that of our repeat market customers, 71 percent said they were eating more fruits and vegetables. Sixty-three percent were eating new and different fruits and vegetables.

Convenience is part of what our market offers. But I think people caught the spirit of it for another reason. It's one thing for your primary-care doctor to say, "You know, you really should be eating a healthier diet." But it's a lot more convincing when your medical center hosts a farmers' market where you can fill a bag with fresh, delicious produce. Our market proved that we, as doctors, not only talk the talk, we walk the walk. And that goes a long way toward convincing people—not just patients but everyone in our community—that we really believe in the importance of making healthy food choices.

Encouraging people to shop at farmers' markets also encourages them to cook, and I firmly believe that's another key to good health. When you prepare your own meals, it's much easier to take charge of exactly what you eat. Take the example of salt. Too much of it can raise blood pressure, which in turn increases the risk of heart disease and stroke. Where does most of the salt in the average diet come from? Processed foods. When people cook their own food (as opposed to relying on these processed foods), they typically consume less salt without even having to think about it. And the recipes in this book are all vetted by nutritionists; almost all contain less than 750 mg sodium per serving.

Also, when you're in charge of the menu, you can easily serve a more modest-sized portion of meat and add extra servings of fresh vegetables to a salad or a stir-fry, for example. You can also make smart choices, such as serving a whole grain like quinoa or brown rice instead of a refined grain like white rice. You can

FERRY PLAZA FARMERS MARKET
San Francisco, California | cuesa.org

Since it was started in 1992, the Ferry Plaza Farmers Market has become one of the Bay Area's biggest draws. It combines California's bounty and San Francisco's sophistication in a Gilded Age ferry terminal. The Golden State tightly regulates farmers' markets, which ensures you'll buy directly from California producers. And there's plenty to choose from: blackberries from the Sierra slopes, table grapes from the flood zones around the Bay and oysters from windy, desolate Point Reyes, just over the Golden Gate Bridge. Be sure to try Marshall's Farm Natural Honey, run by the wiry, irrepressible Helene Marshall, whose husband drags their thousands of hives to 70 locations all over the state, awaiting the next flowering of star thistle or eucalyptus. And most Saturdays in the north arcade, there's a meet-the-farmer talk in the morning, followed by a seasonal cooking demonstration. —*B.W. & M.S.*

"In the heart of San Francisco, this market has taught me about sustainable agriculture, the difference between eating what's in season and the cardboard fruits and vegetables you get in the supermarket. I have been going for years and if I can't get there on Saturday morning, I feel like I've missed my 'fix.'"

—J. Spielberger, San Francisco, CA

SUNSET VALLEY FARMERS MARKET
Sunset Valley, Texas | sunsetvalleyfarmersmarket.org

This culinary bazaar makes our list of top markets because of its rocket-fire growth, its abundant produce from the Texas Hill Country and the sheer passion of one person: Pamela Boyar, a visionary who built a small market into a community event. All profits are plowed into the farmers' tills and most of the produce is organic or sustainably grown. Don't miss Bella Verdi Farms' sour, herbaceous and irresistible Lilliputian arugula. Check out Spiceburst's hand-blended seasoning mixes, including their banging-hot Chile Lime Saltburst, great on a steak or rimmed on a margarita glass. Melons are an Austin tradition. When the market puts on Melon Mania, stop by and taste some sorbet, learn to carve a watermelon and explore the endless list of heritage varietals, sweetened in the hot Texas sun. Later in the season, the serranos, poblanos and hatch chiles are hot and fresh-roasted at the annual Chile Pepper Fest. —*B. W. & M.S.*

" I went there looking for cucumbers, bison meat and local honey. I left with cucumbers, ground bison meat, bison jerky, local honey, a sage stick made from sage gathered outside of Kerrville, a lavender sachet, lavender mist, and a jar of pickled okra. How a cute little farmers' market can offer everything under the sun is beyond me."

—Robin Blackburn, San Marcos, TX

experiment, as my wife and I have, with fruits and vegetables you weren't familiar with and might just learn to love.

I'll admit, we've been lucky that our son, who trained as a professional chef before enrolling in medical school, taught us some tricks of his trade. When he was home for the summer, we cooked as a family nearly every night and had the tastiest meals I've ever enjoyed. My son showed us how to wield a chef's knife correctly and how to slice and dice quickly. You don't need to go to culinary school to cook at home, of course: the tips at the back of this book and the simple, straightforward recipes will help you feel like a pro. And if you want to learn more, many larger farmers' markets are sponsoring cooking classes. Even if yours doesn't, it is a great place to meet other people who truly love good food—a place where you're more likely to learn about how to choose, store and prepare produce than almost anywhere else.

4. Support Your Community

The benefits of supporting farmers' markets go beyond individual health to something larger: the well-being of an entire community. Prosperous farms help ensure green spaces between towns and cities and con-serve land for agriculture. For many small growers, a thriving local market offers the opportunity to make a decent living from farming, pay their workers a fair wage and plan for the future. At farmers' markets, they can sell directly to customers, earning close to 80 cents on a dollar, on average, compared to just 20 cents if they sell to food distributors who ship their produce to grocery chains.

In large metropolitan areas, such as the San Francisco Bay Area, Chicago or New York City, many small farmers sell exclusively through farmers' markets. They wouldn't be able to survive as small business owners without them. For example, my friend Mr. Rodriguez began selling his organic strawberries at our farmers' market and soon we began offering his spectacular berries to patients at our 19 Northern California hospitals. Now, each season he provides 130 dozen pints per week and, to do that, he has had to hire five new farm workers.

Also, when you buy from a farm or a farmers' market, you are helping ensure that the farm is economically viable and that local produce will be available year after year. I can't speak for everyone, but for me it's worth a lot to know that every spring I can help myself to several different varieties of exquisitely ripe and sweet berries, and that early fall will arrive with fresh figs and beautiful heirloom tomatoes by the basketful. Small farms have played a leading role in re-introducing many unusual varieties of fruits and vegetables that were virtually abandoned when large-scale agriculture came along. Among these so-called heirloom varieties are hundreds of different kinds of apples, pears and tomatoes that were in danger of being lost, fruits and vegetables you would hardly ever find at supermarkets.

And of course there's the simple fact that these local markets are just plain fun. They are places where people can come together to shop, talk, sit on a bench and watch the world go by, listen to music and exchange recipes. Local markets are as old as the oldest human settlements, and they have always been about more than just the buying and selling of goods. They are the heart and soul of a community. With the rise of big-box stores and shopping malls, we've unfortunately lost that feature in many parts of the country.

But today it's being recaptured in the growing number of farmers' markets cropping up in towns and cities large and small, with their colorful stalls and handwritten signs, their bins of hand-picked produce that was often harvested just hours ago.

5. Encourage Sustainable Agriculture

Farmers' markets help keep not only our communities healthy but our environment too. Small farms have been leaders in adapting sustainable agricultural techniques that protect water and build healthy soils. They have revived growing techniques that don't require as many chemical fertilizers and pesticides as some large operations do, and adapted to specific local growing conditions. Their hard work has helped prevent contamination of rivers, streams, lakes and oceans and often prevented farm workers from being exposed to chemicals that are known to pose health hazards.

Many small farms, whether they are certified "organic" or not, use sustainable approaches: the farmers you meet at these community markets often have only 20 or 30 acres or less and don't have the option of moving their operations to new locations when the soil becomes unworkable. Their livelihood, and the health of the towns they live in, depends on sustainable growing techniques that preserve and replenish the fertility of their small patch of soil. Local growers protect our communities in another way. They typically plant a wide variety of crops, in contrast to some large industrial farms, which grow hundreds or thousands of acres of the same crop. Crop diversity is a good defense against the spread of damaging insects and plant pathogens. If a problem arises in one crop, it's unlikely to spread to others. That's not true of monocropping, where the spread of a pathogen can be catastrophic.

Finally, local farmers are a small but important part of the solution to the largest environmental challenges we face. We're just beginning to understand the environmental consequences of shipping food long distances. Energy independence has become the rallying cry. Well, every time you buy something locally grown rather than shipped from halfway around the world, you reduce the amount of oil being burned *and* the amount of carbon emitted into the atmosphere. All in all, you end up getting a lot from your food dollar when you spend it at a local farmers' market, and that dollar goes right back into your community.

6. Eat by Season

I sometimes linger at our market simply to listen in on conversations between shoppers and farmers. I learn something new almost every time about how food is grown or how to prepare it, about the vagaries of weather and the details of our local climate. Before we started our market, I didn't know all that much about where the food I ate came from or how it was grown. Now I know many of the local farmers by name. I have new respect for how hard they work. I follow the local weather reports, knowing that too much rain in the spring or an unexpected freeze can endanger their crops. I'm much more aware of the many challenges they face. I understand that farming is by its nature a precarious business, at the mercy of weather and fluctuating prices. But I've also seen firsthand the deep satisfaction farmers take from planting seeds and watching them turn into the foods that nourish us.

By their very nature, farmers' markets encourage us to buy seasonal produce. As every chef knows, the most beautiful, best-tasting and most economical foods are the ones that are in season. Eating with the seasons is all about anticipation and then savoring what is ripe at the moment—the first tangerines of the winter that light up the market, the season of stonefruit, then the arrival of heirloom tomatoes, followed by the wild shapes and colors of squash in the late fall. The bounty on display at a farmers' market at the peak of the season is the very opposite of fast food. It's food that a farmer has spent months nurturing to the moment of perfect ripeness. It is food to be cherished and savored.

7. Change Our Food Systems

When a good idea comes along, it takes root and begins to grow faster and more vigorously than even its biggest advocates ever imagined. Certainly that was true of our small market. We were open for business only a few weeks when I started getting calls from people at other Kaiser Permanente facilities who wanted to start their own farmers' markets. Within a year, five farmers' markets were up and running. Today, our health-care system boasts some 30 markets in four states. And of course, many other hospitals and medical centers have launched their own.

Meanwhile, the success of our farmers' market inspired us to look for other ways to encourage the people we serve to eat healthier foods. One obvious place for a hospital to start is with its patients. The same values that inform our outdoor market, after all, should guide the choice of food we serve to our patients. That means using as much food as we can manage from small local farms growing in sustainable ways. Over the past few years we've been working hard to introduce more locally grown fresh produce onto the menu and to plan around foods that are in season. It's a big undertaking. In 2006 Kaiser Permanente bought about 25 tons of produce from small family farmers to serve at our hospitals. In 2007, we were up to 60 tons.

Building on the enthusiastic reception our market received, we're also experimenting with other ways to get produce to the people. We've started "best of the market" programs, where we put together bags of produce from the market and bring them to people who may be too busy caring for patients to be able to shop themselves. We're investigating ways to grow vegetables on unused land at a few of our medical facilities.

Around the country, farmers' markets are booming. According to the latest tally, there are more than 4,600 farmers' markets in the United States. Almost anywhere you go during the growing season, you'll find one. Each and every one, in its own way, reflects the special character of the places they call home—from the sizzling chiles in Arizona to the tropical fruits on Maui to the wild mushrooms displayed at the Portland Farmers Market in Oregon (*see page 14*).

More and more markets are working to make sure that people at every economic level can take advantage of fresh, locally grown produce. Several states are experimenting with wireless devices that allow people on food stamps to use their swipe cards at local markets. Many neighborhood food banks are forming partnerships with local farmers, arranging to buy up food that might otherwise go to waste in the field and serving it to those in need—a win-win arrangement for everyone. A wonderful group called Urban Farming has been converting abandoned lots in Detroit into small garden plots tended by volunteers, who turn their produce over to local food banks and other meal-assistance programs—an idea that has taken root in dozens of other cities around the country.

Chances are there's a terrific farmers' market near you. Or a community-supported agriculture program that allows customers to buy a certain amount of produce from a local farmer each week—providing farmers more stable revenue and consumers the best of the harvest. I urge you to support them. As a physician, I know there's nothing more important to health than what you eat. As an avid home cook, I know there's no better place to find the healthiest, freshest and best-tasting food than at a farmers' market. The recipe ideas in the following pages offer plenty of inspiration.

Enjoy them in good health.

Dr. Preston Maring, the associate physician-in-chief at Kaiser Permanente's Oakland (CA) Medical Center, is a crusader for local, healthy food and a national advocate for the small family farm. Peter Jaret won a James Beard Foundation journalism award for his article "The Search for the Anti-Aging Diet" (EATINGWELL *Magazine, November/December 2007). His most recent book is* Nurse: A World of Care *(Emory University Press, 2008).*

5 Ways to Eat Local Beyond the Farmers' Market

Join a CSA

If you like to cook and like to try new foods, get a community supported agriculture (CSA) share from a local farm. You pay up front, which helps the farmer pay for early-season costs in exchange for farm-fresh produce each week. Typically pick-ups are at the farm or a central location like a local business. If you work for a large company and your fellow employees are interested as well, ask if the farm will do a workplace drop-off. Before you commit, ask about the amount of produce to expect in a typical pick-up to see if it's manageable. You may also find you get produce you're not familiar with (rutabaga, anyone?). But that provides a great opportunity to get ideas from your farmer and other CSA members. And, of course, the recipes in this book will inspire you as well.

Find a CSA near you at *localharvest.org* **or ask farmers at the market if they have CSA shares.**

Buy the Cow

Don't just buy a burger, buy the cow—or a pig or a lamb. Small farms are increasingly selling "animal shares": a whole animal or portion of one. The farm takes care of processing, USDA inspection and packaging. Buying an animal is a great way to save money if you are committed to eating locally raised meat, as prices are lower per pound (usually $3 to $5, depending on type of animal and how much you're buying). Make sure you have adequate freezer space before purchasing an animal. If the amount of meat seems daunting, ask friends or family to go in on a share with you.

Find a local farm where you can buy meat direct at *localharvest.org* **or check your local classified ads.**

Start a Kitchen Garden

A kitchen garden is a great way to supplement your trips to the grocery store. Whether you grow a pot of herbs on your windowsill or replace a bed of flowers with dark leafy greens, your kitchen garden will inspire you to celebrate fresh flavors. Start by making a list of foods, focusing on crops that you can't always buy fresh. Lettuce is easy to sow and quick to grow.

Fresh herbs pack lively flavors, and edible flowers serve as pretty garnishes. Plant your seeds in rich, organic soil supplemented with organic compost, usually found at garden centers, to give plants a

boost. Mail-order seed sources offer a wide selection, or go to local nurseries for heirloom tomatoes and ornamental edibles, such as rainbow chard and Tuscan kale.

Learn how to start a successful garden at *gardeners.com* **or** *seedsofchange.com.*

Join a Community Garden

If you want to garden but don't have space where you live, get involved in a community garden. A community garden can be as small as a simple bed next to a building or an acre of land in a park. The garden may be divvied into small plots, each worked by an individual. Other gardens are worked collectively and all involved share the bounty.

To start your own community garden, go to *communitygarden.org.*

Pick Your Own

Enjoy the sunshine while gathering berries, apples or citrus fruit at a local pick-your-own farm. Some farms even give you the opportunity to dig potatoes or cut flowers. Freeze extra berries and stone fruit or try making freezer jam (*see page 234*). Both are great ways to enjoy summer-ripe fruit all year long.

Find a you-pick farm near you at *pickyourown.org.*

Frost-kissed curly kale

Ripe sour cherries in July

Afternoon sun on apples

Tatsoi in early spring

Savoring the Seasons

At EATINGWELL, what's fresh from the farm inspires our recipes all year long

BY JESSIE PRICE

Here at EATINGWELL, staying in touch with the seasons is a way of life. Our office in Charlotte, Vermont, a rural town of about 3,500, is located in the midst of farm fields. We have dairy cows across the street and a flock of woolly sheep just down the road. The compost from our Test Kitchen feeds a pair of black pigs at a nearby farm. Each spring we plant big pots of herbs, chard and kale outside the front door. And all summer, we stop by the Charlotte Berry Farm after work to pick strawberries, raspberries and blueberries or head down to a local "secret spot" to forage for chanterelles.

As the food editor at EATINGWELL, I am passionate about savoring seasonal produce. In May it's asparagus seven nights a week, and then in October I give myself stomachaches from eating too many apples. In early July I rush to my mom's house to pick sour cherries before the birds eat them. When those cherries are in season, it means weeks of cherry tarts, cherry preserves, cherry pie and even sour-cherry cocktails with dark rum.

And I'm not the only one here who's so crazy about seasonal produce. Test Kitchen Manager Stacy Fraser ran a small organic vegetable farm when she first moved to Charlotte. People around town still miss the amazing blend of salad greens she and her husband sold at their farmstand, back before you could find mesclun in plastic boxes at every supermarket. Now she puts her green thumb to work as the coordinator of the vegetable garden at her son's school. Associate Editor Carolyn Malcoun is especially partial to dark leafy greens, which she tenderly refers to as "DLGs." She gets DLGs from her CSA, grows them in her garden and one of her favorite stops on Saturday mornings is Pete's Greens' stand at her local farmers' market. At Pete's she picks up some of Vermont's finest greens, from wild arugula to Italian dandelion. (*See page 154 for more on Pete.*)

This wealth of wonderful fresh fruits and vegetables surrounding us inspires and informs our recipes at EATINGWELL every day. When I'm looking for ideas for an easy summer recipe, the first place I turn is my backyard garden. I got the idea for the Poblano & Skirt Steak Fajitas on page 103 when I was harvesting scallions and hot peppers from my garden. Carolyn had no problem coming up with recipe ideas for dark leafy greens. You'll find her recipe for Chard & Feta Tart on page 129.

Besides the inspiration that these fabulous local ingredients provide, they also happen to synch perfectly with our mission—to help people make healthy eating a way of life. After all, there's no more enjoyable and delicious way to eat healthfully than to cook and eat whatever produce is best at the moment. Of course we also pepper in lean meats, cheeses, whole grains and dairy products. But the tart Honeycrisp apples in October and the ripe tomatoes in July are what make cooking exciting and make our recipes taste great.

And we strive to make these recipes as easy as possible so that eating well in season is a joy rather than a chore. In our Test Kitchen we test each recipe, on average, seven times to make sure that you get the same great results when you cook our recipes at home. Plus we stick with simple methods and easy-to-find ingredients to keep our recipes streamlined.

This book is a collection of some of our favorite recipes that highlight the best produce of the year. We've organized the recipes by season so you'll find, for example, that the dishes in the Summer chapter feature produce that "peaks" during the summer months. Our Seasonal Produce Chart (*page 242*) shows how we've organized the produce by season. You can also reference the top corner of each recipe page to see what fresh fruit or vegetable is highlighted in that recipe. In some cases a fruit or vegetable spans several seasons and you'll find it in more than one chapter. Eggplant, for example, appears in both the Summer and Fall chapters.

Of course, "peak" season is different depending on where you live. So what's ripe around you locally at the moment is your best guide to what to cook next.

You'll find recipes for the most iconic seasonal vegetables, such as peas in spring or citrus in winter, in this collection. And we've also included some more underappreciated seasonal beauties (just the sort of thing you might pick up at your farmers' market), such as dandelion greens in spring or celery root in winter. And of course, I wouldn't leave out the sour cherries. You can turn to page 119 to enjoy our delicious sour cherry slump. Just thinking of it, I can hardly wait for July.

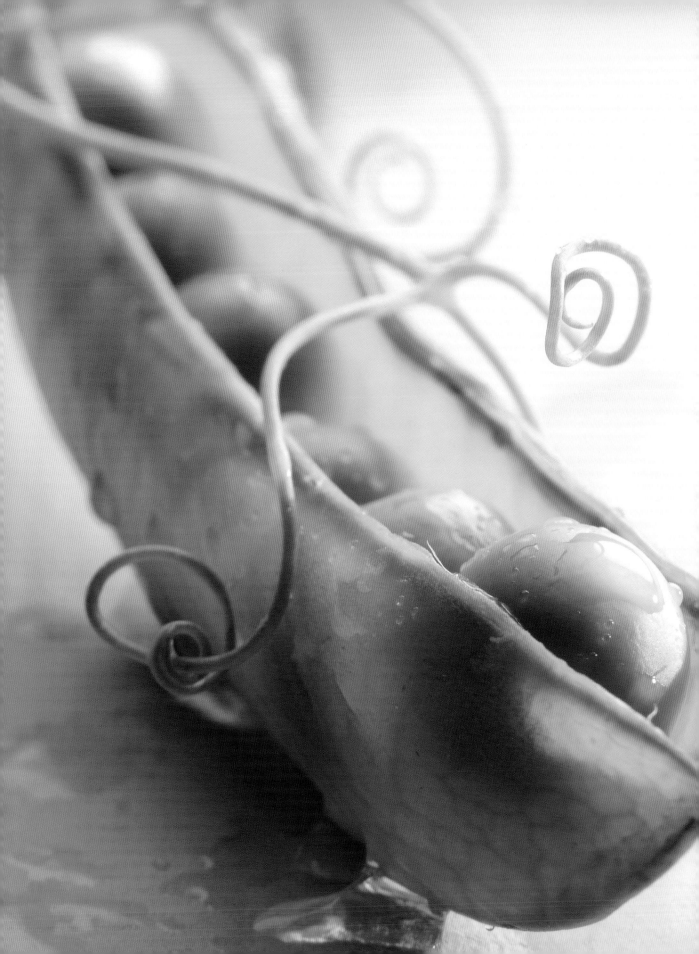

SPRING

MENUS

BRUNCH SEASON

SPRING DINNER

❝ Spring delights us with its bounty of fresh
sweet green vegetables: artichokes,
asparagus, baby leeks and—above all—tiny
peas, with their crunchy pods and delicate
curling tendrils of vine. **❞**

— BARBARA KAFKA, FROM
HER BOOK *VEGETABLE LOVE*

Asparagus delivers a healthy dose of folate, a vitamin that
helps produce DNA and form healthy new cells.

ASPARAGUS

Garden-Fresh Asparagus Soup

*When the weather is just right, asparagus can shoot up 10 inches in one day—now
that's robust! Of course, it has an assertive flavor to match. This lemony asparagus soup
is spiced with a touch of curry and gets added richness from "lite" coconut milk and
creamy red potatoes. Top it with a dollop of crème fraîche or plain yogurt and serve
warm or chilled.*

2	tablespoons butter
2	tablespoons extra-virgin olive oil
1	medium onion, finely chopped
½	teaspoon salt, divided
½	teaspoon curry powder
¼	teaspoon ground ginger
	Zest and juice of 1 lemon, divided
2	cups diced peeled red potatoes
3	cups vegetable broth *or* reduced-sodium chicken broth
1	cup "lite" coconut milk
2	cups ½-inch pieces trimmed asparagus (about 1 bunch)
	Freshly ground pepper to taste
¼	cup crème fraîche *or* reduced-fat sour cream (*see Note*)
¼	cup finely chopped scallion greens *or* fresh chives

1. Melt butter and oil in a large saucepan over medium heat. Add onion and
   ¼ teaspoon salt and cook, stirring often, until golden, about 5 minutes.
   Stir in curry powder, ginger, lemon zest and potatoes and simmer, stirring
   occasionally, for 5 minutes. Stir in broth, coconut milk and asparagus. Bring
   to a simmer over medium heat, partially cover and continue to cook until
   the potatoes are tender, about 15 minutes.

2. Puree the soup with an immersion blender or a regular blender (in batches)
   until smooth. (Use caution when pureeing hot liquids.) Season with the
   remaining ¼ teaspoon salt and pepper.

3. Whisk crème fraîche (or sour cream), lemon juice and scallion greens
   (or chives) in a small bowl and garnish with a swirl of it.

   MAKES 6 APPETIZER SERVINGS, 1 GENEROUS CUP EACH.

ACTIVE TIME: 35 minutes

TOTAL TIME: 50 minutes

PER SERVING:

203 calories; 13 g fat (6 g sat,
4 g mono); 14 mg cholesterol;
19 g carbohydrate; 4 g protein;
3 g fiber; 444 mg sodium;
154 mg potassium

NUTRITION BONUS:

Vitamin C (35% daily value)
Vitamin A (20% dv)

L ⬇ C

NOTE: **Crème fraîche** is a tangy,
thick, rich cultured cream
commonly used in French
cooking. Find it in the dairy
section of large supermarkets,
usually near other specialty
cheeses. **Sour cream** can be
used as a substitute, or you can
make your own lower-fat version
by combining equal portions
of reduced-fat sour cream and
nonfat plain yogurt.

Spinach Soup with Rosemary Croutons

In temperate climates, rosemary will last right through the winter so it's usually one of the first herbs available in a spring herb garden. Although it does have a strong flavor, it offers only a subtle hint in this soup that blends nicely with the greens. If you like, any seasonal greens you have on hand can be substituted for the spinach.

ACTIVE TIME: 30 minutes

TOTAL TIME: 1 hour

PER SERVING:

176 calories; 7 g fat (2 g sat, 4 g mono); 8 mg cholesterol; 21 g carbohydrate; 7 g protein; 2 g fiber; 301 mg sodium; 202 mg potassium

NUTRITION BONUS:

Vitamin A (35% daily value)
Vitamin C (30% dv)
Folate (16% dv)

H✕W   L↓C   H♥H

CROUTONS

2	cups ½-inch cubes country-style sourdough bread
2	tablespoons extra-virgin olive oil
1	clove garlic, minced
1	tablespoon finely chopped fresh rosemary *or* 1 teaspoon dried

SOUP

1	tablespoon butter
1	medium onion, coarsely chopped
1	clove garlic, minced
1	tablespoon finely chopped fresh rosemary *or* 1 teaspoon dried
¼	teaspoon salt
	Freshly ground pepper to taste
2	cups diced peeled red potatoes
4	cups reduced-sodium chicken broth, vegetable broth *or* water
6	cups fresh spinach *or* chard leaves, tough stems removed
	Freshly grated nutmeg for garnish

1. **To prepare croutons:** Preheat oven to 375°F.

2. Toss bread cubes, oil, garlic and rosemary in a large bowl until well combined. Spread in a single layer on a large baking sheet. Bake until golden and crisp, 12 to 15 minutes.

3. **Meanwhile, to prepare soup:** Melt butter in a large saucepan over medium heat. Add onion, garlic, rosemary, salt and pepper, reduce heat to medium-low and cook, stirring occasionally, for 5 minutes. Stir in potatoes and cook, stirring occasionally, for 3 minutes. Pour in broth (or water). Bring to a simmer over medium heat and cook until the potatoes are soft, about 15 minutes. Stir in spinach (or chard) and continue to simmer until the greens are tender, about 10 minutes more. Puree the soup with an immersion blender or regular blender (in batches), leaving it a little chunky if desired. (Use caution when pureeing hot liquids.)

4. Serve the soup garnished with nutmeg, if desired, and topped with the croutons.

MAKES 6 APPETIZER SERVINGS, 1 CUP EACH.

Escarole & Rice Soup with Chicken

Unlike other members of the endive family, escarole has only a mild peppery bitterness. It tolerates cold and heat extremely well so it grows from very early spring to late fall. Here it adds an assertive bite to an Italian-themed dish that would otherwise be just another chicken and rice soup.

1	tablespoon extra-virgin olive oil
1	small onion, chopped
1	head escarole, thinly sliced
7	cups reduced-sodium chicken broth, divided
½	cup arborio *or* other short-grain rice
12	ounces boneless, skinless chicken breasts, trimmed and cut into ½-inch cubes
1	14-ounce can whole tomatoes, drained, seeded and chopped
¼	teaspoon salt
	Freshly ground pepper to taste
2	tablespoons grated Asiago *or* Parmesan cheese

1. Heat oil in a Dutch oven over medium-high heat. Add onion and cook, stirring, until golden, 2 to 3 minutes. Add escarole and 1 cup broth. Bring to a boil. Reduce heat to low, cover and simmer for 15 minutes.

2. Stir in the remaining 6 cups broth and bring to a simmer. Add rice and simmer, covered, for 10 minutes. Add chicken and tomatoes and cook, covered, until the rice is tender and the chicken is no longer pink inside, about 5 minutes longer. Season with salt and pepper. Ladle into bowls and top with cheese.

MAKES 6 SERVINGS.

ACTIVE TIME: 20 minutes

TOTAL TIME: 45 minutes

PER SERVING:

173 calories; 5 g fat (2 g sat, 2 g mono); 41 mg cholesterol; 13 g carbohydrate; 20 g protein; 3 g fiber; 386 mg sodium; 492 mg potassium

NUTRITION BONUS:

Vitamin A (39% daily value)
Folate (32% dv)
Vitamin C (17% dv)

H)(W L↓C H♥H

Watercress & Sugar Snap Salad with Warm Sesame-Shallot Vinaigrette

The peppery flavor of watercress is due to the presence of mustard oil in the leaves. In this Asian-inspired salad, watercress is paired with another emblematic spring vegetable—sugar snap peas. Tossed with a warm dressing made with caramelized onions, rice vinegar and toasted sesame oil, this salad is the perfect antidote to the chill of early spring. For the best-tasting watercress, look for supple, thin stems (not woody stalks) with small, heart-shaped, dark green leaves that have no yellow blemishes.

8	ounces fresh sugar snap peas, trimmed (about 2 cups; *see photo, page 228*)
2	large bunches watercress, woody stems trimmed (4 ounces *or* 4 loosely packed cups)
2	tablespoons peanut oil *or* canola oil
4	large shallots, thinly sliced into rings
2	tablespoons rice vinegar
2	teaspoons toasted sesame oil
¼	teaspoon salt
2	ounces hard, aged goat cheese *or* Asiago, crumbled

1. Bring a small pot of water to a boil. Add peas and cook until bright green, 30 seconds. Drain in a colander and rinse with cold water until cool. Transfer to a large bowl, add watercress and toss to combine.

2. Heat peanut (or canola) oil in a medium nonstick skillet over low heat; add shallots and cook very slowly, stirring frequently, until caramelized, about 15 minutes. Stir in vinegar, sesame oil and salt; cook until fragrant, about 10 seconds. Pour the warm dressing over the peas and watercress; toss well. Top with cheese and serve.

MAKES 4 SERVINGS, 1½ CUPS EACH.

ACTIVE TIME: 25 minutes

TOTAL TIME: 25 minutes

PER SERVING:

183 calories; 14 g fat (5 g sat, 5 g mono); 15 mg cholesterol; 8 g carbohydrate; 7 g protein; 2 g fiber; 208 mg sodium; 150 mg potassium

NUTRITION BONUS:

Vitamin A (40% daily value)
Vitamin C (30% dv)
Calcium (20% dv)

L ⬇ C

Peas are higher in protein and fiber than most vegetables: 1/2 cup provides 4 grams of each.

PEAS

Green Salad with Asparagus & Peas

Here's a salad where we've combined two stars of the spring garden, asparagus and peas. Since the asparagus goes into the mix raw, you'll want to look for the freshest, most tender spears you can find and slice them into very thin rounds.

2	teaspoons freshly grated lemon zest
1/4	cup lemon juice
1/4	cup canola oil *or* extra-virgin olive oil
1	teaspoon sugar
1/2	teaspoon salt
1/4	teaspoon freshly ground pepper
2	heads Boston *or* Bibb lettuce, torn into bite-size pieces
2	cups very thinly sliced fresh asparagus (about 1 bunch)
2	cups shelled fresh peas (about 3 pounds unshelled)
1	pint grape *or* cherry tomatoes, halved
2	tablespoons minced fresh chives *or* scallion greens

Combine lemon zest and juice, oil, sugar, salt and pepper in a large salad bowl. Add lettuce, asparagus, peas, tomatoes and chives (or scallion greens); toss to coat.

MAKES 8 SERVINGS, ABOUT 2 CUPS EACH.

ACTIVE TIME: 35 minutes

TOTAL TIME: 35 minutes

TO MAKE AHEAD: Cover and refrigerate the dressing for up to 5 days.

PER SERVING:

113 calories; 7 g fat (1 g sat, 4 g mono); 0 mg cholesterol; 10 g carbohydrate; 3 g protein; 3 g fiber; 152 mg sodium; 339 mg potassium

NUTRITION BONUS:

Vitamin A & Vitamin C (45% daily value)
Folate (19% dv)

H✖W   L↓C   H♥H

Mango Salad with Ginger-Raisin Vinaigrette

Mangoes are available year-round, but some of the highest quality, which come from Florida, come into season in early May. In this recipe, the juicy tropical fruit is paired with fresh ginger plus an unusual combination of golden raisins and malt vinegar, which adds great complexity to an otherwise basic mixed green salad.

ACTIVE TIME: 35 minutes

TOTAL TIME: 35 minutes

PER SERVING:

117 calories; 7 g fat (1 g sat, 5 g mono); 0 mg cholesterol; 14 g carbohydrate; 1 g protein; 2 g fiber; 58 mg sodium; 222 mg potassium

NUTRITION BONUS:

Vitamin C (76% daily value)
Vitamin A (30% dv)

H✝W L↓C H♥H

DRESSING

¼	cup golden raisins
1	cup boiling water
3	tablespoons extra-virgin olive oil
2	tablespoons malt vinegar *or* red-wine vinegar
1	tablespoon finely chopped fresh cilantro leaves and tender stems
1	teaspoon minced fresh ginger
1	fresh green Thai, serrano *or* small jalapeño chile, stemmed and finely chopped (*see Note*)
⅛	teaspoon salt

SALAD

8	cups mesclun *or* other mixed baby salad greens (5 ounces)
1	large ripe, firm mango, peeled and diced (*see photos, page* 225)
1	medium red bell pepper, thinly sliced

1. **To prepare dressing:** Place raisins and boiling water in a small bowl. Let soften for 30 minutes. Drain; transfer the raisins to a blender. Add oil, vinegar, cilantro, ginger, chile and salt. Puree, scraping the sides as needed, until smooth. Set aside 1 tablespoon of the dressing.

2. **To prepare salad:** Place greens in a large bowl and toss with the remaining dressing. Divide among 6 plates. Place mango and bell pepper in the bowl; add the reserved tablespoon of dressing and toss to coat. Top the greens with the mango mixture. Serve immediately.

MAKES **6** SERVINGS.

NOTE: Fresh and dried **chiles** vary widely in spiciness depending on variety and seasonality. Smaller varieties are generally hotter. The compound that makes chiles hot, capsaicin, is found in the inner membrane and seeds. Add chiles with caution when cooking, tasting as you go.

Asparagus & Potato Frittata

A frittata makes a perfect lunch or light supper, especially when served with a salad of spring greens and some good, crusty bread. This version calls for cooked asparagus and a few small potatoes but in a pinch, you can use just about any vegetables you have on hand.

3	teaspoons canola oil, divided
1	small onion, thinly sliced
1	clove garlic, finely chopped
1	teaspoon chopped fresh rosemary *or* 1/4 teaspoon dried
1	tomato, seeded and chopped, divided
2	small cooked potatoes, cut into 1/2-inch dice
10-12	cooked asparagus stalks, cut into 2-inch pieces
1/2	teaspoon salt
1/2	teaspoon freshly ground pepper, plus more to taste
4	large eggs
4	large egg whites
1/4	cup freshly grated Parmesan *or* Gruyère cheese
2	tablespoons chopped fresh chives *or* scallions

1. Preheat the broiler. Heat 2 teaspoons oil in a large, ovenproof, nonstick skillet over medium heat. Add onion, garlic, rosemary and half of the tomato; cook, stirring, until the onion is tender, about 8 minutes.

2. Add potatoes and cook, stirring, until they start to brown, about 4 minutes. Add asparagus and cook until heated through. Remove the vegetables from the pan; season with salt and pepper.

3. Wipe out the pan, brush with the remaining 1 teaspoon oil, and return it to low heat.

4. Lightly whisk whole eggs, egg whites and cheese in a medium bowl. Add the vegetables to the egg mixture and pour into the pan, gently stirring to distribute the vegetables. Cook over low heat until the underside is light golden, 5 to 8 minutes.

5. Place the pan under the broiler and broil until the top of the frittata is puffed and golden brown, 1 to 2 minutes. Loosen the frittata and slide it onto a platter. Garnish with chives (or scallions) and the remaining chopped tomato.

MAKES **4** SERVINGS.

ACTIVE TIME: 35 minutes

TOTAL TIME: 35 minutes

PER SERVING:

186 calories; 10 g fat (3 g sat, 5 g mono); 216 mg cholesterol; 11 g carbohydrate; 14 g protein; 2 g fiber; 507 mg sodium; 419 mg potassium

NUTRITION BONUS:

Selenium (37% daily value)
Folate (24% dv)
Vitamin A & Vitamin C (20% dv)

H✖W   L⬇C   H♥H

An Organic Oasis on the Central Coast

One of California's oldest organic farms raises a traditional crop of white asparagus

Fifty years ago, the rich seaside plains west of Goleta, 10 miles outside Santa Barbara, were planted with fields, orange and avocado groves. Today, much of the surrounding landscape has been paved or built upon. But a 12-acre oasis remains. Established in 1895, Fairview Gardens is one of California's oldest organic farms and serves as a reminder of the way things were and an example of what's still possible.

The West Coast was once a hotbed for white asparagus, but with rising land and labor costs, most commercial white-asparagus farms are now based in Peru. At Fairview, whose mission is to preserve agricultural traditions, farmers still plant about an acre of white asparagus a year, carefully piling mounds of earth on the rows that will become white asparagus. Then they cover the mounds with plastic covers—tunnel-like archways that deflect the sun's rays. When the asparagus stalks break through the mounds in the spring, they are clipped at the very bottom of the mound—the result being white stalks where photosynthesis never had the opportunity to occur.

Santa Barbara's chefs and regular customers make up a loyal fan base, and the tender, mild-tasting white asparagus never lingers long on the farmstand's counters. "It is gone in a matter of minutes," says Fairview's Tiffany Cooper (*right*). Although agriculture struggles for survival amidst the developments that creep along the coast, Cooper knows that protecting the region's farming heritage requires a forgiving climate and people who will buy their produce. Goleta, California, offers both. —*Mark Aiken*

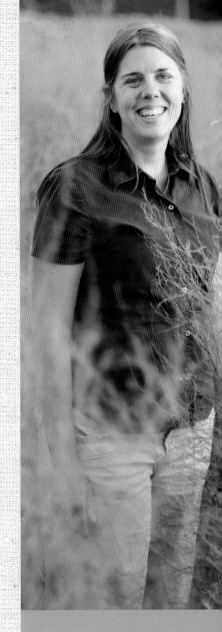

Fairview Gardens
Goleta, California
(805) 967-7369
fairviewgardens.org

Sun-Dried Tomato & Feta Stuffed Artichokes

Flavorful sun-dried tomatoes and tangy feta add depth to the stuffing for these artichokes.

STUFFING

2¼	cups coarse dry whole-wheat dry breadcrumbs (*see Note*)
1	cup finely crumbled feta cheese
⅔	cup oil-packed sun-dried tomatoes, rinsed and finely chopped
½	cup minced fresh basil
2	cloves garlic, minced
¼	teaspoon salt
¼	teaspoon freshly ground pepper
1	tablespoon extra-virgin olive oil

ARTICHOKES

4	large artichokes (2½-3½ pounds total)
6	teaspoons extra-virgin olive oil, divided
3	cloves garlic, minced
2	cups reduced-sodium chicken broth
1	tablespoon lemon juice

1. Preheat oven to 375°F.

2. **To prepare stuffing:** Combine breadcrumbs, feta, tomatoes, basil, garlic, salt, pepper and oil in a medium bowl.

3. **To prepare artichokes (*see photos, page 219*):** Cut off the top 1 inch of leaves from an artichoke. Remove the outer layer of small, tough leaves from the stem end. Snip all remaining spiky tips from the outer leaves. Cut off the stem to make a flat bottom. (Discard the stem.) Starting at the outer layers and progressing inward, pull the leaves apart to loosen. Pull open the leaves at the center until you see the spiky, lighter leaves around the heart. Pull out those lighter leaves to expose the fuzzy choke. Scoop out the choke with a melon baller or grapefruit spoon and discard. Repeat this step with the remaining artichokes.

4. Spoon ½ cup stuffing into the center of an artichoke. Stuff an additional ½ cup stuffing between the outer leaves, toward the base, using a small spoon. Repeat with the remaining artichokes and stuffing. Divide any remaining stuffing among the artichokes.

5. Heat 2 teaspoons oil in a Dutch oven over medium-high heat. Add garlic and cook, stirring often, until fragrant, about 30 seconds. Add broth and lemon juice; bring to a simmer. Carefully stand the artichokes upright in the pan. Drizzle each artichoke with 1 teaspoon oil.

6. Cover, transfer the pot to the oven and bake until tender when pierced down through the center with a knife, about 50 minutes. Uncover and continue baking until the stuffing is slightly browned, about 10 minutes more. Remove from the braising liquid and serve. Use the braising liquid for dipping if desired.

MAKES **4** SERVINGS.

ACTIVE TIME: 1 hour

TOTAL TIME: 2 hours

TO MAKE AHEAD: Cover and refrigerate stuffing (Step 2) for up to 1 day. Prep and stuff artichokes (Steps 3-4) up to 1 hour ahead.

PER SERVING:

412 calories; 18 g fat (6 g sat, 9 g mono); 28 mg cholesterol; 50 g carbohydrate; 16 g protein; 12 g fiber; 709 mg sodium; 757 mg potassium

NUTRITION BONUS:

Vitamin C (55% daily value)
Folate (27% dv)
Calcium & Iron (23% dv)
Potassium (22% dv)

H ⬆ F

NOTE: We like Ian's brand of **whole-wheat dry breadcrumbs** labeled "Panko breadcrumbs." Find them in the natural-foods section of large supermarkets. To make your own, trim crusts from whole-wheat bread. Tear bread into pieces and process in a food processor until coarse crumbs form. Spread on a baking sheet and bake at 250°F until crispy, about 15 minutes. One slice of fresh bread makes about ⅓ cup dry crumbs. Or use prepared coarse dry breadcrumbs.

Spring Vegetable Stew

Morel mushrooms are one of the treasures that can be foraged from the woods each spring. This rich, satisfying vegetarian entree actually calls for dried morels (you can use fresh if you're lucky enough to have some), which have a more intense smoky flavor. For a truly in-dulgent flair, omit the butter at the end and drizzle each serving with a little truffle oil.

½	ounce dried morels (*see Note*) *or* porcini mushrooms (¼ cup)
1	cup warm water
1	large lemon
6	large artichokes
1	tablespoon extra-virgin olive oil
4	medium leeks, white part only, cleaned and cut into ½-inch dice
1	cup baby carrots
12	cloves garlic, peeled
1	tablespoon finely chopped fresh thyme *or* 1 teaspoon dried
½	cup dry white wine
2½	cups reduced-sodium vegetable broth
½	teaspoon salt
1	cup baby lima beans, fresh *or* frozen
1	cup shelled fresh peas (about 1½ pounds unshelled) *or* frozen peas
4	teaspoons butter
	Freshly ground pepper to taste
¼	cup chopped fresh chives
¼	cup chopped fresh parsley

1. Cover mushrooms with warm water in a small bowl. Let stand for 30 minutes. Strain, reserving liquid. Rinse the mushrooms well under cold water; drain and chop. Strain the reserved liquid through a coffee filter or paper towel to remove any dirt.

2. Meanwhile, fill a large bowl with water; juice the lemon and, reserving half the juice, add the rest along with the lemon halves to the water. Pull off outer leaves from an artichoke. Using a small, sharp knife, remove the leaves down to the heart. Trim the bottom of the stem, then peel the stem. Scrape out the choke with a melon baller or spoon. Cut the heart into quarters and place in the lemon water to prevent browning. Repeat with the remaining artichokes.

3. Heat oil in a large deep skillet or Dutch oven over medium heat. Add leeks, carrots, garlic, thyme, mushrooms and the artichoke hearts; cook, stirring often, until the vegetables start to brown, about 5 minutes. Add wine and cook until slightly reduced, 2 to 3 minutes. Add broth, salt and the reserved mushroom liquid. Cover and cook over low heat until the artichoke hearts and carrots are almost tender, 30 to 40 minutes.

4. Stir in lima beans and peas. Increase heat to medium, cover and cook for 10 minutes more. Stir in butter and the reserved lemon juice. Season with pepper. Serve the stew in shallow bowls, garnished with chives and parsley.

MAKES 6 SERVINGS, ABOUT 1 CUP EACH.

ACTIVE TIME: 1 hour 20 minutes

TOTAL TIME: 2 hours

PER SERVING:

271 calories; 6 g fat (2 g sat, 2 g mono); 7 mg cholesterol; 45 g carbohydrate; 11 g protein; 14 g fiber; 646 mg sodium; 1,005 mg potassium

NUTRITION BONUS:

Vitamin A (110% daily value)
Vitamin C (90% dv)
Folate (50% dv)
Iron (30% dv)
Magnesium & Potassium (29% dv)
Calcium (15% dv)

H✖W   H↑F   H♥H

NOTE: **Morel mushrooms** are cone-shaped, with a honeycombed structure and a smoky flavor. Fresh wild morels are found at gourmet shops or specialty stores in the spring; they are sold dried year-round.

Sugar Snap Pea &
Cherry Tomato Pasta Salad

This fresh garden pasta salad has a creamy dressing that's made with a puree of low-fat cottage cheese and buttermilk rather than heavy mayonnaise. The recipe calls for cherry tomatoes, which tend to be some of the earliest to ripen, but other larger tomatoes from later in the season can be diced and used in the salad as well.

½	cup low-fat cottage cheese
½	cup nonfat buttermilk (*see Tip, page 239*)
1	tablespoon extra-virgin olive oil
2	tablespoons chopped fresh dill
2	tablespoons chopped fresh parsley
2½	tablespoons freshly grated Parmesan cheese
1	teaspoon freshly grated lemon zest
1	teaspoon lemon juice
¼	teaspoon salt
	Freshly ground pepper
8	ounces whole-wheat bowtie pasta
8	ounces fresh sugar snap peas, trimmed (about 2 cups; *see photo, page 228*)
2	cups red and yellow cherry tomatoes, halved
4	scallions, trimmed and thinly sliced

1. Bring a large pot of salted water to a boil for cooking pasta.

2. Meanwhile, puree cottage cheese until smooth in a blender or mini food processor. Add buttermilk and oil; process until smooth. Scrape into a storage container and stir in dill, parsley, Parmesan, lemon zest and lemon juice. Season with salt and pepper. Cover and set aside in the refrigerator.

3. Cook pasta in boiling water until just al dente, about 10 minutes. Add peas and cook until crisp-tender, about 1 minute. Drain and rinse under cold running water.

4. Place pasta and peas in a large storage container and toss with tomatoes and scallions. Season with salt and pepper.

5. Just before serving, toss salad with dressing.

MAKES **6** SERVINGS.

ACTIVE TIME: 30 minutes

TOTAL TIME: 30 minutes

TO MAKE AHEAD: Cover and refrigerate the dressing and salad separately for up to 8 hours.

PER SERVING:

213 calories; 4 g fat (1 g sat, 2 g mono); 3 mg cholesterol; 35 g carbohydrate; 11 g protein; 5 g fiber; 182 mg sodium; 217 mg potassium

NUTRITION BONUS:

Selenium (40% daily value)
Vitamin C (30% dv)
Vitamin A (20% dv)

H W   H F   H H

Caramelized Onion & White Bean Flatbread

Forget the traditional tomato or pesto sauce base that you'd normally put on a pizza. Here mashed beans are combined with herbs and cooked onion to make a tasty puree that can be spread right on top of the dough. Topped with plum tomatoes, sweet caramelized onions and some shredded Gouda, this tasty flatbread will have you rethinking pizza toppings. This pizza is wonderful with fresh spring sweet onions, but works with whatever onions you have on hand any time of the year.

3	tablespoons extra-virgin olive oil
1	large onion, thinly sliced lengthwise
¼	teaspoon salt
20	ounces prepared whole-wheat pizza dough (*see Note*), thawed if frozen
2	tablespoons minced fresh oregano *or* 2 teaspoons dried
½	teaspoon freshly ground pepper
1	15-ounce can white beans, rinsed (*see Tip, page 239*)
3	tablespoons water
2	teaspoons white-wine vinegar
2	plum tomatoes, thinly sliced
1	cup finely shredded smoked Gouda *or* Cheddar cheese
2	tablespoons pepitas (*see Note*), optional

1. Place oven rack in the lowest position; preheat to 450°F. Coat a large noninsulated baking sheet with cooking spray.

2. Combine oil, onion and salt in a medium saucepan. Cover and cook over medium-high heat, stirring often, until the onion is softened, 5 to 7 minutes. Reduce heat to medium-low, uncover and cook, stirring occasionally, until very soft and golden, 5 to 8 minutes more.

3. Meanwhile, roll out dough on a lightly floured surface to the size of the baking sheet. Transfer to the baking sheet. Bake until puffed and lightly crisped on the bottom, 8 to 10 minutes.

4. Stir oregano and pepper into the onion. Transfer half the onion to a small bowl. Add beans to the remaining onion; cook over medium heat, stirring often, until heated through, 2 to 3 minutes. Transfer the bean mixture to a food processor, add water and vinegar and pulse until a coarse paste forms.

5. Spread the bean paste over the pizza crust. Top with the reserved onion, tomatoes, cheese and pepitas, if using. Bake on the bottom rack until the crust is crispy and golden and the cheese is melted, 11 to 13 minutes. Slice and serve.

MAKES 6 SERVINGS.

ACTIVE TIME: 30 minutes

TOTAL TIME: 45 minutes

PER SERVING:

365 calories; 11 g fat (3 g sat, 5 g mono); 10 mg cholesterol; 51 g carbohydrate; 13 g protein; 6 g fiber; 576 mg sodium; 296 mg potassium

NUTRITION BONUS:

Fiber (24% daily value)

H↑F H♥H

NOTES: Look for **whole-wheat pizza-dough** balls at your supermarket. Check the ingredient list to make sure the dough doesn't contain any hydrogenated oils. Or visit *eatingwell.com* for an easy pizza-dough recipe.

Hulled pumpkin seeds, also known as **pepitas**, are dusky green and have a delicate nutty flavor. They can be found in the natural-food or bulk sections of many supermarkets.

Chicken & Asparagus with Melted Gruyère

For this elegant dish, boneless chicken breast and asparagus are smothered in a luxurious white-wine sauce with just the right amount of melted Gruyère cheese. Tarragon and lemon add a delicious light flavor that is perfect with asparagus.

8	ounces asparagus, trimmed and cut into 1-inch pieces
2/3	cup reduced-sodium chicken broth
2	teaspoons plus 1/4 cup all-purpose flour, divided
4	boneless, skinless chicken breasts (1-1 1/4 pounds), trimmed
1/4	teaspoon salt
1/2	teaspoon freshly ground pepper
1	tablespoon canola oil
1	shallot, thinly sliced
1/2	cup white wine
1/3	cup reduced-fat sour cream
1	tablespoon chopped fresh tarragon *or* 1 teaspoon dried
2	teaspoons lemon juice
2/3	cup shredded Gruyère cheese

1. Place a steamer basket in a large saucepan, add 1 inch of water and bring to a boil. Add asparagus; cover and steam for 3 minutes. Uncover, remove from the heat and set aside.

2. Whisk broth and 2 teaspoons flour in a small bowl until smooth. Set aside.

3. Place the remaining 1/4 cup flour in a shallow dish. Sprinkle chicken with salt and pepper and dredge both sides in the flour, shaking off any excess.

4. Heat oil in a large skillet over medium heat. Add the chicken and cook until golden brown, 3 to 4 minutes per side, adjusting heat as needed to prevent scorching. Transfer to a plate and cover to keep warm.

5. Add shallot, wine and the reserved broth mixture to the pan; cook over medium heat, stirring, until thickened, about 2 minutes. Reduce heat to medium-low; stir in sour cream, tarragon, lemon juice and the reserved asparagus until combined. Return the chicken to the pan and turn to coat with the sauce. Sprinkle cheese on top of each piece of chicken, cover and continue cooking until the cheese is melted, about 2 minutes.

MAKES **4** SERVINGS.

ACTIVE TIME: 35 minutes

TOTAL TIME: 35 minutes

PER SERVING:

306 calories; 15 g fat (6 g sat, 6 g mono); 91 mg cholesterol; 7 g carbohydrate; 31 g protein; 1 g fiber; 298 mg sodium; 343 mg potassium

NUTRITION BONUS:

Selenium (36% daily value)
Calcium (25% dv)

L↓C

Spice-Rubbed Game Hens with Rhubarb-Date Chutney

Tart rhubarb simmered in cider vinegar with chopped dates, brown sugar and cinna-mon makes an excellent chutney to accompany tender game hens. The chutney would be delightful with pork as well. It freezes well, so if you like, you can make extra to enjoy throughout the year.

ACTIVE TIME: 20 minutes

TOTAL TIME: 1 hour 20 minutes

EQUIPMENT: Kitchen string (optional)

PER SERVING:

250 calories; 5 g fat (1 g sat, 2 g mono); 146 mg cholesterol; 17 g carbohydrate; 33 g protein; 1 g fiber; 160 mg sodium; 551 mg potassium.

NUTRITION BONUS:

Selenium (41% daily value)

H✳W L↓C H♥H

NOTE: Cornish game hens, a naturally smaller breed of chicken, are a cross between Plymouth Rock and Cornish chickens. Usually weighing less than 2 pounds, one bird will comfortably serve two. If you can't find fresh hens, look for them in the freezer section. To retain moisture, hens should be prepared with the skin on, but to reduce fat and calories, remove the skin before eating.

HENS		CHUTNEY	
1	orange	1/3	cup cider vinegar
4	Cornish game hens, about 1½ pounds each (*see Note*)	1/4	cup packed light brown sugar
		1	tablespoon minced fresh ginger
1	tablespoon light brown sugar	1/4	teaspoon ground cinnamon
1/4	teaspoon ground cinnamon	2	cups fresh rhubarb, trimmed and sliced into 1-inch pieces
1/2	teaspoon kosher salt		
1/4	teaspoon freshly ground pepper	1/2	cup pitted dates, chopped

1. **To prepare hens:** Preheat oven to 400°F. Using a vegetable peeler, remove a 2-inch strip of zest from the orange, then cut the orange in half, squeezing juice out of one half and cutting the remaining half into 4 wedges. Place 2 tablespoons juice and the strip of zest in a medium saucepan for Step 4. Tuck an orange wedge into the cavity of each game hen. Sprinkle the remaining orange juice over the hens and place breast side up in a large roasting pan, leaving plenty of space between them.

2. Stir together 1 tablespoon brown sugar, cinnamon, salt and pepper. Rub the mixture over the hens and tie the legs together with kitchen string, if desired.

3. Roast the hens until the juices run clear and an instant-read thermometer registers 165°F when inserted into the thickest part of the thigh, about 1 hour. Let rest for 5 minutes before serving.

4. **Meanwhile, to prepare chutney:** Add vinegar, 1/4 cup brown sugar, ginger and cinnamon to the orange juice and zest in the saucepan. Bring to a boil over medium-high heat. Reduce heat to low and simmer for 5 minutes. Add rhubarb and dates, increase heat to medium-high and return to a boil. Reduce heat to low and simmer gently until the rhubarb is tender, about 5 minutes. Remove from the heat and let cool. Just before serving, remove orange zest.

5. To serve, remove string (if necessary) and skin from each hen. Turn breast-side down and slice in half lengthwise using a large heavy knife, cutting straight through to the breast side. Serve each portion with 1/4 cup of the chutney.

MAKES **8** SERVINGS.

A ½-cup serving of radishes contains 14% of the recommended daily value for vitamin C and only 9 calories.

RADISHES

Beef Tataki

Tataki is a typical Japanese preparation in which beef or fish is seared on the outside, left very rare inside, thinly sliced and served with a citrusy soy sauce. In this version, a springy salad of crisp radishes and carrot matchsticks combined with sliced onion provides textural contrast to the flavorful steak. Serve this dish over a bed of buckwheat soba noodles to make it a meal.

1	cup matchstick-cut red radishes *or* peeled daikon radish (*see Note*)
1	cup matchstick-cut carrots
½	cup thinly sliced onion
¼	cup reduced-sodium soy sauce
2	tablespoons plus 2 teaspoons lemon juice
2	tablespoons finely chopped scallions
2	teaspoons finely grated fresh ginger
1	pound boneless sirloin steak, ¾-1 inch thick, trimmed
¼	teaspoon salt
¼	teaspoon freshly ground pepper
2	teaspoons canola oil

1. Place radishes (or daikon), carrot and onion in a medium bowl. Cover with cold water and let soak for 5 minutes. Drain.

2. Combine soy sauce, lemon juice, scallions and ginger in a small bowl. Add 2 tablespoons of the mixture to the drained vegetables and toss. Set aside the remaining sauce.

3. Season steak on both sides with salt and pepper. Heat oil in a large nonstick skillet over medium-high heat. Cook the steak 3 to 4 minutes per side for medium-rare. Let rest on a cutting board for 5 minutes, then thinly slice and serve with the vegetables, drizzled with the reserved sauce.

MAKES 4 SERVINGS.

ACTIVE TIME: 40 minutes

TOTAL TIME: 40 minutes

PER SERVING:

196 calories; 7 g fat (2 g sat, 3 g mono); 42 mg cholesterol; 8 g carbohydrate; 24 g protein; 2 g fiber; 617 mg sodium; 551 mg potassium

NUTRITION BONUS:

Vitamin A (110% daily value)
Zinc (27% dv)
Vitamin C (20% dv)

H�W L↓C H♥H

NOTE: **Daikon** is a long, white radish; it can be found in Asian groceries and most natural-foods stores.

Steak & Purple-Potato Salad

This hearty steak and potato salad is inspired by salpicón, *a favorite dish in Chile. The purple potatoes add vibrant color but you can substitute any young "new" potatoes that are harvested early in the season—even small fingerlings would work. Serve on a bed of spicy mesclun greens to round out the meal. This recipe can easily be doubled.*

1	teaspoon lime juice
1	teaspoon chili powder
½	teaspoon salt, divided
1	clove garlic, mashed into a paste
8	ounces sirloin steak, trimmed
¾	pound small purple potatoes (*see Tip*), scrubbed
2	tablespoons sherry vinegar
1	tablespoon extra-virgin olive oil
½	teaspoon ground cumin
¼	teaspoon freshly ground pepper
4	large radishes, sliced
3	scallions, thinly sliced
¼	cup chopped fresh cilantro

1. Mix lime juice, chili powder, ¼ teaspoon salt and garlic in a small bowl to form a paste; rub onto both sides of steak. Refrigerate the steak.

2. Place potatoes in a large pot, cover with water and bring to a boil over high heat. Cook until tender when pierced with a fork, 15 to 20 minutes, depending on the size of the potatoes. Drain, let cool for 10 minutes, then quarter.

3. While the potatoes cool, preheat grill or grill pan over medium-high heat. Oil the grill rack (*see photo, page 239*) or pan. Grill the steak, turning once, until an instant-read meat thermometer inserted into the thickest part registers 140°F, about 10 minutes total on the grill or 16 to 20 minutes in a grill pan. Let rest for 5 minutes, then cut into ¼-inch-thick slices.

4. Whisk vinegar, oil, cumin, pepper and the remaining ¼ teaspoon salt in a large bowl. Add the steak and any accumulated juices, the potatoes, radishes, scallions and cilantro; gently toss to coat.

MAKES 2 SERVINGS, ABOUT 2½ CUPS EACH.

ACTIVE TIME: 15 minutes

TOTAL TIME: 40 minutes

TO MAKE AHEAD: Prepare through Step 3, cover and refrigerate for up to 1 day. Toss the steak and potatoes with the dressing and vegetables (Step 4) just before serving.

PER SERVING:

360 calories; 12 g fat (3 g sat, 7 g mono); 42 mg cholesterol; 34 g carbohydrate; 27 g protein; 4 g fiber; 660 mg sodium; 413 mg potassium

NUTRITION BONUS:

Vitamin C (70% daily value)
Zinc (27% dv)
Iron (20% dv)
Vitamin A (15% dv)

H ♥ H

TIP: Look for **purple potatoes** in well-stocked markets or substitute small yellow-fleshed potatoes, such as Yukon Golds.

Vietnamese Steak Salad

Crisp spring greens, crunchy carrots and cucumbers are tossed with plenty of fresh herbs (a signature of Vietnamese cuisine) and a savory lemongrass vinaigrette in this refreshing salad. Topped with slices of grilled, marinated flank steak that are reminiscent of the street food of Hanoi, this dish makes an excellent lunch or light supper. Add a few slices of crusty baguette (also a Vietnamese tradition) to finish the plate.

ACTIVE TIME: 30 minutes

TOTAL TIME: 4½ hours (including 4 hours marinating time)

TO MAKE AHEAD: Marinate the steak (Step 1) for up to 8 hours. The vinaigrette (Step 2) will keep in the refrigerator for up to 1 day.

PER SERVING:

224 calories; 8 g fat (3 g sat, 3 g mono); 48 mg cholesterol; 10 g carbohydrate; 28 g protein; 2 g fiber; 715 mg sodium; 749 mg potassium.

NUTRITION BONUS:

Vitamin A (127% daily value)
Vitamin C (63% dv)
Selenium (39% dv)
Zinc (32% dv)
Potassium (21% dv)
Iron (18% dv)

H✻W L↓C

NOTE: Fish sauce is a pungent Southeast Asian condiment made from salted, fermented fish. Find it in the Asian section of large supermarkets and in Asian specialty markets. We use Thai Kitchen fish sauce, lower in sodium than other brands (1,190 mg per tablespoon), in our nutritional analyses.

STEAK

1	tablespoon lime juice
1	teaspoon fish sauce (*see Note*)
1	teaspoon reduced-sodium soy sauce
½	teaspoon hot chile oil
12	ounces flank steak, trimmed

SALAD

8	cups watercress *or* spinach, trimmed, rinsed and dried
1	cucumber, peeled, seeded and thinly sliced
1	carrot, cut into matchsticks
¼	cup fresh cilantro leaves
¼	cup fresh mint leaves

LEMONGRASS VINAIGRETTE

¾	cup reduced-sodium chicken broth
2	small stalks lemongrass, trimmed and chopped
4	tablespoons chopped shallot, divided
2	tablespoons lime juice
1	tablespoon fish sauce
1	tablespoon reduced-sodium soy sauce
1½	teaspoons sugar
1	teaspoon hot chile oil
2	tablespoons finely chopped fresh cilantro
2	tablespoons finely chopped fresh mint

1. **To prepare steak:** Combine lime juice, fish sauce, soy sauce and chile oil in a large sealable plastic bag. Add steak and seal the bag, turning to coat the meat with the marinade. Marinate in the refrigerator, turning the bag occasionally, for 4 hours.

2. **Meanwhile, prepare vinaigrette:** Combine broth, lemongrass and 2 tablespoons shallot in a small saucepan. Cook over medium heat until reduced to ¼ cup, about 10 minutes. Remove from the heat and let stand for 10 minutes. Strain into a small bowl, discarding solids. Add the remaining 2 tablespoons shallot, lime juice, fish sauce, soy sauce, sugar and chile oil; whisk to combine. Just before serving, stir in cilantro and mint.

3. Preheat grill to high.

4. Remove the steak from the marinade (discard marinade). Grill the steak, 4 to 5 minutes per side for medium-rare. Transfer to a clean cutting board and let rest for 5 minutes. Slice thinly on the diagonal, across the grain.

5. **To prepare salad:** Toss watercress (or spinach), cucumber, carrot, cilantro and mint with ½ cup of the vinaigrette in a large shallow bowl. Arrange the steak over the greens. Spoon the remaining vinaigrette over the top and serve.

MAKES **4** SERVINGS.

Smoky Pea & Artichoke Pasta

In California, spring is the peak of the artichoke harvest. However, artichokes continue to be available throughout the year, with a second major harvest in the fall. Here they are combined with smoky ham and fresh peas to create a pasta dish that tastes richer than it actually is. Serve with a green salad with a simple dressing of lemon juice and extra-virgin olive oil.

1	lemon, halved
2	large artichokes
1	tablespoon extra-virgin olive oil
1	clove garlic, minced
2	cups shelled fresh peas (about 3 pounds unshelled) *or* frozen peas
½	cup thinly sliced prosciutto *or* ham (2 ounces)
1	14-ounce can reduced-sodium chicken broth
2	tablespoons finely chopped fresh parsley
¼	teaspoon salt
	Freshly ground pepper to taste
1	pound whole-wheat orecchiette *or* penne
½	cup freshly grated Parmesan cheese, divided

1. Put a large pot of water on to boil for cooking pasta.

2. Fill a medium bowl with cold water. Squeeze the lemon juice into the water and add lemon halves. Snap off all the outer leaves of the artichokes. With a paring knife, trim the bottom ¼ inch off the stems. Pare away the fibrous green portions, down to the hearts. With a melon baller or spoon, scoop out the fuzzy chokes. Cut stems and hearts into ¼-inch-thick slices and drop into lemon water.

3. Heat oil in a large nonstick skillet over medium heat. Add garlic and cook, stirring, until fragrant, about 1 minute. Drain the artichokes and add to the pan. Cook, stirring, until lightly browned, 4 to 5 minutes. Add peas, ham and broth. Cover and simmer until the artichokes are tender, 8 to 10 minutes. Stir in parsley and season with salt and pepper.

4. Meanwhile, cook pasta until just tender, 8 to 10 minutes or according to package directions. Drain and place in a large warmed bowl. Add the pea mixture and ¼ cup Parmesan and toss. Pass remaining cheese separately.

MAKES **6** SERVINGS.

ACTIVE TIME: 35 minutes

TOTAL TIME: 35 minutes

PER SERVING:

421 calories; 8 g fat (2 g sat, 2 g mono); 15 mg cholesterol; 67 g carbohydrate; 20 g protein; 10 g fiber; 588 mg sodium; 434 mg potassium

NUTRITION BONUS:

Vitamin C (41% daily value)
Calcium (18% dv)
Iron (16% dv)

H↑F H♥H

Grilled Pork Tenderloin & Apricot Salad

If you're an apricot lover, look no further. This grilled pork dish offers a triple hit of the fruit with an apricot preserve glaze for the tenderloin plus a grilled apricot and watercress salad with an apricot-spiked vinaigrette. Serve with grilled whole-grain country bread and a chilled Chardonnay, which will harmonize beautifully with the smoky-sweetness of grilled apricots.

1	pound pork tenderloin, trimmed
1/2	teaspoon salt, divided
1/4	teaspoon freshly ground pepper, plus more to taste
3	tablespoons apricot preserves, divided
4	ripe but firm fresh apricots *or* nectarines, halved and pitted
2	tablespoons white-wine vinegar
2	tablespoons minced shallot
2	tablespoons canola oil
1	4- to 5-ounce bag watercress *or* baby arugula (about 8 cups)

1. Preheat grill to high.

2. Sprinkle pork with 1/4 teaspoon salt and pepper. Oil the grill rack (*see photo, page 239*). Grill the pork, turning occasionally, for 10 minutes. Brush the pork with 2 tablespoons preserves and continue grilling until an instant-read thermometer inserted into the thickest part registers 145°F, 2 to 5 minutes more. Grill apricot (or nectarine) halves on the coolest part of the grill, turning occasionally, until tender and marked, about 4 minutes. Transfer the pork and apricots to a clean cutting board and let rest for 5 minutes.

3. Meanwhile, whisk the remaining 1 tablespoon preserves, vinegar, shallot, oil, 1/4 teaspoon salt and pepper to taste in a large bowl. Cut the fruit into wedges and add to the dressing along with watercress (or arugula); toss to coat. Thinly slice the pork. Serve the salad with the sliced pork.

MAKES 4 SERVINGS.

ACTIVE TIME: 40 minutes

TOTAL TIME: 40 minutes

PER SERVING:

247 calories; 10 g fat (1 g sat, 5 g mono); 74 mg cholesterol; 15 g carbohydrate; 25 g protein; 1 g fiber; 363 mg sodium; 653 mg potassium

NUTRITION BONUS:

Selenium (47% daily value)
Vitamin A (40% dv)
Vitamin C (30% dv)
Potassium (18% dv)

H✕W L↓C H♥H

Onions contain several antioxidant compounds that have been linked to improving blood pressure and heart health.

ONIONS

Jumbo Prawns & Balsamic-Orange Onions

The arrival of the first sweet onions of the season is an event to be celebrated, and this dish does just that. The onions are slow-cooked in the oven—which brings out even more sweetness—and then combined with both orange zest and juice, plus some balsamic vinegar to balance the flavors. Jumbo shrimp are added here, but sweet scallops would be delicious as well. Serve with warmed flour tortillas so this luscious dish can be eaten taco-style.

2	large sweet onions, sliced
2	tablespoons extra-virgin olive oil
1	teaspoon kosher salt
1	teaspoon freshly grated orange zest
	Juice of 1 orange
2	tablespoons balsamic vinegar
1	teaspoon finely chopped fresh rosemary *or* ¼ teaspoon dried
	Pinch of crushed red pepper
12	raw shrimp (6-8 per pound; *see Note, page 241*), peeled and deveined
¼	cup sliced scallion greens

1. Preheat oven to 400°F.

2. Toss onions, oil and salt in a 9-by-13-inch baking pan until coated. Cover with foil. Bake until softened and juicy, about 45 minutes.

3. Remove foil, stir and continue baking, uncovered, until the onions around the edges of the pan are lightly golden, 25 to 30 minutes.

4. Stir in orange zest, orange juice, vinegar, rosemary and crushed red pepper. Bake until most of the liquid has evaporated, about 30 minutes.

5. Stir in shrimp and bake until cooked through, 20 to 25 minutes. Stir in scallion greens and serve.

MAKES **4** SERVINGS.

ACTIVE TIME: 25 minutes

TOTAL TIME: 2 hours 20 minutes

PER SERVING:

314 calories; 10 g fat (2 g sat, 6 g mono); 259 mg cholesterol; 18 g carbohydrate; 36 g protein; 2 g fiber; 550 mg sodium; 581 mg potassium

NUTRITION BONUS:

Vitamin C (40% daily value)
Iron (26% dv)
Magnesium (20% dv)
Potassium (17% dv)

H✖W L⬇C H♥H

Thai Red Curry Mussels

Watercress thrives in the damp meadows and saturated streambeds that are typical of late spring. It is prized in Asian cuisine for its peppery flavor and in this dish stands up to the sweet spiciness of the mussels in a coconut-laced red curry sauce. If you can find it in your market, use Thai basil for the garnish—it adds a unique sweet anise flavor that will make the dish taste all the more authentic.

ACTIVE TIME: 40 minutes

TOTAL TIME: 40 minutes

PER SERVING:

273 calories; 13 g fat (6 g sat, 2 g mono); 48 mg cholesterol; 16 g carbohydrate; 24 g protein; 1 g fiber; 582 mg sodium; 438 mg potassium

NUTRITION BONUS:

Selenium (108% daily value)
Vitamin A & Vitamin C (60% dv)
Iron (35% dv)
Folate (19% dv)
Good source of omega-3s

L↓C

2	teaspoons peanut oil *or* canola oil
2	medium cloves garlic, minced
2	scallions, thinly sliced, whites and greens separated
	Zest and juice of 1 lime
1-2	teaspoons Thai red curry paste (*see Note*)
1	14-ounce can "lite" coconut milk
1	tablespoon brown sugar
2	teaspoons fish sauce (*see Note*)
4	pounds mussels, scrubbed and debearded (*see Tip*)
6	cups trimmed watercress (1-2 bunches) *or* trimmed spinach
2	tablespoons thinly sliced fresh basil for garnish

1. Heat oil in a large high-sided skillet or Dutch oven over medium-high heat. Add garlic, scallion whites, lime zest and curry paste to taste; cook until fragrant and the paste is sizzling, 1 to 3 minutes. Add lime juice, coconut milk, brown sugar and fish sauce. Bring to a boil and let cook for 2 minutes.

2. Add mussels, return to a simmer, cover and cook for 6 minutes. Spread watercress (or spinach) over the mussels, cover and cook until slightly wilted, about 4 minutes; stir into the mussels. (Discard any unopened mussels.) Serve garnished with scallion greens and basil.

MAKES 4 SERVINGS.

NOTE: **Red curry paste** and **fish sauce**, typical Thai ingredients, can be found in the Asian food section of large supermarkets.

TIP: To clean **mussels**, scrub with a stiff brush under cold running water. Scrape off any barnacles using the shell of another mussel. Pull off the fuzzy "beard" from each one (some mussels may not have a beard). (*See photo, page 239.*)

Sautéed Spinach with Red Onion, Bacon & Blue Cheese

Bacon and blue cheese transform spinach into a stellar side. Popeye would be jealous.

2	teaspoons extra-virgin olive oil
½	cup thinly sliced red onion
2	cloves garlic, minced
1	10-ounce bag fresh spinach, tough stems removed
2	strips center-cut bacon, cooked and crumbled
1	tablespoon crumbled blue cheese

Heat oil in a large nonstick skillet or Dutch oven over medium-high heat. Add onion and cook, stirring, until beginning to soften, about 1 minute. Add garlic and cook, stirring, until fragrant, about 30 seconds more. Add spinach and cook, stirring, until just wilted, about 2 minutes. Remove from heat; stir in bacon and sprinkle cheese on top. Serve immediately.

MAKES 2 SERVINGS.

ACTIVE TIME: 15 minutes

TOTAL TIME: 15 minutes

PER SERVING:

127 calories; 8 g fat (3 g sat, 6 g mono); 11 mg cholesterol; 8 g carbohydrate; 7 g protein; 4 g fiber; 300 mg sodium; 796 mg potassium

NUTRITION BONUS:

Vitamin A (170% daily value)
Folate (44% dv), Vitamin C (40% dv)
Magnesium (28% dv)
Potassium (22% dv), Iron (20% dv)
Calcium (15% dv)

H✕W L↓C H♥H

Sautéed Spinach with Pine Nuts & Golden Raisins

Pine nuts and sweet golden raisins brighten up sautéed spinach, making any "eat your spinach" urgings a thing of the past.

2	teaspoons extra-virgin olive oil	2	teaspoons balsamic vinegar
2	tablespoons golden raisins	⅛	teaspoon salt
1	tablespoon pine nuts	1	tablespoon shaved Parmesan cheese
2	cloves garlic, minced		Freshly ground pepper to taste
1	10-ounce bag fresh spinach, tough stems removed		

Heat oil in a large nonstick skillet or Dutch oven over medium-high heat. Add raisins, pine nuts and garlic; cook, stirring, until fragrant, about 30 seconds. Add spinach and cook, stirring, until just wilted, about 2 minutes. Remove from heat; stir in vinegar and salt. Serve immediately, sprinkled with Parmesan and pepper.

MAKES 2 SERVINGS.

ACTIVE TIME: 15 minutes

TOTAL TIME: 15 minutes

PER SERVING:

154 calories; 9 g fat (2 g sat, 5 g mono); 2 mg cholesterol; 15 g carbohydrate; 6 g protein; 4 g fiber; 311 mg sodium; 808 mg potassium

NUTRITION BONUS:

Vitamin A (170% daily value)
Folate (42% dv)
Vitamin C (40% dv)
Magnesium (29% dv)
Potassium (23% dv)
Calcium & Iron (20% dv)

H✕W L↓C H♥H

For only 17 calories, a ½-cup serving of cooked dandelion greens provides 150% of the recommended daily value for vitamin A, which helps keep your immune system strong.

DANDELION GREENS

Warm Dandelion Greens

Dandelion greens are a favorite springtime wild edible, but if you don't get them early enough, they begin to toughen. Here, the peppery-tasting leaves are simply sautéed with olive oil and garlic and then tossed with balsamic vinegar plus some crisped Canadian bacon. If large, store-bought dandelion greens are used, blanch them for 1 to 2 minutes in boiling water before sautéing.

2	ounces lean back bacon *or* Canadian bacon (three 3-by-¼-inch slices), diced
2	teaspoons extra-virgin olive oil
1	clove garlic, minced
12	cups young dandelion greens, rinsed well and briefly shaken dry
2	tablespoons balsamic *or* rice-wine vinegar
6	dandelion flowers and 12 small, whole leaves for garnish (optional)

1. Fry bacon in a large cast-iron skillet or Dutch oven over medium heat until edges curl, 2 to 3 minutes. Remove from the pan and drain on paper towels.

2. Pour off excess fat from the pan and add oil. Add garlic and cook, stirring occasionally, until light brown, 1 to 2 minutes. Add still-damp greens, stir to coat them with the oil, cover pan and steam until just limp, about 3 minutes.

3. Add vinegar and the cooked bacon, toss lightly and serve garnished with flowers and small leaves (if using).

MAKES 6 SERVINGS.

ACTIVE TIME: 20 minutes

TOTAL TIME: 20 minutes

PER SERVING:

119 calories; 6 g fat (2 g sat, 3 g mono); 10 mg cholesterol; 11 g carbohydrate; 7 g protein; 4 g fiber; 303 mg sodium; 496 mg potassium

NUTRITION BONUS:

Vitamin A (109% daily value)
Vitamin C (61% dv)
Calcium (21% dv)
Iron (20% dv)

Grilled Artichokes

Artichokes are most often served steamed, but grilling them adds a smoky dimension to their flavor. If you can get them, first-of-the-season baby artichokes will yield extra-tender results—double the number of artichokes and reduce the cooking time as needed.

2	lemons
4	large artichokes (3-3½ pounds total)
1	tablespoon extra-virgin olive oil
¼	teaspoon salt
	Freshly ground pepper to taste

1. **To prepare artichokes (*see photos, page 219*):** Fill a Dutch oven with water; add the juice of 1 lemon. Trim leaves from the top of an artichoke. Remove the outer layer(s) of leaves from the stem end and snip all remaining spiky tips from the outer leaves. Trim an inch off the bottom of the stem and use a vegetable peeler to remove the fibrous outer layer. As each artichoke is prepared, drop it into the lemon water to prevent it from turning brown.

2. When all the artichokes are prepared, cover the pan and bring to a boil. Boil until the base of the stem can be pierced with a fork, 12 to 15 minutes. Transfer to a cutting board and let stand until cool enough to handle, about 10 minutes.

3. Meanwhile, preheat grill to medium. Slice the artichokes in half lengthwise. Scoop out the choke and first few inner layers in the center until the bottom is revealed. Brush each half with oil and sprinkle with salt and pepper. Grill the artichokes until tender and lightly charred, about 5 minutes per side. Transfer to a serving platter, squeeze half a lemon over them and garnish with the remaining lemon half cut into 4 wedges. Serve warm, at room temperature or chilled.

MAKES 4 SERVINGS.

ACTIVE TIME: 30 minutes

TOTAL TIME: 50 minutes

TO MAKE AHEAD: Grilled artichokes will keep, covered, in the refrigerator for up to 1 day and may be served chilled.

PER SERVING:

109 calories; 4 g fat (1 g sat, 3 g mono); 0 mg cholesterol; 17 g carbohydrate; 5 g protein; 9 g fiber; 298 mg sodium; 604 mg potassium

NUTRITION BONUS:

Vitamin C (35% daily value)
Folate (27% dv)
Magnesium (24% dv)
Potassium (17% dv)

H✕W L↓C H↑F H♥H

VARIATION: For **boiled artichokes**, add 5 minutes to the cooking time in Step 2. Serve whole or cut in half and scoop out the chokes.

New Potatoes & Peas

This simple side is a triple treat of spring delights: new potatoes, spring onions and fresh green peas. The flavors are so delicate that all that's needed to finish the dish is just a touch of butter, a few grinds of black pepper and some chopped fresh mint.

1	pound new potatoes, scrubbed
12	spring onions *or* scallions, bulbs whole, tops chopped (optional)
2	cups shelled fresh peas (about 3 pounds unshelled) *or* frozen peas
2	teaspoons butter
1/2	teaspoon coarsely ground pepper
2	tablespoons chopped fresh mint, or more to taste

Place potatoes and onions (or scallions, if using) in a small saucepan, barely cover with water and bring to a boil. Cook over medium heat until just tender, 5 to 6 minutes. Add peas, cover and cook until tender, about 1 minute. Drain, add butter, pepper and mint. Heat for 1 minute, tossing gently.

MAKES **6** SERVINGS.

ACTIVE TIME: 20 minutes

TOTAL TIME: 20 minutes

PER SERVING:

98 calories; 1 g fat (1 g sat, 0 g mono); 3 mg cholesterol; 17 g carbohydrate; 4 g protein; 3 g fiber; 57 mg sodium; 470 mg potassium

NUTRITION BONUS:

Vitamin C (45% daily value)
Vitamin A (20% dv)

H✖W L⬇C H♥H

RADISHES

ACTIVE TIME: 20 minutes

TOTAL TIME: 20 minutes

TO MAKE AHEAD: Prepare through Step 1, cover and refrigerate for up to 1 day. Stir in the radishes just before serving.

PER SERVING:

43 calories; 0 g fat (0 g sat, 0 g mono); 0 mg cholesterol; 11 g carbohydrate; 0 g protein; 1 g fiber; 80 mg sodium; 135 mg potassium

NUTRITION BONUS:

Vitamin C (35% daily value)

H✖W L⬇C H♥H

Mango-Radish Salsa

Crisp, peppery diced radishes, sweet, juicy mango and tart lime juice have opposing flavors that come together here to create salsa nirvana. Serve with grilled fish, steak or chicken or just put out a dish of it with some crisp baked corn chips.

3	cups diced mango (about 2 large)
1/4	cup chopped cilantro
1	tablespoon lime juice
1/4	teaspoon salt
1	cup diced radishes (about 1 bunch)

1. Toss mangoes, cilantro, lime juice and salt in a bowl.

2. Stir in radishes just before serving.

MAKES **8** SERVINGS, 1/2 CUP EACH.

Double Strawberry Pie

What better way to showcase this beautiful fruit than to have a strawberry pie...topped
with strawberries. A light cornmeal-and-flour crust uses low-fat milk and just enough
butter to give it the richness you want. Serve the pie with a dab of reduced-fat sour
cream to balance the sweetness.

FILLING

2½	pints fresh strawberries
¾	cup sugar
⅓	cup lemon juice
1	cup water
2	teaspoons unflavored gelatin

CRUST

½	cup all-purpose flour
¼	cup cornmeal
2	tablespoons sugar
¾	teaspoon baking powder
¼	teaspoon salt
2	tablespoons cold butter, cut into pieces
3	tablespoons low-fat milk

1. **To prepare filling:** Choose 2 cups of strawberries as close to the same size as possible; hull and set aside. Hull and dice the remaining berries.

2. Mix the diced berries, ¾ cup sugar and lemon juice in a bowl. Let stand for 20 minutes. Drain the berries well in a sieve set over a medium saucepan. Return the berries to the bowl and set aside.

3. Add water and gelatin to the strawberry liquid in the saucepan and heat over medium heat, stirring, until the gelatin is completely dissolved. Remove from the heat and stir into the reserved diced berries. Refrigerate, stirring occasionally, until the filling has thickened slightly and mounds when dropped from a spoon, 3 to 4 hours.

4. **To prepare crust:** Preheat oven to 350°F.

5. Stir together flour, cornmeal, 2 tablespoons sugar, baking powder and salt in a large bowl. Cut butter into dry ingredients using a pastry cutter, 2 forks or your fingers until crumbly. Stir in milk with a fork, 1 tablespoon at a time, just until dough comes together.

6. Turn dough out onto a floured surface and knead 7 to 8 times. Roll out into an 11-inch circle with a floured rolling pin. Drape dough over rolling pin and fit into a 9-inch pie pan. Fold edges under and crimp with the tines of a fork.

7. Prick bottom of crust with a fork and line with foil or parchment paper. Fill with pie weights (or use rice or dried beans). Bake for 10 minutes. Remove foil and weights and bake until lightly browned, 8 to 10 minutes more. Place on a wire rack to cool.

8. **To assemble pie:** Arrange reserved whole berries, pointed ends up, in crust. Spoon filling over whole berries. Refrigerate until firm, at least 2 hours, before slicing.

MAKES 8 SERVINGS.

ACTIVE TIME: 30 minutes

TOTAL TIME: 6 hours (including chilling time)

PER SERVING:

185 calories; 3 g fat (2 g sat, 0 g mono); 8 mg cholesterol; 38 g carbohydrate; 2 g protein; 2 g fiber; 116 mg sodium; 159 mg potassium

NUTRITION BONUS:

Vitamin C (96% daily value)

H✕W   H♥H

Apricot-Almond Clafouti

Originally from the Limousin region of France, clafouti is sort of a cross between a flan and a fruit-filled pancake. This one embraces apricots instead of the traditional cherries, but any fruit can be used, including apples, pears, peaches and plums. It will puff up dramatically during baking, then collapse; let it cool slightly before serving so you can truly enjoy the flavors. Leftovers make a delicious breakfast treat.

1	pound fresh apricots (about 8 medium), pitted and cut into wedges
¼	cup almond liqueur, such as amaretto, *or* orange juice
1	lemon
1	tablespoon plus ⅓ cup sugar, divided
2	large eggs
1	large egg white
1	cup low-fat milk
⅔	cup all-purpose flour
½	teaspoon almond extract
	Pinch of salt
1	tablespoon sliced almonds
	Confectioners' sugar for dusting

1. Combine apricots and almond liqueur (or orange juice) in a large bowl. Grate 2 teaspoons zest from the lemon and set aside. Juice the lemon and stir 2 teaspoons of the juice into the apricots. Let stand for at least 1 hour.

2. Preheat oven to 350°F. Coat a 10-inch round baking dish or oval casserole with cooking spray. Sprinkle 1 tablespoon sugar evenly over the bottom. Drain the apricots (reserving the syrup) and arrange in the baking dish.

3. Combine whole eggs, egg white and the remaining ⅓ cup sugar in a medium bowl. Beat with an electric mixer on medium speed until pale yellow. Add milk, flour, almond extract, salt, the reserved lemon zest and the reserved syrup; beat well to blend. Pour the batter over the apricots; sprinkle with almonds.

4. Bake the clafouti until puffed and golden, 45 to 55 minutes. Let cool for about 20 minutes. Sprinkle with confectioners' sugar and serve warm.

MAKES **12** SERVINGS.

ACTIVE TIME: 30 minutes

TOTAL TIME: 2½ hours

EQUIPMENT: 10-inch ceramic quiche dish or oval casserole

PER SERVING:

116 calories; 2 g fat (0 g sat, 1 g mono); 37 mg cholesterol; 20 g carbohydrate; 3 g protein; 1 g fiber; 40 mg sodium; 34 mg potassium

NUTRITION BONUS:

Vitamin A (15% daily value)

H✖W L↓C H♥H

Strawberry Cream

Here's a delicious way to use your harvest of fresh, sweet strawberries. This deluxe chilled dessert gets creaminess and a touch of tanginess from reduced-fat sour cream. Topped with some ruby-red diced strawberries, it makes a perfect ending to any meal.

ACTIVE TIME: 15 minutes

TOTAL TIME: 3¼ hours (including 3 hours chilling time)

TO MAKE AHEAD: Prepare through Step 2, cover and refrigerate for up to 3 days. Add topping just before serving.

PER SERVING:

232 calories; 6 g fat (3 g sat, 2 g mono); 18 mg cholesterol; 43 g carbohydrate; 4 g protein; 4 g fiber; 24 mg sodium; 336 mg potassium

NUTRITION BONUS:

Vitamin C (180% daily value)

H≻≺W L↓C H↑F

CREAM

3	tablespoons cold water
1	envelope unflavored gelatin
4	cups hulled strawberries
½	cup sugar
1	teaspoon vanilla extract
¾	cup reduced-fat sour cream

TOPPING

1	cup hulled strawberries, cut into ¼-inch dice
2	teaspoons sugar

1. **To prepare cream:** Stir together water and gelatin in a small heatproof cup or bowl. Microwave, uncovered, on High until the gelatin has completely dissolved but the liquid is not boiling, 20 to 30 seconds. (*Alternatively, bring ½ inch water to a gentle simmer in a small skillet. Set the bowl with the gelatin mixture in the simmering water until the gelatin has dissolved completely.*) Stir the mixture until smooth.

2. Place strawberries, sugar and vanilla in a food processor and puree. Add sour cream; pulse to combine. With the motor running, slowly add the dissolved gelatin. Pour the cream into four 8-ounce bowls or wineglasses. Cover and refrigerate until set, about 3 hours.

3. **To prepare topping & serve:** Toss diced strawberries and sugar in a small bowl; let stand until slightly juicy, about 2 minutes. Divide among the creams.

MAKES 4 SERVINGS.

Strawberry-Rhubarb Cobbler

Strawberries and rhubarb are one of the great flavor combinations of springtime. Here the duo stars in a traditional cobbler, redolent with the aromas of cinnamon, ginger and nutmeg. If you must, you can top it with a scoop of vanilla frozen yogurt or a dollop of whipped cream but quite honestly, it doesn't need it.

ACTIVE TIME: 20 minutes

TOTAL TIME: 1 hour

EQUIPMENT: 9-inch deep-dish pie pan

PER SERVING:

249 calories; 3 g fat (2 g sat, 0 g mono); 8 mg cholesterol; 52 g carbohydrate; 6 g protein; 3 g fiber; 329 mg sodium; 237 mg potassium

NUTRITION BONUS:

Vitamin C (75% daily value)

H ♥ H

TIP: No **buttermilk**? You can use buttermilk powder prepared according to package directions. Or make "sour milk": mix 1 tablespoon lemon juice or vinegar to 1 cup milk.

FILLING

2	pints strawberries, hulled and thickly sliced
8	ounces rhubarb, trimmed and cut into $1/2$-inch pieces (2 cups)
$1/2$	cup sugar
2	tablespoons quick-cooking tapioca *or* 1 tablespoon cornstarch
$1/8$	teaspoon ground cinnamon
$1/8$	teaspoon ground ginger
$1/8$	teaspoon ground nutmeg

TOPPING

$1^{1/2}$	cups all-purpose flour
$1/4$	cup plus 1 tablespoon sugar, divided
$1^{1/2}$	teaspoons baking powder
$1/2$	teaspoon baking soda
$1/2$	teaspoon salt
$1/4$	teaspoon ground cinnamon
$1/4$	teaspoon ground ginger
$1/4$	teaspoon ground nutmeg
2	tablespoons cold butter, cut into pieces
1	cup nonfat buttermilk (*see Tip*)

1. **To prepare filling:** Combine strawberries, rhubarb, $1/2$ cup sugar, tapioca (or cornstarch), $1/8$ teaspoon cinnamon, $1/8$ teaspoon ginger and $1/8$ teaspoon nutmeg in a 9-inch deep-dish pie pan and let stand for 20 minutes.

2. Preheat oven to 400°F.

3. **To prepare topping:** Stir together flour, $1/4$ cup sugar, baking powder, baking soda, salt, $1/4$ teaspoon cinnamon, $1/4$ teaspoon ginger and $1/4$ teaspoon nutmeg in a large bowl. Cut butter into dry ingredients with a pastry cutter, 2 forks or your fingers until crumbly. Use a fork to stir in buttermilk just until combined.

4. Using a large spoon, drop the dough in 8 dollops over the filling. Sprinkle with the remaining 1 tablespoon sugar. Bake the cobbler until browned and bubbling, 40 to 50 minutes. (Cover with foil if the top is browning too quickly.) Cool slightly on a wire rack. Serve warm.

MAKES 8 SERVINGS.

Rhubarb Waffles with Rhubarb Sauce

Rhubarb is the early bird of spring edibles, so it seems fitting that it be included in a lovely meal to start your day with. Light and crispy waffles made with whole-wheat flour and egg whites make a perfect partner for this easy-to-make, sweet and tangy sauce that goes beautifully drizzled over a scoop of frozen yogurt as well.

RHUBARB SAUCE

| 1¼ | pounds rhubarb, trimmed and cut into ¼-inch pieces (5 cups) |
| 1½ | cups sugar |

WAFFLES

3	large egg whites
1¼	cups nonfat milk
1½	tablespoons canola oil
1½	cups all-purpose flour
¼	cup whole-wheat flour
3	tablespoons sugar
1	tablespoon baking powder
¼	teaspoon salt

1. **To prepare sauce:** Combine rhubarb and 1½ cups sugar in a medium saucepan and bring to a simmer over medium-low heat. Cook until the rhubarb is tender and translucent. Transfer about 1 cup of the rhubarb to a small bowl with a slotted spoon, and reserve for the waffle batter. Boil the remaining rhubarb in syrup over medium heat, stirring occasionally, until slightly thickened, about 5 minutes.

2. **To prepare waffles:** Whisk egg whites in a large bowl until frothy. Whisk in milk and oil. Stir in the reserved 1 cup cooked rhubarb. Sift all-purpose flour, whole-wheat flour, 3 tablespoons sugar, baking powder and salt into a medium bowl. Gently stir the dry ingredients into the egg-milk mixture just until moistened.

3. Preheat a waffle iron to medium-high. (If your waffle iron is not nonstick, brush it lightly with oil.) Fill the iron about two-thirds full. Close and cook the waffles until they are nicely browned, about 4 minutes. Repeat with the remaining batter, coating the waffle iron lightly with oil, if necessary, before cooking each batch. Serve hot, topped with the rhubarb sauce.

MAKES 6 SERVINGS.

ACTIVE TIME: 30 minutes

TOTAL TIME: 30 minutes

TO MAKE AHEAD: The sauce (Step 1) can be prepared ahead and stored, covered, in the refrigerator for up to 4 days. Bring to room temperature or heat before serving.

PER SERVING:

434 calories; 4 g fat (0 g sat, 2 g mono); 1 mg cholesterol; 93 g carbohydrate; 8 g protein; 3 g fiber; 431 mg sodium; 459 mg potassium

NUTRITION BONUS:

Selenium (29% daily value)
Folate (26% dv)
Calcium (21% dv)

H ♥ H

SUMMER

" Part of the joy of eating is the anticipation of seasonal foods. For me the first asparagus of spring or the first raspberries in the summer are a cause for celebration. Eating with the seasons helps ground us and reminds us of our connections to the earth. "

—JOHN ASH, FROM HIS BOOK
FROM THE EARTH TO THE TABLE

Honeydew melon is a good source of potassium, a nutrient important for maintaining healthy blood pressure.

HONEYDEW MELON

White Sangria

OK, so it's kind of a contradiction for a sangria, which is named for its blood-red color, to be made with white wine, but once you've tasted this festive thirst quencher it won't matter a bit. Pieces of mixed summer melons are the perfect match for a crisp Sauvignon Blanc.

1½	cups mixed colorful bite-size melon pieces, such as cantaloupe, honeydew, Ogen *or* Charentais
⅓	cup sugar
1	750-ml bottle crisp white wine, such as Sauvignon Blanc *or* Pinot Grigio
¼	cup brandy
2	tablespoons Triple Sec *or* other orange-flavored liqueur
¾	cup sparkling water *or* club soda
	Ice cubes
	Lime *or* starfruit slices for garnish
	Small mint sprigs for garnish

1. Stir melon and sugar together in a large pitcher. Let stand for 15 to 30 minutes to draw out the juices.

2. Just before serving, stir wine, brandy, Triple Sec (or other orange liqueur) and sparkling water (or club soda) into the pitcher. Add ice cubes to 6 glasses. Fill the glasses with the sangria, spooning some of the fruit into each glass. Garnish each drink with a slice of lime (or starfruit) and a sprig of mint.

MAKES 6 SERVINGS, 1 CUP EACH.

ACTIVE TIME: 10 minutes

TOTAL TIME: 30 minutes

TO MAKE AHEAD: Prepare through Step 1, cover and refrigerate for up to 1 day. Finish with Step 2 just before serving.

PER SERVING:

198 calories; 0 g fat (0 g sat, 0 g mono); 0 mg cholesterol; 20 g carbohydrate; 0 g protein; 0 g fiber; 14 mg sodium; 191 mg potassium

NUTRITION BONUS:

Vitamin C (20% daily value)
Vitamin A (15% dv)

| Eggplant contains soluble fiber, the kind that may help lower blood cholesterol levels.

Baba Ganouj

The peak season for eggplant is toward the end of the summer—but good things are worth waiting for. Here, it is grilled and pureed along with garlic, lemon juice and tahini to make a lighter version of the classic Middle Eastern dip. If you can't find ground sumac for the garnish, chopped pistachios are traditional as well. Serve with pita wedges or use as a spread for sandwiches.

ACTIVE TIME: 20 minutes

TOTAL TIME: 40 minutes

TO MAKE AHEAD: Cover and refrigerate for up to 3 days.

EQUIPMENT: Skewer

PER SERVING:

32 calories; 1 g fat (0 g sat, 1 g mono); 0 mg cholesterol; 5 g carbohydrate; 1 g protein; 2 g fiber; 245 mg sodium; 163 mg potassium

H✕W L↓C H♥H

2	medium eggplants (about 1 pound each)
4	cloves garlic, unpeeled
1/4	cup lemon juice
2	tablespoons tahini (*see Note*)
1 1/4	teaspoons salt
	Extra-virgin olive oil for garnish
	Ground sumac for garnish (*see Note*)

1. Preheat grill to high.

2. Prick eggplants all over with a fork. Thread garlic cloves onto a skewer. Grill the eggplants, turning occasionally, until charred and tender, 10 to 12 minutes. Grill the garlic, turning once, until charred and tender, 6 to 8 minutes.

3. Transfer the eggplants and garlic to a cutting board. When cool enough to handle, peel both. Transfer to a food processor. Add lemon juice, tahini and salt; process until almost smooth. Drizzle with oil and sprinkle with sumac, if desired.

MAKES **12** SERVINGS, ABOUT 1/4 CUP EACH.

NOTES: **Tahini** is a thick paste of ground sesame seeds. Look for it in large supermarkets in the Middle Eastern section or near other nut butters.

The tart berries of a particular variety of **sumac** bush add a distinctive element to many Middle Eastern dishes. Find them whole or ground in Middle Eastern markets or online at *kalustyans.com* or *lebaneseproducts.com.*

Garlic & White Bean Dip

Roasting or poaching garlic mellows out its flavor and make the cloves turn soft and creamy. For this simple-as-can-be dip, the rich-tasting garlic is pureed with convenient canned beans, a little bit of onion and a dash of lemon juice. Use it as a dip for crudités, a topping for bruschetta or even as a spread for a sandwich.

ACTIVE TIME: 20 minutes

TOTAL TIME: 20 minutes

TO MAKE AHEAD: Cover and refrigerate the dip for up to 3 days.

PER 2-TABLESPOON SERVING:

123 calories; 8 g fat (1 g sat, 5 g mono); 0 mg cholesterol; 12 g carbohydrate; 3 g protein; 2 g fiber; 139 mg sodium; 173 mg potassium

½	cup Roasted-Garlic Oil (*recipe follows*)
1½	cups chopped onion
½	teaspoon salt
1	15-ounce can cannellini beans, rinsed (*see Tip, page 239*)
½	cup Oil-Poached Garlic Puree (*recipe follows*)
1	teaspoon lemon juice

Put oil, onion and salt in a large skillet and cook over medium heat until the onion is softened but not browned, 6 to 9 minutes. Stir in beans and cook until heated through, about 2 minutes. Transfer to a food processor. Add garlic puree and lemon juice and puree until smooth. Serve warm or cold.

MAKES 2 CUPS.

Oil-Poached-Garlic Puree & Roasted-Garlic Oil

ACTIVE TIME: 30 minutes

TOTAL TIME: 2½ hours

TO MAKE AHEAD: Refrigerate puree for up to 1 week or freeze for up to 6 months; refrigerate oil for no more than 1 week.

PER TABLESPOON (PUREE):

94 calories; 5 g fat (0 g sat, 3 g mono); 0 mg cholesterol; 12 g carbohydrate; 2 g protein; 1 g fiber; 6 mg sodium; 148 mg potassium

NUTRITION BONUS:

Vitamin C (20% daily value)

PER TABLESPOON (OIL):

105 calories; 12 g fat (1 g sat, 8 g mono); 0 mg cholesterol; 0 g carbohydrate; 0 g protein; 0 g fiber; 0 mg sodium; 0 mg potassium

This process for preparing garlic yields two culinary treasures: a rich-tasting puree that can be enjoyed on its own or used as a cooking ingredient as well as an infused oil.

1. Bring 4 cups of water to a boil in a medium saucepan. Remove from the heat, add the separated but unpeeled cloves of 4 heads of garlic, stir to submerge the cloves and let sit until the garlic skins are softened and cool enough to handle, about 50 minutes. Strain the garlic, remove the skins and cut off the hard nub where the clove was attached to the head.

2. Place the garlic, 1½ cups canola oil and ½ cup extra-virgin olive oil in a medium saucepan; bring to a gentle simmer over medium-low heat. Reduce the heat to low and maintain a very gentle simmer (it may be necessary to slide the pan to the edge of the burner). Simmer until the cloves are golden and very soft when pressed with a fork, 40 to 50 minutes. Let cool for 30 minutes.

3. Transfer the cooled garlic to a sieve to drain, reserving the oil. Transfer the garlic to a food processor and puree until smooth, scraping down the sides occasionally. Store the puree and the oil separately in the refrigerator.

MAKES ½-⅔ CUP PUREE (DEPENDING ON THE SIZE OF THE GARLIC) & 2 CUPS GARLIC-INFUSED OIL.

Grilled Shrimp Cocktail with Yellow Tomato Salsa

Yellow tomatoes have a lower acidity than their red cousins and several varieties are among the earliest in the season to ripen. Here they combine with cool cucumber and yellow bell peppers in a refreshing salsa. Grilled shrimp make this dish a more full-flavored and elegant version of shrimp cocktail.

4	medium yellow tomatoes (1 pound), seeded and finely chopped
1	yellow bell pepper, finely chopped
1	medium cucumber, peeled, seeded and finely chopped
1	stalk celery, finely chopped
½	small red onion, finely chopped
2	tablespoons minced fresh chives
2	tablespoons white-wine vinegar
2	tablespoons lemon juice
1	tablespoon Worcestershire sauce
½	teaspoon freshly ground pepper
¼	teaspoon salt
	Several dashes hot sauce, to taste
1	pound raw shrimp (21-25 per pound; *see Note, page 241*), peeled and deveined
2	cloves garlic, minced
2	tablespoons minced fresh thyme

1. Mix tomatoes, bell pepper, cucumber, celery, onion, chives, vinegar, lemon juice, Worcestershire sauce, pepper, salt and hot sauce in a large bowl. Cover and chill for at least 20 minutes or up to 1 day.

2. Mix shrimp, garlic and thyme in a medium bowl; cover and refrigerate for 20 minutes.

3. Coat a grill pan with cooking spray and heat over medium-high heat or preheat the grill to medium-high and oil the grill rack (*see photo, page 239*). Cook the shrimp until pink and firm, about 2 minutes per side. Serve the shrimp with the salsa in martini glasses or bowls.

MAKES **4** SERVINGS.

ACTIVE TIME: 40 minutes

TOTAL TIME: 1 hour

TO MAKE AHEAD: Prepare through Step 1. Cover and refrigerate for up to 1 day.

PER SERVING:

136 calories; 1 g fat (0 g sat, 0 g mono); 168 mg cholesterol; 11 g carbohydrate; 20 g protein; 2 g fiber; 419 mg sodium; 717 mg potassium

NUTRITION BONUS:

Vitamin C (130% daily value)
Iron (25% dv)
Potassium (19% dv)
Folate (15% dv)

H�W L↓C H♥H

Serrano Ham with Crusty Tomato Bread

For this classic tapas morsel, plum tomatoes are called for because they contain less water and therefore have a more intense flavor when they are slow-roasted. The resulting sweet and garlicky tomato spread is the perfect companion for thin slices of salty, dry-cured Spanish ham.

ACTIVE TIME: 30 minutes

TOTAL TIME: 2½ hours

TO MAKE AHEAD: Cover and refrigerate the roasted tomatoes (Steps 1-2) for up to 3 days. Bring to room temperature before serving.

PER SERVING:

152 calories; 7 g fat (1 g sat, 4 g mono); 8 mg cholesterol; 14 g carbohydrate; 9 g protein; 3 g fiber; 484 mg sodium; 221 mg potassium

NUTRITION BONUS:

Vitamin C (15% daily value)

H✂W   L↓C   H♥H

12	plum tomatoes
4	tablespoons garlic oil (*see Note*), divided
2	teaspoons dried oregano
¾	teaspoon kosher salt
1	whole-grain baguette, cut into 24 slices, *or* 12 pieces whole-grain bread, cut in half
6	ounces thinly sliced Serrano ham (about 24 slices; *see Note*)

1. **To prepare tomatoes:** Preheat oven to 300°F. Coat a large rimmed baking sheet with cooking spray.

2. Cut tomatoes in half lengthwise and place on the prepared baking sheet. Sprinkle each half with some oil, some oregano and salt. Roast for 2 hours. When cool enough to handle, coarsely chop the tomatoes and transfer (with juices) to a serving bowl.

3. **To serve tapas:** Shortly before serving, preheat oven to 350°F.

4. Place bread on a baking sheet and brush with some of the remaining garlic oil. Bake until slightly crispy, but not hard, 2 to 4 minutes per side. Let cool slightly. To serve, arrange the bread on a large platter with ham and the bowl of tomato mixture for spreading.

MAKES **12** SERVINGS.

NOTES: Garlic oil is oil that has been infused with fresh garlic. We like to use it for salad dressings, as dipping oil with crusty bread, in marinades or to simply drizzle over steamed vegetables. Find it at well-stocked supermarkets, at *boyajianinc.com* or see page 78 for a recipe to make it.

Serrano ham is full-flavored, savory dry-cured ham made from specific breeds of white pigs. It is traditionally enjoyed very thinly sliced, like its Italian cousin prosciutto. Find it in well-stocked supermarkets, specialty stores or online at *tienda.com*.

Chilled Tomato Soup with Cilantro-Yogurt Swirl

Here's a fresh take on gazpacho, that's spiked with chopped chipotle peppers, which add a deep, smoky heat to the dish. The cilantro-yogurt swirl balances the heat from the chiles and makes a beautiful garnish. Serve this soup as a starter for dinner on a warm summer evening.

2	teaspoons ground cumin
2	pounds ripe tomatoes, coarsely chopped (about 5 cups)
1/2	cup chopped red onion
2	tablespoons plus 1/4 cup chopped fresh cilantro, divided
2	teaspoons chopped chipotle pepper in adobo sauce (*see Note*)
1	cup fresh corn kernels (from about 2 ears; *see photo, page* 223)
1	cup ice water
2	tablespoons lime juice, or to taste
1	teaspoon kosher salt
1	cup low-fat plain yogurt

1. **To prepare soup:** Toast cumin in a small skillet over low heat, stirring, until just fragrant, 1 to 2 minutes.

2. Combine tomatoes, onion, 2 tablespoons cilantro and chipotle in a blender or food processor. Puree until smooth. Transfer to a large bowl. Add the toasted cumin, corn, ice water, lime juice and salt; stir to combine. Refrigerate until chilled, about 1 hour or until ready to serve.

3. **To prepare cilantro yogurt:** Puree yogurt and the remaining 1/4 cup cilantro in a blender or food processor until smooth. Refrigerate until ready to serve (it will thicken slightly as it stands).

4. To serve, divide the soup among 4 bowls and garnish each with a generous swirl of cilantro yogurt.

   MAKES 4 SERVINGS, 1 1/4 CUPS EACH.

ACTIVE TIME: 25 minutes

TOTAL TIME: 1 hour 25 minutes

TO MAKE AHEAD: Refrigerate the soup and cilantro yogurt in separate containers for up to 1 day.

PER SERVING:

128 calories; 2 g fat (1 g sat, 0 g mono); 4 mg cholesterol; 24 g carbohydrate; 7 g protein; 5 g fiber; 667 mg sodium; 827 mg potassium

NUTRITION BONUS:

Vitamin C (110% daily value)
Vitamin A (30% dv)
Potassium (22% dv)
Calcium (15% dv)

H✖W　L⬇C　H⬆F　H♥H

NOTE: Chipotle chiles in adobo sauce are smoked jalapeños packed in a flavorful sauce. Look for the small cans with the Mexican foods in large supermarkets. Once opened, they'll keep up to 2 weeks in the refrigerator or 6 months in the freezer.

Tomatillo Gazpacho

Tomatillos have a flavor that's a bit like green tomatoes with apple and citrus notes. In this chilled soup their tartness provides a mouthwatering contrast to sweet shrimp and salty olives. Although you can get tomatillos sporadically throughout the year, they do especially well in the heat of summer. And this chilled soup is a true cooler on a sweltering-hot day, particularly since your stove is on for less than 5 minutes. If you want to make this vegetarian, opt for vegetable broth over chicken broth and replace the shrimp with diced feta or halloumi cheese.

2	tablespoons extra-virgin olive oil, divided
3	cloves garlic, chopped
1	English cucumber, halved lengthwise and seeded
1	avocado, halved and pitted
1	pound tomatillos (*see Tip*), husks removed, chopped
1	green bell pepper, chopped
1-2	jalapeño peppers, seeded and chopped
1	15-ounce can reduced-sodium chicken broth *or* vegetable broth
1	teaspoon sugar
¼	teaspoon salt
12	ounces cooked and peeled shrimp, chopped
¼	cup green olives, chopped
2	scallions, sliced

1. Heat 1 tablespoon oil in a small nonstick skillet over medium heat. Add garlic and cook, stirring, until just beginning to brown, 1 to 2 minutes. Remove from the heat.

2. Coarsely chop half the cucumber and half the avocado and place in a food processor. Add tomatillos, bell pepper, jalapeño to taste and the garlic. Process until smooth. Transfer to a large bowl; stir in broth, sugar and salt.

3. Dice the remaining cucumber and avocado and place in a medium bowl. Add shrimp, olives and scallions. Drizzle with the remaining 1 tablespoon oil; gently toss to combine.

4. Ladle the gazpacho into bowls and top each portion with about ¾ cup of the shrimp salad.

MAKES **4** SERVINGS.

ACTIVE TIME: 30 minutes

TOTAL TIME: 30 minutes

TO MAKE AHEAD: Cover and refrigerate the gazpacho (Step 2) and the shrimp salad (Step 3) in separate bowls for up to 1 hour.

PER SERVING:

329 calories; 19 g fat (2 g sat, 12 g mono); 174 mg cholesterol; 18 g carbohydrate; 26 g protein; 7 g fiber; 597 mg sodium; 962 mg potassium

NUTRITION BONUS:

Vitamin C (90% daily value)
Potassium (28% dv)
Iron (20% dv)
Vitamin A (15% dv)

H✖W L↓C H↑F H♥H

TIP: **Tomatillos** are tart, plum-size green fruits that look like small, husk-covered green tomatoes. Find them in the produce section near the tomatoes. Remove outer husks and rinse well before using.

Arugula Salad with Honey-Drizzled Peaches

You can get peaches from early spring to early fall but they absolutely taste their best in midsummer. Creamy goat cheese, nutty pecans and peppery arugula in a lemony dressing highlight the sweetness of juicy ripe peaches in this special salad. A sweet ribbon of honey ties the whole thing together.

ACTIVE TIME: 20 minutes

TOTAL TIME: 20 minutes

PER SERVING:

294 calories; 16 g fat (5 g sat, 7 g mono); 13 mg cholesterol; 36 g carbohydrate; 8 g protein; 3 g fiber; 253 mg sodium; 404 mg potassium

NUTRITION BONUS:

Vitamin C (35% daily value) Vitamin A (25% dv)

TIP: To **toast chopped pecans**, cook in a small dry skillet over medium-low heat, stirring constantly, until fragrant and lightly browned, 2 to 4 minutes.

¼	cup finely chopped toasted pecans (*see Tip*)
½	teaspoon kosher salt, divided
	Freshly ground pepper to taste
1	4-ounce log goat cheese
6	cups baby arugula (about 4 ounces)
1	tablespoon extra-virgin olive oil
	Zest and juice of 1 lemon
4	ripe but firm peaches, halved and pitted
4	tablespoons honey

1. Place pecans in a shallow dish. Season with ¼ teaspoon salt and pepper. Roll goat cheese log in the pecans to coat. Refrigerate the log until firm, if necessary, then cut into 8 rounds.

2. Place arugula in a medium bowl. Add oil, lemon zest and juice and toss to coat; season with the remaining ¼ teaspoon salt and pepper.

3. Divide the arugula among 4 shallow bowls. Nestle 2 peach halves into each portion of greens, top each half with a round of pecan-crusted goat cheese and drizzle each salad with 1 tablespoon honey.

MAKES **4** SERVINGS.

Bean & Tomato Salad with Honey Vinaigrette

This beautiful salad combines fresh tomatoes, green beans, red onions and dried heirloom beans. Recently harvested beans (and thus freshly dried) cook more quickly than the kind you buy year-round at the market. In the latter part of the summer, farmers' markets begin to sell a fresh crop of heirloom varieties that would be perfect for this salad. (Photograph: front cover.)

ACTIVE TIME: 35 minutes

TOTAL TIME: 1 hour 35 minutes (not including soaking time)

TO MAKE AHEAD: Prepare through Step 3, cover and refrigerate for up to 1 day.

PER SERVING:

134 calories; 1 g fat (0 g sat, 0 g mono); 0 mg cholesterol; 26 g carbohydrate; 7 g protein; 7 g fiber; 298 mg sodium; 565 mg potassium

NUTRITION BONUS:

Vitamin C (27% daily value)
Folate (25% dv)
Vitamin A (22% dv)
Potassium (16% dv)

H✂W   H↑F   H♥H

TIP: To **quick-soak beans**, place in a large saucepan with enough cold water to cover them by 2 inches. Bring to a boil. Boil for 2 minutes. Remove from the heat, cover and let stand for 1 hour. Proceed with Step 2.

1¼ cups dried beans, preferably heirloom, *or* 2 15-ounce cans white beans, rinsed (*see Tip, page 239*)	½ teaspoon freshly ground pepper, or to taste
1 teaspoon salt, divided	8 ounces green beans, trimmed and cut into 2-inch pieces
½ cup minced red onion	1 pint cherry *or* grape tomatoes, halved or quartered
¼ cup cider vinegar	½ cup fresh basil leaves, thinly sliced
4 teaspoons honey	1 pound tomatoes, sliced
1 teaspoon peanut *or* canola oil	

1. If using canned beans, skip to Step 3. If using dried beans, rinse and pick over for any stones, then place in a large bowl, cover with 3 inches of cold water and soak at room temperature for at least 6 hours or overnight. (*Alternatively, use our quick-soak method: see Tip.*)

2. Drain the soaked beans, rinse and transfer to a large saucepan. Add 6 cups cold water. Bring to a simmer, partially cover, and simmer gently, stirring once or twice, until tender but not mushy, 20 minutes to 1 hour, depending on the freshness of the dried beans. (If you're using heirloom beans, be sure to check them after 20 minutes—they tend to cook more quickly than conventional beans.) If at any time the liquid level drops below the beans, add 1 cup water. When the beans are about three-fourths done, season with ½ teaspoon salt. When the beans are tender, remove from the heat and drain.

3. Combine the beans (cooked or canned), the remaining ½ teaspoon salt, onion, vinegar, honey, oil and pepper in a large bowl. Stir, cover and refrigerate to marinate for at least 1 hour or overnight.

4. Cook green beans in a large pot of boiling water until crisp-tender, about 5 minutes. Drain, rinse with cold water, and drain again. Pat dry and add to the marinated beans. Stir in cherry (or grape) tomatoes and basil. Season with pepper.

5. To serve, arrange tomato slices around the edge of a serving platter or shallow salad bowl and spoon the bean salad into the center.

MAKES 8 SERVINGS, ABOUT 1 CUP EACH.

Grilled Smoky Eggplant Salad

Eggplant seems to take on smoky flavors quite well and that's definitely the case in this decidedly Spanish salad. The mellow grilled eggplant melds perfectly with the smoked paprika and tart sherry vinegar that define the flavor of the dressing. Curls of mild Manchego complete the Spanish theme. If you can't find smoked paprika, substitute Hungarian paprika—the grilled eggplant brings some smoke to the salad on its own.

2	small eggplants (about 1 pound total)
¾	teaspoon kosher salt, divided
	Olive oil cooking spray
¼	cup extra-virgin olive oil
1	tablespoon sherry vinegar
1	small plum tomato, diced
1	small clove garlic, chopped
1½	teaspoons smoked paprika (*see Note*)
3	cups mixed baby salad greens
2	ounces Manchego cheese, cut into thin curls with a vegetable peeler (*see Note*)

1. Preheat grill to medium.

2. Cut stripes in each eggplant's peel by running a vegetable peeler down the length of it and repeating at about 1-inch intervals. Slice the eggplants into rounds ⅓ to ½ inch thick. Lay them on a baking sheet and sprinkle lightly with ½ teaspoon salt. Let stand for about 5 minutes.

3. Blot the eggplant slices with paper towels and lightly coat both sides with olive oil cooking spray. Grill the eggplant, flipping halfway through, until soft and browned on both sides, 9 to 11 minutes total.

4. Puree oil, vinegar, tomato, garlic, paprika and the remaining ¼ teaspoon salt in a blender until well combined.

5. Toss salad greens with half the vinaigrette in a medium bowl. Arrange the eggplant slices on 6 salad plates. Drizzle with the remaining vinaigrette. Place the salad greens over and between the eggplant slices, then scatter the cheese curls on top of each salad. Serve warm or at room temperature.

MAKES **6** SERVINGS.

ACTIVE TIME: 45 minutes

TOTAL TIME: 45 minutes

TO MAKE AHEAD: Prepare eggplant and vinaigrette (Steps 1-4), cover and refrigerate separately for up to 1 day. Bring to room temperature before serving.

PER SERVING:

141 calories; 12 g fat (3 g sat; 7 g mono); 7 mg cholesterol; 6 g carbohydrate; 3 g protein; 3 g fiber; 280 mg sodium; 287 mg potassium

NUTRITION BONUS:

Vitamin A (25% daily value)
Vitamin C (15% dv)

L ↓ C

NOTE: To experience the full flavor of this salad, it's worth seeking out the two signature Spanish ingredients: mild-flavored, smooth sheep-milk **Manchego cheese** and **smoked paprika**. If you can't find them, substitute Parmigiano-Reggiano and Hungarian paprika.

Middle Eastern Chickpea Platter

Here's a dish that's perfectly suited to warm-weather entertaining. A chickpea and eggplant salad that combines the flavors of two Middle Eastern favorites—hummus and baba ganouj—is plated with a refreshing salad of tomatoes, red onions, olives and feta cheese. Guests can take pieces of pita bread and pick and choose from the salad as they like. Serve with grilled chicken breast to make this a more substantial meal.

1	tablespoon extra-virgin olive oil
1	small eggplant (about 12 ounces), cubed
2	cloves garlic, minced
1/4	teaspoon salt, divided
2	tablespoons tahini (*see Note*)
3	tablespoons lemon juice
1	tablespoon water
1	15- *or* 19-ounce can chickpeas *or* cannellini beans, rinsed (*see Tip, page 239*)
3	tablespoons chopped fresh parsley, plus more for garnish
2	medium tomatoes, sliced
1/2	medium red onion, thinly sliced
1/4	cup crumbled feta
1/4	cup halved pitted briny black olives, such as Kalamata (optional)
4	whole-wheat pita breads, warmed and cut in half or into wedges

1. Heat oil in a large nonstick skillet over medium heat. Add eggplant, garlic and 1/8 teaspoon salt and cook, stirring occasionally, until the eggplant is soft and beginning to brown, about 8 minutes.

2. Meanwhile, whisk tahini, lemon juice, water and the remaining 1/8 teaspoon salt in a medium bowl. Stir in chickpeas (or beans), parsley and the eggplant.

3. Arrange the chickpea-eggplant salad, tomatoes, onion, feta, olives (if using) and pitas on a platter. Serve at room temperature or chilled and sprinkled with more parsley, if desired.

MAKES **4** SERVINGS.

ACTIVE TIME: 25 minutes

TOTAL TIME: 25 minutes

PER SERVING:

313 calories; 11 g fat (3 g sat, 5 g mono); 8 mg cholesterol; 46 g carbohydrate; 11 g protein; 10 g fiber; 648 mg sodium; 622 mg potassium

NUTRITION BONUS:

Vitamin C (40% daily value)
Folate (28% dv)
Magnesium & Potassium (18% dv)
Iron (15% dv)

H✕W H↑F H♥H

NOTE: Tahini is a thick paste of ground sesame seeds. Look for it in large supermarkets in the Middle Eastern section or near other nut butters.

Gnocchi with Zucchini Ribbons & Parsley Brown Butter

Zucchini can be so plentiful by the end of the summer that they're hard to even give away. For this recipe, convenient store-bought potato gnocchi are tossed with delicate ribbons of zucchini, shallots and cherry tomatoes that have all been sautéed in nutty, browned butter. After you taste this dish you'll think twice before giving your zucchini away again.

1	pound fresh *or* frozen gnocchi
2	tablespoons butter
2	medium shallots, chopped
1	pound zucchini (about 3 small), very thinly sliced lengthwise (*see Tip*)
1	pint cherry tomatoes, halved
½	teaspoon salt
¼	teaspoon grated nutmeg
	Freshly ground pepper to taste
½	cup grated Parmesan cheese
½	cup chopped fresh parsley

1. Bring a large saucepan of water to a boil. Cook gnocchi until they float, 3 to 5 minutes or according to package directions. Drain.

2. Meanwhile, melt butter in a large skillet over medium-high heat. Cook until the butter is beginning to brown, about 2 minutes. Add shallots and zucchini and cook, stirring often, until softened, 2 to 3 minutes. Add tomatoes, salt, nutmeg and pepper and continue cooking, stirring often, until the tomatoes are just starting to break down, 1 to 2 minutes. Stir in Parmesan and parsley. Add the gnocchi and toss to coat. Serve immediately.

MAKES **4** SERVINGS, 1½ CUPS EACH.

ACTIVE TIME: 20 minutes

TOTAL TIME: 20 minutes

PER SERVING:

424 calories; 10 g fat (6 g sat, 0 g mono); 25 mg cholesterol; 66 g carbohydrate; 17 g protein; 5 g fiber; 753 mg sodium; 539 mg potassium

NUTRITION BONUS:

Vitamin C (75% daily value)
Vitamin A (35% dv)
Calcium (28% dv)

H F

TIP: To make "ribbon-thin" **zucchini**, slice lengthwise with a vegetable peeler or a mandoline slicer.

Summer Squash & White Bean Sauté

Protein-rich white beans turn a quick sauté of bountiful summer vegetables— zucchini, summer squash, fresh tomatoes—into a satisfying vegetarian entree. The dish is quite versatile so if you like, substitute any other fresh vegetables you have on hand. Serve with whole-wheat pasta, couscous or rice and a mixed green salad.

ACTIVE TIME: 30 minutes

TOTAL TIME: 30 minutes

PER SERVING:

195 calories; 6 g fat (2 g sat, 4 g mono); 5 mg cholesterol; 25 g carbohydrate; 11 g protein; 8 g fiber; 600 mg sodium; 726 mg potassium

NUTRITION BONUS:

Vitamin C (50% daily value)
Folate & Potassium (21% dv)
Calcium, Magnesium &
Vitamin A (15% dv)

H✂W   H↑F   H♥H

1	tablespoon extra-virgin olive oil
1	medium onion, halved and sliced
2	cloves garlic, minced
1	medium zucchini, halved lengthwise and sliced
1	medium yellow summer squash, halved lengthwise and sliced
1	tablespoon chopped fresh oregano *or* 1 teaspoon dried
¼	teaspoon salt
¼	teaspoon freshly ground pepper
1	15- *or* 19-ounce can cannellini *or* great northern beans, rinsed (*see Tip*)
2	medium tomatoes, chopped
1	tablespoon red-wine vinegar
⅓	cup finely shredded Parmesan cheese

1. Heat oil in a large nonstick skillet over medium heat. Add onion and garlic and cook, stirring, until beginning to soften, about 3 minutes. Add zucchini, summer squash, oregano, salt and pepper and stir to combine. Reduce heat to low, cover and cook, stirring once, until the vegetables are tender-crisp, 3 to 5 minutes.

2. Stir in beans, tomatoes and vinegar; increase heat to medium and cook, stirring, until heated through, about 2 minutes. Remove from the heat and stir in Parmesan.

MAKES 4 SERVINGS, ABOUT 1¼ CUPS EACH.

TIP: While we love the convenience of **canned beans**, they tend to be high in sodium. Give them a good rinse before adding to a recipe to rid them of some of their sodium (up to 35 percent) or opt for low-sodium or no-salt-added varieties. (These recipes are analyzed with rinsed, regular canned beans.) Or, if you have the time, cook your own beans from scratch. You'll find our Bean Cooking Guide at *eatingwell.com/guides.*

Sweet Georgia Peaches

Picked fresh, this luscious fruit brings a taste of summer to the table

You have never been hot until you've been peach picking in the middle of a Georgia summer. Rumor has it that hell is cooler. The air is thick and stifling. Gnats and mosquitoes buzz about incessantly. Peach fuzz covers your arms and wrists. Still, in the midst of picking, we'd take a break, rub the downy fuzz off on our shirts and bite into the ripest peaches, the sweet juices running down our arms, each mouthful more precious than gold.

I grew up in the heart of Georgia's peach country and my favorite farmers are the Pearsons, a family that has grown peaches around Fort Valley since Moses Winlock Pearson planted the first trees over a century ago. "For us," says Al Pearson (*right*), who now runs the farm, "peach season starts in May with the Flavorich, a clingstone peach, and goes through August with Big Red, a large freestone." Peach flesh clings to the pit (stone) of clingstone peaches and pulls away easily in freestones.

In a good year, one tree on the Pearson farm produces between 100 and 150 pounds of peaches. Peach farming, however, is hard work, particularly when Mother Nature doesn't cooperate—and the Pearsons have been there. "With the constant threat of hail, freeze, tornadoes and drought," says Pearson, "it always seems a miracle that a crop is ever harvested." Good peach farmers, he says, must have the right blend of art, talent, hard work and faith.

I no longer live down the road from the Pearsons, but when I need especially juicy and fresh peaches, I know where to turn. When I open a box of their peaches, I know they'll be the best quality, and I can feel good about supporting a family farm and people I know. —*Virginia Willis*

Pearson Farm
Fort Valley, Georgia
(888) 423-7374
pearsonfarm.com

93

Pecan-Crusted Turkey Tenderloin with Grilled Peach Salsa

Down South, many orchards grow peaches in the spring and summer and harvest pecans in the fall so it seems natural for the two to be paired in this recipe. Fresh whole-wheat breadcrumbs and finely chopped pecans make a rich-tasting crust on cutlets of turkey tenderloin that have been buttermilk-marinated. If you like, you can substitute boneless, skinless chicken breast for the turkey.

ACTIVE TIME: 1 hour

TOTAL TIME: 1¼ hours

PER SERVING:

474 calories; 22 g fat (2 g sat, 11 g mono); 45 mg cholesterol; 40 g carbohydrate; 37 g protein; 6 g fiber; 390 mg sodium; 368 mg potassium

NUTRITION BONUS:

Vitamin C (25% daily value)
Iron (15% dv)

H F   H H

1	pound turkey tenderloin, cut crosswise into 4 equal portions
2	cups nonfat buttermilk (*see Tip, page 239*)
2	tablespoons kosher salt
1	tablespoon sugar
¼	cup all-purpose flour
¼	teaspoon paprika
¼	teaspoon freshly ground pepper
2	large egg whites
1	tablespoon Dijon mustard
1	cup fresh breadcrumbs, preferably whole-wheat (*see Tip, page 239*)
½	cup finely chopped pecans
2	tablespoons canola oil, divided

GRILLED PEACH SALSA

1¼	pounds ripe peaches (3-4 medium), halved and pitted
1	teaspoon canola oil
2	tablespoons finely chopped onion, preferably Vidalia
1	small jalapeño pepper, seeded and finely chopped
	Zest and juice of 1 lime
¼	cup coarsely chopped fresh cilantro
2	tablespoons chopped fresh mint

1. Place one portion of turkey at a time between sheets of plastic wrap and pound with a meat mallet or heavy skillet until flattened to an even thickness, slightly thicker than ¼ inch.

2. Pour buttermilk in a large sealable plastic bag. Add salt and sugar; seal and shake to dissolve. Add the turkey and seal the bag, pressing out as much air as possible; refrigerate to marinate for 30 minutes (but no longer or it may be too salty).

3. **Meanwhile, prepare salsa:** Preheat grill to medium. Brush cut sides of peaches with oil. Grill the peaches until softened and browned in spots, 3 to 5 minutes per side. Let cool. Chop the peaches into ¼-inch pieces and place in a medium bowl. Add onion, jalapeño, lime zest and juice, cilantro and mint.

4. Preheat oven to 350°F. Place a wire rack on a rimmed baking sheet.

5. Remove the turkey from the marinade (discard marinade) and thoroughly dry with paper towels. Combine flour, paprika and pepper in a shallow dish. Beat egg whites and mustard in a second shallow dish. Combine breadcrumbs and pecans in a third shallow dish. Dredge each cutlet in the flour mixture, shaking off excess. Then, dip both sides in the egg mixture, allowing excess to drip back into the dish to ensure a very thin coating. Then, dredge both sides in the breadcrumb mixture, pressing the crumbs onto each piece to evenly coat.

6. Heat 1 tablespoon oil in a large nonstick skillet over medium heat. Place half the turkey gently in the pan without crowding; cook until golden brown, 1 to 2 minutes per side. Transfer to the wire rack on the baking sheet. Wipe out the pan and repeat with the remaining oil and turkey, adjusting the heat as necessary to prevent burning. Transfer the baking sheet to the oven. Bake until an instant-read thermometer inserted into the center of a cutlet registers 165°F, 12 to 15 minutes. Serve the turkey with the salsa.

MAKES 4 SERVINGS.

Grilled Chicken Ratatouille

The classic Provençal dish ratatouille is truly a celebration of summer vegetables (bell pepper, eggplant, zucchini, tomato). For this variation we've infused the dish with a welcome smokiness by grilling the vegetables before chopping and combining them with fresh basil and marjoram. Grilled chicken elevates the dish from side to entree. Serve with grilled slices of polenta and a glass of Pinot Noir.

ACTIVE TIME: 45 minutes

TOTAL TIME: 45 minutes

PER SERVING:

324 calories; 13 g fat (2 g sat, 9 g mono); 82 mg cholesterol; 16 g carbohydrate; 36 g protein; 7 g fiber; 687 mg sodium; 1,063 mg potassium

NUTRITION BONUS:

Vitamin C (100% daily value)
Vitamin A (35% dv)
Potassium (30% dv)
Folate & Magnesium (20% dv)

H❌W L⬇C H⬆F H❤H

3	tablespoons extra-virgin olive oil
3	tablespoons chopped fresh basil
1	tablespoon chopped fresh marjoram
1	teaspoon salt
	Canola *or* olive oil cooking spray
1	red bell pepper, halved lengthwise, stemmed and seeded
1	small eggplant, cut into ½-inch-thick rounds
1	medium zucchini, halved lengthwise
4	plum tomatoes, halved lengthwise
1	medium red onion, cut into ½-inch-thick rounds
4	boneless, skinless chicken breasts (about 1¼ pounds), trimmed and tenders removed (*see Note*)
¼	teaspoon freshly ground pepper
1	tablespoon red-wine vinegar

1. Preheat grill to medium-high.

2. Combine oil, basil, marjoram and salt in a small bowl and reserve 1 tablespoon of the mixture in another small bowl; set aside.

3. Coat both sides of bell pepper, eggplant, zucchini, tomato and onion pieces with cooking spray. Grill the vegetables, turning once, until soft and charred in spots, about 5 minutes per side for the pepper, 4 minutes per side for the eggplant and zucchini and 3 minutes per side for the tomatoes and onion. As the vegetables finish cooking, place them in a large bowl. Cover the bowl with plastic wrap.

4. Rub the tablespoon of reserved herb mixture on both sides of chicken and sprinkle with pepper. Grill the chicken until cooked through and no longer pink in the center, 4 to 5 minutes per side.

5. Meanwhile, transfer the grilled vegetables to a cutting board and chop into 1-inch pieces. Return to the bowl and toss with vinegar and the remaining herb mixture. Serve the grilled chicken with the ratatouille.

MAKES **4** SERVINGS.

NOTE: It's difficult to find an individual **chicken breast** small enough for one portion. Removing the thin strip of meat from the underside of a 5-ounce breast—the "tender"—removes about 1 ounce of meat and yields a perfect 4-ounce portion. Wrap and freeze the tenders and when you have gathered enough, use them in a stir-fry or for oven-baked chicken fingers.

Cherries are rich in anthocyanins and quercetin, phytochemicals that may bolster immune defenses and help regulate blood pressure.

Grilled Chicken with Cherry-Chipotle Barbecue Sauce

Fresh cherries can be a chore to pit but this recipe makes it worth the effort. Chopped cherries combine with cherry preserves and smoky, hot chipotle peppers for an unusual marinade and sauce. The cherry sauce is delicious here with chicken but is also great with pork chops or steak.

1	cup fresh *or* frozen (thawed) dark sweet cherries, pitted and chopped (*see Tips*)
½	cup reduced-sodium chicken broth
⅓	cup cherry preserves
⅓	cup ketchup
2	tablespoons cider vinegar
1½	teaspoons minced canned chipotle chiles in adobo sauce (*see Note, page 240*), or more to taste
1¼	teaspoons dried thyme
½	teaspoon ground allspice
2	pounds boneless, skinless chicken breasts, trimmed

1. Stir cherries, broth, preserves, ketchup, vinegar, chipotle peppers, thyme and allspice in a small deep bowl. Transfer to a shallow nonreactive dish (*see Note*) large enough to hold chicken. Add chicken and turn to coat well. Cover and marinate in the refrigerator for at least 2 hours or overnight.

2. Preheat grill to high. Oil the grill rack (*see Tip, page 239*). Remove the chicken from the marinade. Transfer the marinade to a medium skillet.

3. Bring the marinade to a boil. Reduce heat to a simmer and cook until the sauce is reduced by about half, 12 to 15 minutes.

4. Meanwhile, reduce the grill heat to medium and grill the chicken until cooked through and no longer pink in the middle, 7 to 9 minutes per side. Let the chicken cool slightly; serve with the sauce.

MAKES **8** SERVINGS.

ACTIVE TIME: 30 minutes

TOTAL TIME: 2¾ hours (including 2 hours marinating time)

TO MAKE AHEAD: Prepare through Step 1. Cover and refrigerate for up to 1 day.

PER SERVING:

180 calories; 3 g fat (1 g sat, 1 g mono); 63 mg cholesterol; 15 g carbohydrate; 24 g protein; 1 g fiber; 179 mg sodium; 272 mg potassium

NUTRITION BONUS:

Selenium (29% daily value)

H✷W L↓C H♥H

TIPS: Be sure to measure **frozen cherries** while still frozen, then thaw. (Drain juice before using.)

To **pit a cherry**, halve it with a paring knife then pry out the pit with the tip of the knife, or use a cherry pitter (*see Tool Smarts, page 237*).

NOTE: A **nonreactive pan**—stainless steel, enamel-coated or glass—is best for acidic foods, such as lemon, to prevent the food from reacting with the pan. Reactive pans, such as aluminum and cast-iron, can impart an off color and/or off flavor in acidic foods.

Capicola & Grilled Vegetable Sandwiches

On days when you're trying to beat the heat, a sandwich can be the perfect choice for a light supper. Here, grilled eggplant and red bell peppers are paired with thin slices of garlicky capicola (a dry-cured rolled pork shoulder) and spicy arugula, all on grilled Italian bread. To round out this meal, start with a bowl of Chilled Tomato Soup with Cilantro-Yogurt Swirl (page 81).

1	small eggplant (about 12 ounces), cut into ¼-inch-thick slices
1	teaspoon salt
1	tablespoon extra-virgin olive oil
2	tablespoons balsamic vinegar, divided
2	cloves garlic, minced, divided
2	large red bell peppers, roasted (*see photos, page 228*) and sliced, *or* two 6-ounce jars roasted red peppers, drained, rinsed and sliced
	Freshly ground pepper to taste
8	½-inch-thick slices Italian bread, preferably whole-grain
4	ounces thinly sliced capicola (*see Note*)
1	bunch arugula, trimmed (4 cups)

1. Preheat grill or broiler.

2. Place eggplant slices in a large colander over a bowl. Sprinkle with salt and let stand for 15 minutes. Rinse well under running water and pat dry.

3. Brush oil lightly over both sides of the eggplant slices. Grill or broil the eggplant until tender, 3 to 4 minutes per side. Place in a bowl and toss with 1 tablespoon vinegar and half of the minced garlic.

4. Toss peppers in a separate bowl with the remaining 1 tablespoon vinegar and garlic. Season with pepper.

5. Grill or broil bread until lightly browned, 1 to 2 minutes per side.

6. To assemble sandwiches, layer capicola, the eggplant, the red peppers and arugula between toasted bread slices.

MAKES **4** SERVINGS.

ACTIVE TIME: 45 minutes

TOTAL TIME: 1 hour

PER SERVING:

191 calories; 6 g fat (1 g sat, 3 g mono); 15 mg cholesterol; 26 g carbohydrate; 9 g protein; 7 g fiber; 566 mg sodium; 596 mg potassium

NUTRITION BONUS:

Vitamin C (190% daily value)
Vitamin A (60% dv)

H✱W L↓C H↑F H♥H

NOTE: **Capicola** is rolled pork shoulder cured like ham. It can be found in the deli section of most large supermarkets or Italian markets.

Grilled Steak & Escarole with Tomato Vinaigrette

On a hot day it's nice to spend as much time as possible outdoors and out of the kitchen. This quick recipe encourages that philosophy. Tender filet mignon is grilled to perfection alongside wedges of peppery-tasting escarole. The only part that needs to be prepared indoors is the tomato-Parmesan vinaigrette that dresses the whole dish. Of course, you could always bring the blender out to the deck.

1	cup grape tomatoes
2	tablespoons extra-virgin olive oil, divided
2	tablespoons finely shredded Parmesan cheese, divided
1	tablespoon balsamic vinegar
1	tablespoon chopped fresh basil
3/4	teaspoon salt, divided
1/2	teaspoon freshly ground pepper, divided
1	clove garlic, minced
2	large heads escarole *or* romaine lettuce, outermost leaves removed
1	pound beef tenderloin (filet mignon) *or* sirloin steak, trimmed and cut into 4 steaks, 1-1½ inches thick

1. Preheat grill to medium-high.

2. Place tomatoes, 1 tablespoon oil, 1 tablespoon Parmesan, vinegar, basil, ¼ teaspoon salt and ¼ teaspoon pepper in a food processor or blender; pulse until coarsely chopped. Set aside. Combine the remaining 1 tablespoon oil and garlic in another small bowl.

3. Leaving the root ends intact, cut escarole (or romaine) heads into quarters (the root will keep the leaves from falling apart); brush the cut sides with the garlic-oil mixture and sprinkle with ¼ teaspoon salt. Season both sides of steak with the remaining ¼ teaspoon salt and ¼ teaspoon pepper. Pat the remaining 1 tablespoon Parmesan onto both sides of the steak.

4. Oil the grill rack (*see Tip*). Grill the escarole (or romaine), turning occasionally, until the inner leaves have softened and the outer leaves have begun to char, about 4 minutes total. Transfer to a cutting board to cool. Grill the steaks, turning once, until desired doneness, 8 to 12 minutes total for medium.

5. Cut the root ends off the escarole (or romaine) and discard. Chop the leaves into bite-size pieces. Serve the steak and grilled greens drizzled with the reserved tomato vinaigrette.

MAKES **4** SERVINGS.

ACTIVE TIME: 30 minutes

TOTAL TIME: 30 minutes

PER SERVING:

302 calories; 16 g fat (4 g sat, 9 g mono); 78 mg cholesterol; 11 g carbohydrate; 30 g protein; 8 g fiber; 601 mg sodium; 1,299 mg potassium

NUTRITION BONUS:

Vitamin A (120% daily value)
Folate (96% dv)
Vitamin C (35% dv)
Iron (25% dv)
Calcium (20% dv)

H⊁W L↓C H↑F

TIP: To **oil the grill rack**: oil a folded paper towel, hold it with tongs and rub it over the rack (*see photo, page 239*). Do not use cooking spray on a hot grill.

Poblano & Skirt Steak Fajitas

*Dark green poblano chiles ripen to red later in the summer. They are often dried and
then called anchos. This variation on fajitas uses both fresh poblanos and dried ground
ancho chile. The poblanos are grilled along with steak and scallions and served wrapped
in corn tortillas. Skirt steak has fabulous flavor but tends to be chewy, so slice it thinly
across the grain.*

2	ripe avocados, pitted
1/2	cup chopped fresh cilantro
3	tablespoons lime juice, divided, plus lime wedges for garnish
1 1/2	teaspoons kosher salt, divided
1/2	teaspoon freshly ground pepper, divided
2	bunches scallions, trimmed
3	poblano peppers (*see Note*)
3	teaspoons extra-virgin olive oil, divided
1	teaspoon ground ancho chile (*see Note*)
1/2	teaspoon ground cumin
1-1 1/4	pounds skirt steak, trimmed
	Hot sauce for serving
12	6-inch corn tortillas, warmed (*see Tip, page 239*)

1. Preheat grill to high.

2. Mash avocados in a medium bowl with a fork. Stir in cilantro, 2 tablespoons
   lime juice, 3/4 teaspoon salt and 1/4 teaspoon pepper.

3. Brush scallions and poblanos with 2 teaspoons oil. Combine ancho chile,
   cumin, 1/2 teaspoon salt and the remaining 1/4 teaspoon pepper in a small
   bowl. Rub both sides of steak with the remaining 1 teaspoon oil and the
   spice mixture.

4. Oil the grill rack (*see photo, page 239*). Grill the poblanos, turning often, until
   softened and charred, 8 to 12 minutes. Transfer to a medium bowl and cover
   with a plate or plastic wrap to trap the heat. Grill the scallions, turning frequently,
   until softened and lightly charred, 2 to 4 minutes. Grill the steak 2 to 3 minutes
   per side for medium-rare. Transfer the steak to a cutting board, tent with foil
   and let rest.

5. Meanwhile, slice the scallions into 1-inch pieces and transfer to a serving dish.
   Peel as much skin as possible from the peppers, discard the stems and seeds,
   and slice into 1/2-inch-wide strips; transfer to the serving dish. Add the remaining 1 tablespoon lime juice and 1/4 teaspoon salt to the vegetables and toss to
   combine. Slice the steak very thinly, then chop into small pieces. Serve the steak
   and vegetables with the guacamole, lime wedges, hot sauce and tortillas.

MAKES 6 SERVINGS, 2 TORTILLAS, 2 OUNCES STEAK, 1/4 CUP VEGETABLES
& 3 TABLESPOONS GUACAMOLE EACH.

ACTIVE TIME: 1 hour

TOTAL TIME: 1 hour

PER SERVING:

395 calories; 20 g fat (5 g sat,
12 g mono); 39 mg cholesterol;
33 g carbohydrate; 23 g protein;
9 g fiber; 366 mg sodium;
818 mg potassium

NUTRITION BONUS:

Vitamin C (120% daily value)
Zinc (40% dv)
Potassium (24% dv)
Folate (23% dv)
Iron (20% dv)

H ↑ F

NOTE: **Poblano peppers** can be
fiery or relatively mild; there's no
way to tell until you taste them.
Ancho chile peppers, one of the
most popular dried chiles used
in Mexico, are dried poblano
peppers. They have a mild, sweet,
spicy flavor. Ground ancho chile
pepper can be found in the
specialty-spice section of large
supermarkets, or substitute
ground chili powder plus a pinch
of cayenne.

Nectarine & Prosciutto Grilled Pizza

Here sweet ripe nectarines and salty prosciutto ham are arranged on a crust slathered with basil pesto and sprinkled with assertive blue and provolone cheeses. If you haven't tried pizza on the grill, you're missing one of the joys of outdoor cooking. Once you've mastered this technique, use it with any selection of toppings that float your boat.

ACTIVE TIME: 35 minutes

TOTAL TIME: 35 minutes

PER SERVING:

299 calories; 11 g fat (5 g sat, 4 g mono); 23 mg cholesterol; 37 g carbohydrate; 15 g protein; 4 g fiber; 695 mg sodium; 234 mg potassium

NUTRITION BONUS:

Folate (28% daily value)
Calcium (20% dv)
Iron (15% dv)

H✷W

TIPS: Look for **whole-wheat pizza-dough** balls at your supermarket. Check the ingredient list to make sure the dough doesn't contain any hydrogenated oils. Or visit *eatingwell.com* for an easy pizza-dough recipe.

¾	cup shredded provolone cheese
¼	cup crumbled blue cheese
	Yellow cornmeal for dusting
1	pound whole-wheat pizza dough (*see Tip*), thawed if frozen
3	tablespoons prepared basil pesto
½	cup thinly sliced prosciutto (about 2 ounces)
1	large ripe nectarine *or* peach *or* 2 fresh apricots, pitted and thinly sliced
1	tablespoon aged balsamic vinegar
¼	teaspoon freshly ground pepper

1. Preheat grill to low.

2. Mix provolone and blue cheese in a medium bowl; set aside.

3. Sprinkle cornmeal onto a pizza peel or large baking sheet. When you're ready to get your pizzas on the grill, turn the dough out onto a lightly floured surface. Dust the top with flour; dimple with your fingertips to shape into a thick, flattened circle—don't worry if it's not perfectly symmetrical. Then use a rolling pin to roll into a circle about 14 inches in diameter. Transfer the dough to the prepared peel or baking sheet, making sure the underside of the dough is completely coated with cornmeal.

4. Slide the crust onto the grill rack; close the lid. Cook until lightly browned, 3 to 4 minutes.

5. Using a large spatula, flip the crust. Spread pesto on the crust, leaving a 1-inch border. Quickly sprinkle three-fourths of the cheese mixture on top. Top with prosciutto, fruit and the remaining cheese.

6. Close the lid again and grill until the cheese has melted and the bottom of the crust has browned, about 8 minutes.

7. Drizzle balsamic vinegar over the pizza and season with pepper just before slicing and serving.

MAKES **6** SERVINGS.

Spaghetti with Clams & Corn

Fresh corn kernels give spaghetti and clams a hint of summer clambake. Look for minced fresh clams or clam strips at the seafood counter in your market. To complete the meal, consider serving this pasta with Arugula Salad with Honey-Drizzled Peaches (page 84).

6	ounces whole-wheat spaghetti
2	tablespoons extra-virgin olive oil
3	cups diced sweet onions
1	teaspoon salt
1	cup fresh corn kernels (about 2 ears; *see photo, page 223*)
6	cloves garlic, minced
1/2	teaspoon dried thyme
1/4	teaspoon freshly ground pepper
1	tablespoon all-purpose flour
2/3	cup dry white wine, such as Pinot Grigio
1	pound fresh minced clams (*see Note*) *or* chopped clam strips
1/2	cup chopped fresh basil
1/2	cup chopped fresh parsley
1	lemon, cut into wedges

1. Cook pasta in boiling water until just tender, about 8 minutes, or according to package directions. Reserve 1/4 cup of the cooking liquid; drain the pasta.

2. Meanwhile, heat oil in a large nonstick skillet over medium-high heat. Add onions and salt, stir to coat, and cook, stirring often, for 2 minutes. Cover, reduce heat to medium-low and cook, stirring occasionally, until very soft and just beginning to brown, 10 to 12 minutes. Uncover, increase heat to medium-high, stir in corn, garlic, thyme and pepper, and cook, stirring, until fragrant, 30 seconds to 1 minute. Sprinkle flour over the vegetables; stir to coat. Stir in wine and bring to a simmer. Remove from the heat.

3. When the pasta is ready, return the pan to medium-high heat. Stir in the reserved cooking liquid and clams (and any juices). Simmer, stirring often, until the clams are cooked through, about 1 minute. Stir in the pasta, basil and parsley. Serve with lemon wedges.

MAKES 4 SERVINGS, 1 1/2 CUPS EACH.

ACTIVE TIME: 40 minutes

TOTAL TIME: 40 minutes

PER SERVING:

428 calories; 9 g fat (1 g sat, 6 g mono); 39 mg cholesterol; 59 g carbohydrate; 24 g protein; 9 g fiber; 666 mg sodium; 840 mg potassium.

NUTRITION BONUS:

Iron (100% daily value)
Vitamin C (70% dv)
Magnesium & Potassium (27% dv)

H↑F H♥H

NOTE: **Fresh clams**, shucked and minced, are available by the pound in the seafood department in large supermarkets. They are superior to canned varieties in both flavor and texture.

Salmon Panzanella

Traditional Italian bread salad gets a flavor and protein boost with the addition of grilled salmon. To round out this complete meal, serve with a glass of American wheat ale.

ACTIVE TIME: 30 minutes

TOTAL TIME: 30 minutes

PER SERVING:

362 calories; 21 g fat (3 g sat, 12 g mono); 72 mg cholesterol; 15 g carbohydrate; 29 g protein; 5 g fiber; 386 mg sodium; 1,002 mg potassium

NUTRITION BONUS:

Selenium (67% daily value)
Vitamin C (30% dv)
Potassium (29% dv)
Vitamin A (20% dv)
Magnesium (18% dv)
Excellent source of omega-3s

L↓C H↑F H♥H

8	Kalamata olives, pitted and chopped
3	tablespoons red-wine vinegar
1	tablespoon capers, rinsed and chopped
¼	teaspoon freshly ground pepper, divided
3	tablespoons extra-virgin olive oil
2	thick slices day-old whole-grain bread, cut into 1-inch cubes (*see Tip*)
2	large tomatoes, cut into 1-inch pieces
1	medium cucumber, peeled (if desired), seeded and cut into 1-inch pieces
¼	cup thinly sliced red onion
¼	cup thinly sliced fresh basil
1	pound center-cut salmon, skinned (*see Tip*) and cut into 4 portions
½	teaspoon kosher salt

1. Preheat grill to high.

2. Whisk olives, vinegar, capers and ⅛ teaspoon pepper in a large bowl. Slowly whisk in oil until combined. Add bread, tomatoes, cucumber, onion and basil.

3. Oil the grill rack (*see photo, page 239*). Season both sides of salmon with salt and the remaining ⅛ teaspoon pepper. Grill the salmon until cooked through, 4 to 5 minutes per side.

4. Divide the salad among 4 plates and top each with a piece of salmon.

MAKES 4 SERVINGS, 2 CUPS SALAD & 3 OUNCES SALMON EACH.

TIPS: If using **fresh bread**, you can grill the bread slices along with the salmon and then cut them into cubes. Alternatively, cut bread into cubes, place on a baking sheet and bake at 300°F until dry.

How to **skin a salmon fillet**: Place salmon fillet on a clean cutting board, skin-side down. Starting at the tail end, slip the blade of a long knife between the fish flesh and the skin, holding down firmly with your other hand. Gently push the blade along at a 30° angle, separating the fillet from the skin without cutting through either. (*See photo, page 239.*)

Zucchini Rice Casserole

This creamy rice casserole uses some of summer's best produce—zucchini, corn and peppers. It serves a crowd and is just as good at room temperature as it is hot, so it's terrific to bring to a summer potluck party.

ACTIVE TIME: 40 minutes

TOTAL TIME: 2 hours

TO MAKE AHEAD: Prepare through Step 4; stir the sausage into the rice. Refrigerate the cheese sauce and rice casserole separately. When ready to serve, continue with Step 5, adding 10 to 20 minutes to the heating time.

PER SERVING:

249 calories; 10 g fat (5 g sat, 2 g mono); 34 mg cholesterol; 29 g carbohydrate; 13 g protein; 3 g fiber; 493 mg sodium; 254 mg potassium.

NUTRITION BONUS:

Vitamin C (56% daily value)
Vitamin A (20% dv)
Calcium (16% dv)

H❋W

1½	cups long-grain brown rice
3	cups reduced-sodium chicken broth
4	cups diced zucchini *and/or* summer squash
2	red *or* green bell peppers, chopped
1	large onion, diced
¾	teaspoon salt
1½	cups low-fat milk
3	tablespoons all-purpose flour
2	cups shredded pepper Jack cheese, divided
1	cup fresh corn kernels (about 2 ears; *see photo, page 223*) or frozen, thawed
2	teaspoons extra-virgin olive oil
8	ounces turkey sausage, casings removed
4	ounces reduced-fat cream cheese (Neufchâtel)
¼	cup chopped pickled jalapeño peppers

1. Preheat oven to 375°F.

2. Pour rice into a 9-by-13-inch baking dish. Bring broth to a simmer in a small saucepan. Stir hot broth, zucchini (and/or squash), bell peppers, onion and salt into the rice. Cover with foil. Bake for 45 minutes. Remove foil and continue baking until the rice is tender and most of the liquid is absorbed, 35 to 45 minutes more.

3. Meanwhile, whisk milk and flour in a small saucepan. Cook over medium heat until bubbling and thickened, 3 to 4 minutes. Reduce heat to low. Add 1½ cups cheese and corn and cook, stirring, until the cheese is melted. Set aside.

4. Heat oil in a large skillet over medium heat and add sausage. Cook, stirring and breaking the sausage into small pieces with a spoon, until lightly browned and no longer pink, about 4 minutes.

5. When the rice is done, stir in the sausage and cheese sauce. Sprinkle the remaining ½ cup cheese on top and dollop cream cheese by the teaspoonful over the casserole. Top with jalapeños. Return the casserole to the oven and bake until the cheese is melted, about 10 minutes. Let stand for 10 minutes before serving.

MAKES **12** SERVINGS, ABOUT **1** CUP EACH.

Garlicky Green Beans

We cook then cool the beans in advance so they can be heated up and seasoned moments before the meal. If you don't like tarragon, substitute dill or leave it out completely.

2	pounds green beans, trimmed
3	tablespoons extra-virgin olive oil
3	tablespoons minced garlic
3	tablespoons minced fresh parsley
1	tablespoon chopped fresh tarragon *or* 2 teaspoons dried
½	teaspoon salt
	Freshly ground pepper to taste

1. Bring a large pot of water to a boil. Place a large bowl of ice water next to the stove.

2. Add half the green beans to the boiling water and cook until tender-crisp, about 4 minutes. Transfer the beans with a slotted spoon to the ice water to cool. Repeat with the remaining beans. Place a kitchen towel on a baking sheet and use a slotted spoon to transfer the beans from the ice water; blot dry with another towel.

3. Just before serving, heat oil in a large Dutch oven or large skillet over medium heat. Add garlic and cook, stirring constantly, until fragrant, about 30 seconds. Add the green beans and stir. Add parsley, tarragon, salt and pepper and cook, stirring, until heated through, 1 to 3 minutes.

MAKES **8** SERVINGS, ABOUT **1** CUP EACH.

ACTIVE TIME: 35 minutes

TOTAL TIME: 45 minutes

TO MAKE AHEAD: Prepare through Step 2 and store in an airtight container in the refrigerator for up to 1 day.

PER SERVING:

92 calories; 6 g fat (1 g sat, 4 g mono); 0 mg cholesterol; 10 g carbohydrate; 2 g protein; 4 g fiber; 148 mg sodium; 186 mg potassium

NUTRITION BONUS:

Vitamin C (25% daily value)
Vitamin A (20% dv)
Fiber (16% dv)

H✻W L↓C H♥H

ACTIVE TIME: 10 minutes

TOTAL TIME: 45 minutes

TO MAKE AHEAD: Cover and refrigerate for up to 10 days.

PER SERVING:

10 calories; 0 g fat (0 g sat, 0 g mono); 0 mg cholesterol; 2 g carbohydrate; 1 g protein; 1 g fiber; 0 mg sodium; 16 mg potassium

Quick Pickles

Here's a way to make better-than-store-bought pickles in under an hour. The secret is pouring the hot vinegar mixture over slices of cold, crisp cucumber. These pickles have the perfect balance of sour and sweet—though closer to a "bread and butter" taste, they still satisfy the vinegar-loving pickle crowd. In our humble opinion, there's no reason to ever buy another jar of pickles. (Photograph: right.)

1¼	pounds pickling cucumbers, trimmed and cut into ¼-inch slices	1	cup light brown sugar
		1	cup slivered onion
1½	teaspoons salt	2	cloves garlic, slivered
1	cup cider vinegar	1	teaspoon dill seed
1	cup white vinegar	1	teaspoon mustard seed

1. Place cucumber slices in a colander set in the sink. Sprinkle with salt; stir to combine. Let stand for 20 minutes. Rinse, drain and transfer to a large heatproof bowl.

2. Meanwhile, combine cider vinegar, white vinegar, brown sugar, onion, garlic, dill and mustard seed in a medium saucepan. Bring to a boil. Reduce heat and simmer for 10 minutes. Pour the hot liquid over the cucumbers; stir to combine. Refrigerate for at least 10 minutes to bring to room temperature.

MAKES **16** SERVINGS, ABOUT ¼ CUP EACH.

PEPPERS

ACTIVE TIME: 20 minutes

TOTAL TIME: 20 minutes

TO MAKE AHEAD: Cover and refrigerate for up to 3 days.

PER SERVING:

107 calories; 7 g fat (1 g sat, 3 g mono); 0 mg cholesterol; 10 g carbohydrate; 1 g protein; 2 g fiber; 330 mg sodium; 331 mg potassium

NUTRITION BONUS:

Vitamin C (200% daily value)

H❋W L↓C H♥H

Grilled Pepper Salad

This bell pepper salad is quite versatile: serve it as a side dish with some diced sheep's-milk feta cheese, toss it with pasta or even use in a sandwich with torn basil leaves and slices of fresh mozzarella.

4	bell peppers (mixed colors), halved, seeded and stemmed
¼	cup halved and pitted oil-cured black olives
¼	cup rinsed and chopped oil-packed sun-dried tomatoes
1	tablespoon extra-virgin olive oil
1	tablespoon balsamic vinegar
⅛	teaspoon salt

Grill peppers on medium-high, turning once, until soft and charred in spots, about 5 minutes per side. When cool enough to handle, chop the peppers; toss with olives, sun-dried tomatoes, oil, vinegar and salt in a large bowl.

MAKES **4** SERVINGS, ABOUT 1 CUP EACH.

Grilled Corn with Chipotle-Lime Butter

Fresh lime and smoky chipotles makes this compound butter the perfect match for sweet corn. When the corn season is over, try a bit melted on some grilled fish or chicken. (Photograph: left.)

4	ears fresh corn, husked
2	tablespoons butter, softened
1/4	teaspoon freshly grated lime zest
1	teaspoon lime juice
1/2	teaspoon minced chipotle chile in adobo sauce plus 1/4 teaspoon adobo sauce (*see Note, page 240*) *or* 1/4 teaspoon ground chipotle pepper
1/2	teaspoon kosher salt

Preheat grill to high. Wrap each ear in foil. Place on the grill and cook, turning frequently, for 10 minutes. Remove from the grill and let stand in the foil while preparing the butter. Combine butter, lime zest, lime juice, chipotle and adobo sauce (or ground chipotle) and salt in a small bowl. Carefully unwrap the corn. Serve with the butter.

MAKES **4** SERVINGS.

ACTIVE TIME: 15 minutes

TOTAL TIME: 15 minutes

PER SERVING:

129 calories; 7 g fat (4 g sat, 0 g mono); 15 mg cholesterol; 17 g carbohydrate; 3 g protein; 2 g fiber; 222 mg sodium; 245 mg potassium

H✳W L↓C

Corn & Tomato Sauté

Corn and tomatoes are one of the great food marriages of all times. If you don't have fresh basil or tarragon, use whatever is best out of your herb garden.

2	teaspoons canola oil
1	cup fresh corn kernels (about 2 ears; *see photo, page* 223)
1/2	cup diced shallots
1	pound tomatoes, diced
1	tablespoon chopped fresh tarragon *or* basil
1/4	teaspoon salt

Heat oil in a medium skillet over medium heat. Add corn and shallots and cook, stirring occasionally, until lightly browned, about 5 minutes. Remove from the heat and let stand for 5 minutes. Stir in tomatoes, tarragon (or basil) and salt.

MAKES **4** SERVINGS, ABOUT **2/3** CUP EACH.

ACTIVE TIME: 20 minutes

TOTAL TIME: 25 minutes

PER SERVING:

87 calories; 3 g fat (0 g sat, 2 g mono); 0 mg cholesterol; 15 g carbohydrate; 3 g protein; 2 g fiber; 159 mg sodium; 422 mg potassium

NUTRITION BONUS:

Vitamin C (30% daily value)
Vitamin A (25% dv)

H✳W L↓C H♥H

ACTIVE TIME: 10 minutes

TOTAL TIME: 10 minutes

PER SERVING:

25 calories; 2 g fat (0 g sat, 1 g mono); 0 mg cholesterol; 3 g carbohydrate; 0 g protein; 1 g fiber; 233 mg sodium; 115 mg potassium

NUTRITION BONUS:

Vitamin C (15% daily value)

H✳W L↓C H↑F H♥H

Tomato & Green Olive Salsa

When the tomato harvest is in full swing it's prime time for salsa making. This zesty spin on standard tomato salsa includes sliced green olives and hot pepper relish. Serve as a dip with toasted pita chips or spoon over grilled fish or chicken.

1¼	pounds diced tomatoes
¼	cup sliced green olives
1	bunch sliced scallions
¼	cup hot pepper relish
1	tablespoon red-wine vinegar
2	teaspoons minced fresh oregano
¼	teaspoon salt
¼	teaspoon pepper

Combine tomatoes, olives, scallions, hot pepper relish, vinegar, oregano, salt and pepper.

MAKES **14** SERVINGS, ¼ CUP EACH.

ACTIVE TIME: 10 minutes

TOTAL TIME: 20 minutes

PER SERVING:

141 calories; 10 g fat (1 g sat, 7 g mono); 2 mg cholesterol; 8 g carbohydrate; 6 g protein; 3 g fiber; 386 mg sodium; 412 mg potassium

NUTRITION BONUS:

Vitamin C (35% daily value)
Vitamin A (30% dv)

H✳W L↓C H♥H

Raw Tomato Sauce

An uncooked sauce is the best way to get maximum garden-fresh flavor. In this recipe the tomatoes marinate in their own juices along with some fresh herbs, garlic, extra-virgin olive oil and red-wine vinegar. Diced fresh mozzarella absorbs the delicious flavors of the whole mélange. Toss with hot or room-temperature pasta.

1½	pounds plum tomatoes, chopped
⅓	cup diced fresh part-skim mozzarella
2	tablespoons chopped Kalamata olives
2	tablespoons red-wine vinegar
2	tablespoons extra-virgin olive oil
1	clove garlic, minced
2	teaspoons chopped fresh basil
2	teaspoons chopped fresh marjoram
¼	teaspoon salt
	Freshly ground pepper to taste

Combine tomatoes, mozzarella, olives, vinegar, oil and garlic. Add basil, marjoram, salt and pepper. Let stand to allow tomatoes to release their juices, about 10 minutes.

MAKES **4** SERVINGS.

One cup of cooked okra has only 34 calories but as much heart-healthy soluble fiber (4 grams) as a cup of oatmeal.

OKRA

Stewed Okra & Tomatoes

Okra (known as gombo in much of West Africa) does especially well in a hot growing season. In this dish, it appears as both vegetable and thickener, as is typical of many of the continent's okra dishes. Serve it over brown rice.

1	pound fresh okra, trimmed		1	habanero *or* 2 jalapeño
2	medium ripe tomatoes, chopped, *or* one 28-ounce can, drained and chopped		¼	peppers, pierced with a fork teaspoon salt Freshly ground pepper to taste

Place okra, tomatoes and chile(s) in a heavy saucepan. Bring to a boil. Cover and cook over medium heat until the okra is tender, 8 to 13 minutes. Season with salt and pepper.

MAKES 4 SERVINGS, ¾ CUP EACH.

ACTIVE TIME: 20 minutes

TOTAL TIME: 20 minutes

PER SERVING:

51 calories; 0 g fat (0 g sat, 0 g mono); 0 mg cholesterol; 11 g carbohydrate; 3 g protein; 5 g fiber; 86 mg sodium; 535 mg potassium

NUTRITION BONUS:

Vitamin A (122% daily value) Vitamin C (61% dv), Folate (29% dv) Magnesium (19% dv)

H✻W   L↓C   H↑F   H♥H

Tomatillo Sauce (Salsa Verde)

Here's a versatile, spicy green sauce that goes well with beef, pork, poultry and fish. And of course, you can spoon it over a couple poached eggs sitting on corn tortillas and melted cheese to make a mean green version of huevos rancheros.

1	pound tomatillos, husked and rinsed (about 16 small)		1	tablespoon canola oil
3	fresh hot chiles, such as jalapeño *or* serrano, stems trimmed		½	teaspoon dried oregano, preferably Mexican
1	small onion, quartered		1	cup reduced-sodium chicken broth
2	cloves garlic, peeled		¼	teaspoon salt

1. Place tomatillos and chiles in a saucepan; add water to cover. Bring to a boil and simmer until tomatillos are very tender, about 15 minutes. Drain.

2. Pulse onion and garlic in a food processor until finely chopped. Add the drained tomatillos and chiles and process until smooth. Heat oil in a large saucepan over medium-low heat. Add the tomatillo mixture and oregano. Cook, stirring constantly, until the mixture darkens and thickens, about 10 minutes. Stir in broth and return to a simmer. Simmer, stirring occasionally, until the sauce is thick enough to coat the back of a spoon, about 20 minutes. Season with salt and let cool to room temperature.

MAKES ABOUT 2 CUPS.

TOMATILLOS

ACTIVE TIME: 25 minutes

TOTAL TIME: 45 minutes

TO MAKE AHEAD: Cover and refrigerate for up to 2 days.

PER TABLESPOON:

11 calories; 1 g fat (0 g sat, 0 g mono); 0 mg cholesterol; 1 g carbohydrate; 0 g protein; 0 g fiber; 14 mg sodium; 45 mg potassium

Raspberry Bars

These bars highlight the tart, lively flavor of raspberries. They're a festive treat for a summer picnic or party.

ACTIVE TIME: 25 minutes

TOTAL TIME: 3¾ hours

TO MAKE AHEAD: Cover and refrigerate for up to 1 day.

PER BAR:

101 calories; 5 g fat (2 g sat, 2 g mono); 6 mg cholesterol; 14 g carbohydrate; 2 g protein; 2 g fiber; 94 mg sodium; 64 mg potassium

H✱W L⬇C H♥H

CRUST

½	cup chopped pecans
2	tablespoons granulated sugar
¾	cup white whole-wheat flour (*see Note, page 241*)
½	teaspoon salt
3	tablespoons cold butter, cut into small pieces
½	teaspoon vanilla extract
2	tablespoons ice water

RASPBERRY FILLING

2	teaspoons unflavored gelatin
2	tablespoons water
3	cups fresh raspberries, divided
½	cup granulated sugar
4	tablespoons nonfat cream cheese, softened
2	tablespoons low-fat milk
1	tablespoon confectioners' sugar

1. **To prepare crust:** Preheat oven to 400°F. Coat an 8-inch-square baking pan with cooking spray.

2. Place pecans, 2 tablespoons granulated sugar, flour and salt in a food processor; process until the nuts are finely ground. Add butter one piece at a time, pulsing once or twice after each addition, until incorporated. Add vanilla and ice water and pulse just until the dough starts to come together. Transfer to the prepared pan. Spread evenly and press firmly into the bottom to form a crust.

3. Bake the crust until it looks set, but not browned, about 15 minutes. Let cool on a wire rack.

4. **To prepare raspberry filling:** Sprinkle gelatin over 2 tablespoons water in a small bowl; let stand, stirring once or twice, while you prepare the rest of the filling.

5. Reserve 16 raspberries. Puree the remaining raspberries in a food processor until smooth. Transfer to a medium saucepan and stir in ½ cup granulated sugar. Cook over medium heat until bubbling. Stir in gelatin mixture and cook, stirring, until the gelatin is melted, about 1 minute.

6. Fill a large bowl with ice water. Pour the raspberry mixture into a medium bowl and set in the bowl of ice water. Refrigerate, stirring occasionally with a rubber spatula, until the mixture thickens to the consistency of loose jam and is beginning to set around the edges, about 30 minutes.

7. Meanwhile, beat cream cheese, milk and confectioners' sugar in a medium bowl with an electric mixer until smooth.

8. Spread the thickened raspberry filling evenly over the crust. Dollop the cream cheese mixture over the filling. Draw the tip of a sharp knife or skewer through the two fillings to create a swirled effect. Nestle the reserved berries into the filling, evenly spacing them so each bar will be topped with a berry when cut. Refrigerate until the bars are completely set, about 3 hours. Cut into 16 bars, one raspberry per bar.

MAKES **16** BARS.

Sour Cherry-Fruit Slump

Simply put, a slump (sometimes called a grunt) is a cobbler with light, puffy steamed dumplings, rather than browned biscuit dough, on the top. This variation calls for tart "pie" cherries as well as an assortment of sweeter summer fruit (berries and plums) to round out the flavor and brighten the sour-cherry color.

FRUIT

- 3/4 cup sugar, plus more to taste
- 2 tablespoons cornstarch
- 1/4 teaspoon ground cinnamon
- 1/2 cup cranberry juice cocktail *or* orange juice
- 1/2 teaspoon freshly grated lemon zest
- 4 cups fresh, frozen (thawed) *or* canned (drained) pitted sour cherries (*see Tips*)
- 1 3/4 cups blueberries, blackberries *and/or* chopped (unpeeled) purple plums

DOUGH

- 1 cup all-purpose flour
- 1/3 cup whole-wheat pastry flour (*see Note, page 241*)
- 1 1/2 tablespoons sugar
- 1 1/4 teaspoons baking powder
- 1/2 teaspoon salt
- 1/4 teaspoon baking soda
- 2 1/2 tablespoons very cold butter, cut into small pieces
- 2 tablespoons canola oil
- 3/4 cup nonfat buttermilk, plus more as needed
- 1 1/2 teaspoons sugar mixed with 1/4 teaspoon ground cinnamon, for garnish

ACTIVE TIME: 30 minutes

TOTAL TIME: 1 hour

TO MAKE AHEAD: Best the first day, but will keep, covered, in the refrigerator for up to 2 days. Serve at room temperature or reheat to slightly warm in a 250°F oven or microwave.

PER SERVING:

302 calories; 8 g fat (3 g sat, 2 g mono); 10 mg cholesterol; 57 g carbohydrate; 4 g protein; 3 g fiber; 295 mg sodium; 178 mg potassium

NUTRITION BONUS:

Vitamin C (30% daily value)
Vitamin A (25% dv)

1. **To prepare fruit:** Stir together 3/4 cup sugar, cornstarch and cinnamon in a 9- to 10-inch nonreactive deep-sided skillet or 3-quart wide-bottomed saucepan or Dutch oven (*see Note, page 240*). Stir in cranberry (or orange) juice and lemon zest, then the cherries and other fruit. Bring the mixture to a gentle simmer over medium heat, stirring. Simmer, stirring, until the mixture thickens slightly, about 2 minutes. Remove from the heat, taste and add up to 2 tablespoons more sugar if desired.

2. **To prepare dough:** Whisk all-purpose flour, whole-wheat flour, 1 1/2 tablespoons sugar, baking powder, salt and baking soda in a medium bowl. Add butter and oil. Using a pastry blender, two knives or a fork, cut in the butter until the mixture resembles coarse meal. Add 3/4 cup buttermilk, mixing with a fork just until incorporated. The dough should be very soft and slightly wet; if necessary, stir in a little more buttermilk. Let the dough stand for 3 to 4 minutes to firm up slightly.

3. **To finish:** Use lightly oiled soup spoons to scoop up the dough, dropping it in 8 portions onto the fruit, spacing them evenly over the surface. Return the slump to the stovetop and adjust the heat so it simmers very gently. Cover the pot tightly, and continue simmering until the dumplings are very puffy and cooked through, 17 to 20 minutes. (Cut into the center dumpling with a paring knife to check for doneness.) Let the slump cool on a wire rack, uncovered, for at least 15 minutes. Sprinkle the cinnamon sugar over the dumplings. Serve warm.

MAKES 8 SERVINGS.

TIPS: Find frozen, canned and dried **sour cherries** at King Orchards, (877) 937-5464, *kingorchards.com*, and The Cherry Stop, (800) 286-7209, *cherrystop.com*.

Be sure to **measure frozen cherries** while still frozen, then thaw. (Drain juice before using.)

To **pit sour cherries**, squeeze them gently until the pit pops out.

Blueberry Tart with Walnut Crust

Wild blueberries are indigenous to the Northeast, and when they're in season, they frequently show up at breakfast, lunch and dinner. Whether wild or cultivated, any ripe blueberries need little extra sweetening. For this tart a few tablespoons of maple syrup does the job and rounds out the flavor of the cream filling.

ACTIVE TIME: 30 minutes

TOTAL TIME: 2 hours (including cooling & chilling time)

TO MAKE AHEAD: Refrigerate for up to 1 day.

EQUIPMENT: 9-inch removable-bottom tart pan

PER SERVING:

177 calories; 11 g fat (4 g sat, 3 g mono); 18 mg cholesterol; 17 g carbohydrate; 4 g protein; 1 g fiber; 138 mg sodium; 103 mg potassium

L ⬇ C

NOTE: To avoid trans fats, look for **graham crackers** without partially hydrogenated vegetable oil. To make crumbs, pulse graham crackers in a food processor or place in a large sealable plastic bag and crush with a rolling pin. (You'll need about 14 whole-wheat graham cracker squares to make 1 cup of crumbs.)

CRUST

½	cup walnuts, lightly toasted (*see Tip, page 239*)
1	cup graham cracker crumbs, preferably whole-wheat (*see Note*)
1	large egg white
1	tablespoon butter, melted
1	tablespoon peanut *or* canola oil
	Pinch of salt

FILLING

8	ounces reduced-fat cream cheese (Neufchâtel), softened
¼	cup reduced-fat sour cream
¼	cup plus 2 tablespoons pure maple syrup, preferably grade B, divided
2	cups fresh blueberries

1. **To prepare crust:** Preheat oven to 325°F.

2. Coarsely chop walnuts in a food processor. Add graham cracker crumbs and process until the mixture looks like fine crumbs.

3. Whisk egg white in a medium bowl until frothy. Add the crumb mixture, butter, oil and salt; toss to combine. Press the mixture into the bottom and ½ inch up the sides of a 9-inch removable-bottom tart pan. Set the pan on a baking sheet. Bake until dry and slightly darker around the edges, about 8 minutes. Cool on a wire rack.

4. **To prepare filling:** Beat cream cheese, sour cream and ¼ cup maple syrup in a medium bowl with an electric mixer on low speed until smooth. When the crust is cool, spread the filling evenly into it, being careful not to break up the delicate crust. Arrange blueberries on the filling, pressing lightly so they set in. Drizzle the remaining 2 tablespoons maple syrup over the berries. Chill for at least 1 hour to firm up.

MAKES **12** SERVINGS.

Watermelon-Yogurt Ice

Inspired by creamy watermelon sherbet, our light and refreshing dessert captures the essence of summer.

¼	cup water
¼	cup sugar
4	cups diced seedless watermelon (about 3 pounds with the rind)
1	cup low-fat vanilla yogurt
1	tablespoon lime juice

1. Combine water and sugar in a small saucepan. Cook, stirring, over high heat until the sugar is dissolved. Transfer to a glass measuring cup and let cool slightly.

2. Puree watermelon in a food processor or blender, in 2 batches, pulsing until smooth. Transfer to a large bowl. Whisk in the cooled sugar syrup, yogurt and lime juice until combined. Pour the mixture through a fine-mesh sieve into another large bowl, whisking to release all juice. Discard pulp. Pour the extracted juices into an ice cream maker and freeze according to manufacturer's directions. (*Alternatively, pour into a shallow metal pan and freeze until solid, about 6 hours or overnight. Remove from freezer to defrost slightly, 5 minutes. Break into small chunks and process in a food processor, in batches, until smooth and creamy.*) Serve immediately or transfer to a storage container and freeze for up to 2 hours.

MAKES 8 SERVINGS, ½ CUP EACH.

ACTIVE TIME: 20 minutes

TOTAL TIME: 1 hour (if using an ice cream maker)

TO MAKE AHEAD: If frozen longer than 2 hours, break into chunks and puree in a food processor until smooth before serving.

PER SERVING:

74 calories; 1 g fat (0 g sat, 0 g mono); 2 mg cholesterol; 16 g carbohydrate; 2 g protein; 0 g fiber; 21 mg sodium; 155 mg potassium

Cantaloupe Ice Pops

Finely slivered mint frozen inside these cantaloupe ice pops adds a delightfully pretty flair.

1	small cantaloupe
½	cup water
¼	cup sugar
1	tablespoon finely slivered fresh mint leaves
¼-⅓	cup lemon juice, depending on the sweetness of the melon

1. Cut cantaloupe in half; remove and discard the seeds. Scoop out the flesh and transfer to a food processor. Puree until smooth; measure 1⅓ cups puree and transfer to a small bowl. (Reserve any remaining puree for another use, such as a smoothie.)

2. Pour water into a small saucepan, add sugar and bring to a boil over high heat. Stir in mint and immediately remove from the heat. Let stand for 1 minute.

3. Stir the mint syrup and lemon juice into the cantaloupe puree. Pour the mixture into 8 individual popsicle molds or small (2-ounce) paper cups.

4. Freeze until beginning to set, about 1 hour. Insert frozen-treat sticks and freeze until completely firm. Dip the molds briefly in hot water before unmolding.

MAKES EIGHT 2-OUNCE POPS.

ACTIVE TIME: 20 minutes

TOTAL TIME: 1 ½ hours

EQUIPMENT: 8 popsicle molds or small (2-ounce) paper cups

PER SERVING:

45 calories; 0 g fat (0 g sat, 0 g mono); 0 mg cholesterol; 12 g carbohydrate; 1 g protein; 1 g fiber; 10 mg sodium; 160 mg potassium

NUTRITION BONUS:

Vitamin C (40% daily value)
Vitamin A (35% dv)

H✳W L↓C H♥H

Blackberries are an excellent source of fiber: 1 cup packs 8 grams, nearly a third of the recommended daily dose.

BLACKBERRIES

Berry-Almond Quick Bread

Sometimes it seems like it takes forever for berries to ripen and then suddenly they're all ready to be picked at once and you're inundated. This wholesome quick-bread recipe is just what you need; whatever berries you have on hand go into a versatile, whole-grain buttermilk batter that can be baked into muffins, loaves or even doughnutlike mini Bundts. Problem solved.

1½	cups whole-wheat pastry flour (*see Note, page 241*) *or* whole-wheat flour
1	cup all-purpose flour
1½	teaspoons baking powder
1	teaspoon ground cinnamon
½	teaspoon baking soda
¼	teaspoon salt
2	large eggs
1	cup nonfat buttermilk (*see Tip*)
⅔	cup brown sugar
2	tablespoons butter, melted
2	tablespoons canola oil
1	teaspoon vanilla extract
½	teaspoon almond extract
2	cups fresh *or* frozen berries (whole blackberries, blueberries, raspberries; diced strawberries)
½	cup chopped toasted sliced almonds (*see Tip*), plus more for topping if desired

1. Preheat oven to 400°F for muffins, mini loaves and mini Bundts or 375°F for a large loaf. (*See pan options, right.*) Coat pan(s) with cooking spray.

2. Whisk whole-wheat flour, all-purpose flour, baking powder, cinnamon, baking soda and salt in a large bowl.

3. Whisk eggs, buttermilk, brown sugar, butter, oil, vanilla and almond extract in another large bowl until well combined.

4. Make a well in the center of the dry ingredients, pour in the wet ingredients and stir until just combined. Add berries and almonds. Stir just to combine; do not overmix. Transfer batter to the prepared pan(s). Top with additional almonds, if desired.

5. Bake until golden brown and a wooden skewer inserted into the center comes out clean, 22 to 25 minutes for muffins or mini Bundts, 35 minutes for mini loaves, 1 hour 10 minutes for a large loaf. Let cool in the pan(s) for 10 minutes, then turn out onto a wire rack. Let muffins and mini Bundts cool for 5 minutes more, mini loaves for 30 minutes, large loaves for 40 minutes.

MAKES **12** SERVINGS.

ACTIVE TIME: 25 minutes

TOTAL TIME: 1¼ hours (muffins, mini Bundts), 1½ hours (mini loaves), 2¼ hours (large loaf), including cooling times

TO MAKE AHEAD: Store, individually wrapped, at room temperature for up to 2 days or in the freezer for up to 1 month.

PER SERVING:

220 calories; 7 g fat (2 g sat, 3 g mono); 41 mg cholesterol; 33 g carbohydrate; 6 g protein; 3 g fiber; 183 mg sodium; 81 mg potassium

H✂W H♥H

PAN OPTIONS:
1 large loaf (9-by-5-inch pan)
3 mini loaves (6-by-3-inch pan, 2-cup capacity)
6 mini Bundt cakes (6-cup mini Bundt pan, scant 1-cup capacity per cake)
12 muffins (standard 12-cup, 2½-inch muffin pan)

TIPS: No **buttermilk**? Mix 1 tablespoon lemon juice into 1 cup milk.

To **toast sliced almonds**: cook in a small dry skillet over medium-low heat, stirring constantly, until fragrant and lightly browned, 2 to 4 minutes.

FALL

" There is a sweetness and gentleness to the fall. I love the fragrant smell of apple tarts, making cider, roasting a duck with sweet potatoes, the bursting yellow and red of the maple trees, the tanginess of the Concord grapes, and, finally, the turkey of Thanksgiving, my favorite holiday. **"**

—JACQUES PÉPIN, FROM
HIS BOOK *CHEZ JACQUES*

Chard is a good source of magnesium, a nutrient that helps keep muscles and nerves functioning properly.

CHARD

Chard & Feta Tart

Chard is one of the most beautiful greens: its dark leaves have celerylike ribs that come in a whole rainbow of colors. It's been popular with Mediterranean cooks for almost a thousand years so it's an obvious choice for a Greek-inspired tart that balances the slight bitterness of the leafy greens with fragrant lemon zest, briny olives and salty feta cheese. This is a great option as an appetizer or serve it as a vegetarian main course for 8.

CRUST

¾ cup whole-wheat pastry flour
¾ cup all-purpose flour
1½ tablespoons chopped fresh thyme *or* oregano *or* ½ teaspoon dried
¾ teaspoon salt
¾ teaspoon freshly ground pepper
⅓ cup extra-virgin olive oil
5 tablespoons cold water

FILLING

2 teaspoons extra-virgin olive oil
6 cups chopped chard (about 1 bunch), leaves and stems separated
2 tablespoons minced garlic
2 tablespoons water
2 large eggs
1 cup part-skim ricotta cheese
1 teaspoon freshly grated lemon zest
⅛ teaspoon freshly ground pepper
½ cup chopped pitted kalamata olives
⅓ cup crumbled feta cheese

1. **To prepare crust:** Combine whole-wheat flour, all-purpose flour, thyme (or oregano), salt and ¾ teaspoon pepper in a bowl. Make a well in the center and add ⅓ cup oil and 5 tablespoons water. Gradually stir the wet ingredients into the dry to form a soft dough. Knead on a lightly floured surface until the dough comes together. Wrap in plastic and chill for 15 minutes.

2. Preheat oven to 400°F. Coat a 9-inch tart pan with removable bottom with cooking spray.

3. Roll the dough into a 12-inch circle on a lightly floured surface. Transfer to the prepared pan and press into the bottom and up the sides. Trim any overhanging dough and use it to patch any spots that don't come all the way up the sides. Prick the bottom and sides with a fork in a few places. Bake the crust until firm and lightly brown, 20 to 22 minutes. Let cool on a wire rack for at least 10 minutes.

4. **To prepare filling:** Meanwhile, heat 2 teaspoons oil in a large skillet over medium heat. Add chard stems and cook, stirring, until just tender, about 2 minutes. Add garlic and cook, stirring, until fragrant, about 15 seconds. Add chard leaves and 2 tablespoons water and cook, stirring, until the leaves are just tender and the water has evaporated, 2 to 5 minutes. Transfer the greens to a sieve over a bowl and let drain and cool for 5 minutes. Whisk eggs, ricotta, lemon zest and ⅛ teaspoon pepper in a large bowl. Fold in the greens, olives and feta. Spread the filling into the crust. Bake the tart until the top is lightly browned and a knife inserted in the center comes out clean, 30 to 35 minutes. Let cool for 10 minutes before cutting into wedges.

MAKES **12** SERVINGS.

ACTIVE TIME: 1 hour

TOTAL TIME: 2 hours

TO MAKE AHEAD: Store at room temperature for up to 2 hours.

EQUIPMENT: 9-inch tart pan with removable bottom

PER SERVING:

191 calories; 12 g fat (3 g sat, 8 g mono); 45 mg cholesterol; 14 g carbohydrate; 6 g protein; 1 g fiber; 365 mg sodium; 123 mg potassium

NUTRITION BONUS:

Vitamin A (40% daily value)
Calcium & Vitamin C (15% dv)

H✳W L⬇C

Roasted Beet Crostini

Candy-sweet, shockingly bright beets are truly the gems of all root vegetables and the whole plant is delicious. For these stunning crostini the beets are roasted then pureed with goat cheese for a creamy ruby-red spread. The greens and stems are sautéed with olive oil and garlic for the topping.

1	bunch beets with greens attached (*see Note*)
16	½-inch-thick slices baguette, preferably whole-grain, cut on the diagonal
2	tablespoons extra-virgin olive oil, divided
6	cloves garlic, minced
1	tablespoon sherry vinegar *or* red-wine vinegar
2	tablespoons water
¼	teaspoon salt
4	ounces creamy goat cheese
¼	teaspoon freshly ground pepper

1. Preheat oven to 400°F.

2. Trim greens from beets, reserving stems and greens. Place the beets in a baking pan, cover with foil and roast until very tender when pierced with a knife, 45 minutes to 1½ hours, depending on the size of the beets. Uncover and let cool. Reduce oven temperature to 350°.

3. While the beets cool, arrange baguette slices in a single layer on a large baking sheet. Bake, turning the slices over once halfway through, until toasted but not browned, about 14 minutes.

4. Thinly slice the beet green stems and finely chop the leaves; keep stems and leaves separate. Heat 1 tablespoon oil in a large skillet over medium heat. Add the stems and cook, stirring occasionally, until tender, about 3 minutes. Add the remaining 1 tablespoon oil and garlic and cook, stirring, until fragrant, about 15 seconds. Add the greens, vinegar and water and cook, stirring occasionally, until the greens are tender and the liquid has evaporated, 4 to 5 minutes. Stir in salt and remove from the heat.

5. Peel the cooled beets and cut into 1-inch pieces. Place ¾ cup beet pieces, goat cheese and pepper in a food processor and puree until smooth (reserve the remaining beets for another use).

6. To assemble crostini, spread about 2 teaspoons beet-cheese spread on each slice of toasted baguette and top with sautéed greens.

MAKES 16 CROSTINI.

ACTIVE TIME: 50 minutes

TOTAL TIME: 1½ hours

TO MAKE AHEAD: Prepare through Step 4; store the beet spread and greens separately in the refrigerator for up to 2 days. Bring to room temperature before assembling.

PER CROSTINI:

82 calories; 4 g fat (1 g sat, 2 g mono); 3 mg cholesterol; 10 g carbohydrate; 4 g protein; 2 g fiber; 181 mg sodium; 224 mg potassium

NUTRITION BONUS:

Vitamin A (25% daily value)

H�W L↓C H♥H

NOTE: Look for **bunches of beets** with 2 to 3 medium-to-large beets for this recipe. If you have trouble finding beets with greens still attached, use loose beets plus 3 cups finely chopped chard greens and thinly sliced stems.

Roasted Pear-Butternut Soup with Crumbled Stilton

When pears start appearing in the market, don't be put off if they seem hard and unripe: they are one of the rare fruits that actually develop better flavor and texture after they're picked. Here they are roasted to sweet perfection with butternut squash and pureed to create a creamy soup that gets a luxurious garnish of Stilton cheese. You can serve this as a first course or with a salad and crusty bread for a light autumn supper.

2	ripe pears, peeled, quartered and cored
2	pounds butternut squash, peeled, seeded and cut into 2-inch chunks
2	medium tomatoes, cored and quartered
1	large leek, pale green and white parts only, halved lengthwise, sliced and washed thoroughly
2	cloves garlic, crushed
2	tablespoons extra-virgin olive oil
1/2	teaspoon salt, divided
	Freshly ground pepper to taste
4	cups vegetable broth *or* reduced-sodium chicken broth, divided
2/3	cup crumbled Stilton *or* other blue-veined cheese
1	tablespoon thinly sliced fresh chives *or* scallion greens

1. Preheat oven to 400°F.

2. Combine pears, squash, tomatoes, leek, garlic, oil, 1/4 teaspoon salt and pepper in a large bowl; toss to coat. Spread evenly on a large rimmed baking sheet. Roast, stirring occasionally, until the vegetables are tender, 40 to 55 minutes. Let cool slightly.

3. Place half the vegetables and 2 cups broth in a blender; puree until smooth. Transfer to a large saucepan. Puree the remaining vegetables and 2 cups broth. Add to the pan and stir in the remaining 1/4 teaspoon salt.

4. Cook the soup over medium-low heat, stirring, until hot, about 10 minutes. Divide among 6 bowls and garnish with cheese and chives (or scallion greens).

MAKES 6 SERVINGS, 1 1/3 CUPS EACH.

ACTIVE TIME: 35 minutes

TOTAL TIME: 1 1/4 hours

TO MAKE AHEAD: Cover and refrigerate for up to 3 days or freeze for up to 1 month. Add more broth when reheating, if desired.

PER SERVING:

235 calories; 10 g fat (5 g sat, 5 g mono); 11 mg cholesterol; 34 g carbohydrate; 6 g protein; 6 g fiber; 721 mg sodium; 700 mg potassium

NUTRITION BONUS:

Vitamin A (350% daily value)
Vitamin C (70% dv)
Potassium (21% dv)
Calcium (20% dv)

H✕W   H↑F

Sichuan Carrot Soup

Distinctive flavors from the cuisine of Sichuan province in China—peanut, sesame, hot red pepper, ginger and garlic—play against a backdrop of sweet carrots. The beautiful burnished-orange soup is served chilled, which makes it a nice choice for a warm Indian-summer evening.

ACTIVE TIME: 25 minutes

TOTAL TIME: 1 3/4 hours (including chilling)

TO MAKE AHEAD: Cover and refrigerate for up to 2 days.

PER SERVING:

112 calories; 4 g fat (1 g sat, 2 g mono); 3 mg cholesterol; 15 g carbohydrate; 6 g protein; 3 g fiber; 406 mg sodium; 383 mg potassium

NUTRITION BONUS:

Vitamin A (230% dv)

H✖W L↓C H♥H

1	teaspoon canola oil
1	onion, chopped
1	stalk celery, chopped
1	clove garlic, minced
3	cups reduced-sodium chicken broth
1	pound carrots (5-6 medium), chopped
1	3/4-inch piece ginger, peeled and cut into thin slices
1/4-1/2	teaspoon crushed red pepper
2	tablespoons lime juice
1½	tablespoons reduced-sodium soy sauce
1½	tablespoons smooth natural peanut butter
2-3	teaspoons sugar
1	teaspoon sesame oil
1	cup nonfat milk
1/4	teaspoon salt
	Freshly ground pepper to taste
1	tablespoon chopped scallions for garnish

1. Heat canola oil in a large saucepan over medium heat. Add onion, celery and garlic and cook, stirring, until softened, 3 to 5 minutes. Add broth, carrots, ginger and crushed red pepper and bring to a boil. Reduce heat to low and simmer, covered, until the carrots are very tender, 20 to 30 minutes.

2. Pour the mixture through a strainer set over a large bowl. Transfer the solids to a food processor or blender and add lime juice, soy sauce, peanut butter, sugar and sesame oil; puree, adding some of the cooking liquid as needed for a smooth consistency. Transfer the puree to the bowl of cooking liquid and stir in milk. Season with salt and pepper. Cover and refrigerate until chilled, at least 1 hour. Garnish each portion with scallions.

MAKES **6** SERVINGS.

Pueblo Pumpkin Stew

Pumpkin has been part of the American harvest tradition since Colonial times. Here's a contemporary Southwestern-inspired vegetarian stew of fresh pumpkin, pinto beans and New Mexico chiles that can be served over brown rice as a hearty main dish.

8	fresh New Mexico chiles *or* Cubanelle peppers (*see Note*)
2	tablespoons canola oil
1	large onion, sliced
1	tablespoon minced peeled fresh ginger
2	serrano chiles, chopped
4	large tomatoes, chopped
2	teaspoons ground cumin
2	teaspoons garam masala (*see Note*)
½	teaspoon ground turmeric
2	cups water
5	cups cubed peeled pumpkin (*see Note*) *or* butternut squash
1	15-ounce can pinto beans, rinsed (*see Tip, page 239*)
2	tablespoons freshly grated Parmesan cheese
2	teaspoons salt

1. Preheat broiler. Place New Mexico chiles (or peppers) on a foil-lined baking sheet and broil until blackened, turning so that the sides are evenly charred, 8 to 10 minutes total.

2. Transfer the chiles (or peppers) to a large bowl, cover and let steam until the skins are loosened, 10 minutes. Uncover; when cool enough to handle, remove and discard stems, skins, seeds and ribs; chop the chiles (or peppers).

3. Heat oil in a Dutch oven over medium heat. Add onion, ginger, serrano chiles and the roasted chiles (or peppers) and cook, stirring, until softened, about 4 minutes. Add tomatoes, cumin, garam masala and turmeric and cook, stirring often, until the tomatoes are beginning to break down, about 5 minutes.

4. Add water and pumpkin (or squash). Bring to a boil. Reduce heat to low, cover and simmer until the pumpkin (or squash) is tender, about 30 minutes. Stir in beans and cook until heated through. Stir in Parmesan and salt.

MAKES 8 SERVINGS, ABOUT 1½ CUPS EACH.

ACTIVE TIME: 1 hour

TOTAL TIME: 1½ hours

PER SERVING:

143 calories; 5 g fat (1 g sat, 2 g mono); 1 mg cholesterol; 23 g carbohydrate; 6 g protein; 5 g fiber; 614 mg sodium; 780 mg potassium

NUTRITION BONUS:

Vitamin C (215% daily value)
Vitamin A (130% dv)
Folate & Potassium (22% dv)
Iron (15% dv)

H✕W   H↑F   H♥H

NOTES: The **New Mexico chile** is a long green variety that turns red in the fall; it is similar to the Anaheim. **Cubanelles** are long and light green and sometimes called Italian frying peppers.

Garam masala is a blend of spices used in Indian cooking, usually including cardamom, black pepper, cloves, nutmeg, fennel, cumin and coriander. It is available in the spice section of most supermarkets.

Look for smaller-size **pumpkins**, which have more tender and flavorful flesh than the larger ones, for this recipe. And for food-safety concerns, don't use carved jack-o'-lanterns.

Flavorful fennel is virtually calorie-free: it
contains only 16 calories per ½ cup.

FENNEL

Fennel & Orange Salad with Toasted Pistachios

This delicious combination of fennel and oranges takes you right through late fall and into winter. Every part of the fennel plant can be eaten—bulb, stems, feathery tops and seeds. For this elegant salad, the sweet-tasting bulbs are thinly sliced and tossed with salty, toasted pistachios and tangy lime juice. Jícama or radishes add another layer of texture and earthy flavor.

2	navel oranges, peeled, quartered and thinly sliced
1	small bulb fennel, quartered, cored and very thinly sliced crosswise
1	cup very thinly sliced radishes (about 8 radishes) *or* diced peeled jícama (*see Note*)
¼	cup coarsely chopped fresh cilantro
2	tablespoons extra-virgin olive oil *or* pistachio oil
1	tablespoon plus 1 teaspoon lime juice
¼	teaspoon salt
	Freshly ground pepper to taste
6	tablespoons shelled salted pistachio nuts, toasted and chopped

Combine orange slices, fennel, radishes (or jicama), cilantro, oil, lime juice, salt and pepper in a bowl. Gently toss to mix. Just before serving, sprinkle nuts over the salad.

MAKES 4 SERVINGS, 1 CUP EACH.

ACTIVE TIME: 20 minutes

TOTAL TIME: 25 minutes

PER SERVING:

186 calories; 13 g fat (2 g sat, 8 g mono); 0 mg cholesterol; 17 g carbohydrate; 4 g protein; 5 g fiber; 180 mg sodium; 499 mg potassium

NUTRITION BONUS:

Vitamin C (85% daily value)
Copper (12% dv)
Magnesium (8% dv)

L↓C H↑F H♥H

NOTE: **Jícama** is a round root vegetable with thin brown skin and white crunchy flesh. It has a slightly sweet and nutty flavor.

Crunchy Pear & Celery Salad

The variety of pears you will find at a good farmers' market is impressive. Bartlett or Anjou pears are used in this salad for their crisp texture. The nut and cheese combination is really what defines this dish—white Cheddar and pecans is decidedly American. For an Italian twist, try a good Parmesan with some toasted pine nuts or to go British use crumbled Stilton and toasted walnuts.

4	stalks celery, trimmed and cut in half crosswise
2	tablespoons cider, pear, raspberry *or* other fruit vinegar
2	tablespoons honey
¼	teaspoon salt
2	ripe pears, preferably red Bartlett *or* Anjou, diced
1	cup finely diced white Cheddar cheese
½	cup chopped pecans, toasted (*see Tip*)
	Freshly ground pepper to taste
6	large leaves butterhead *or* other lettuce

1. Soak celery in a bowl of ice water for 15 minutes. Drain and pat dry. Cut into ½-inch pieces.

2. Whisk vinegar, honey and salt in a large bowl until blended. Add pears; gently stir to coat. Add the celery, cheese and pecans; stir to combine. Season with pepper. Divide the lettuce leaves among 6 plates and top with a portion of salad. Serve at room temperature or chilled.

MAKES 6 SERVINGS, 1 CUP EACH.

ACTIVE TIME: 25 minutes

TOTAL TIME: 25 minutes

TO MAKE AHEAD: Prepare salad without pecans up to 2 hours ahead. Stir in pecans just before serving.

PER SERVING:

221 calories; 14 g fat (5 g sat, 4 g mono); 20 mg cholesterol; 20 g carbohydrate; 6 g protein; 4 g fiber; 240 mg sodium; 221 mg potassium

NUTRITION BONUS:

Calcium (15% daily value)

TIP: To toast chopped pecans, cook in a small dry skillet over medium-low heat, stirring constantly, until fragrant and lightly browned, 2 to 4 minutes.

Salad of Mâche & Beets

*Ruby beets and deep green mâche are topped with grated hard-cooked egg in this
stunning salad.*

2	tablespoons finely chopped shallot
2	tablespoons red-wine vinegar
2	tablespoons cranberry juice cocktail *or* water
1	tablespoon whole-grain mustard
2	tablespoons extra-virgin olive oil
¼	teaspoon salt
	Freshly ground pepper to taste
6	small cooked beets (*see Guide, page 220*), peeled and cut into thin sticks
1	hard-boiled egg (*see Tip*), peeled
9	cups mâche (lamb's lettuce) *or* Boston lettuce

1. Whisk shallot, vinegar, cranberry juice (or water) and mustard in a small bowl.
   Slowly whisk in oil. Season with salt and pepper. Pour half of the dressing into
   a separate bowl and set aside. Marinate beets in the remaining dressing for at
   least 1 hour and up to 6 hours.

2. Just before serving, use a rubber spatula to press egg through a coarse strainer
   into a small bowl. Toss the reserved dressing with the mâche (or Boston lettuce).
   Arrange on 6 salad plates. Divide the marinated beets over the lettuce and garnish with some of the sieved egg and a grinding of black pepper.

   MAKES 6 SERVINGS.

ACTIVE TIME: 15 minutes

TOTAL TIME: 1¼ hours (including
1 hour marinating time)

TO MAKE AHEAD: Prepare
through Step 1; cover and
refrigerate for up to 6 hours.

PER SERVING:

110 calories; 6 g fat (1 g sat,
4 g mono); 35 mg cholesterol;
11 g carbohydrate; 4 g protein;
3 g fiber; 227 mg sodium;
490 mg potassium

NUTRITION BONUS:

Vitamin A (57% daily value)
Folate (39% dv)
Vitamin C (17% dv)

H✖W L↓C H♥H

TIP: To hard-boil eggs, place eggs
in a single layer in a saucepan;
cover with water. Bring to a
simmer over medium-high heat.
Reduce heat to low and cook at
the barest simmer for 10 minutes.
Remove from heat, pour out hot
water and cover the eggs with
cold water. Let stand until cool
enough to handle before peeling.

Wheat Berry Salad with Red Fruit

Wheat berries are whole kernels of wheat with just the outer husk removed. When cooked they have a chewy bite and nutty flavor. For this sweet and tart salad, they are blended with cranberries, apples and pecans and tossed in a raspberry vinaigrette—a winning combination. Serve over a bed of peppery arugula for lunch or a light supper.

⅓	cup freshly squeezed orange juice
⅓	cup dried cranberries
3	cups Cooked Wheat Berries (*recipe follows*)
1	large Fuji apple, unpeeled, diced
½	cup pecan halves, toasted (*see Tip, page 239*) and coarsely chopped
3	tablespoons raspberry vinegar
3	tablespoons extra-virgin olive oil
¼	teaspoon salt
¼	teaspoon freshly ground pepper

1. Combine orange juice and cranberries in a small bowl. Let stand for 15 minutes.

2. Combine wheat berries, apple and pecans in a large bowl; stir gently. Drain the cranberries, reserving the juice. Stir the cranberries into the wheat berry mixture.

3. Whisk the reserved orange juice, vinegar and oil in a small bowl until combined. Season with salt and pepper. Pour over the salad and stir gently to coat. Refrigerate for at least 30 minutes to allow the flavors to combine. Serve cold or at room temperature.

MAKES 6 SERVINGS, ABOUT 1 CUP EACH.

ACTIVE TIME: 20 minutes

TOTAL TIME: 1 hour

TO MAKE AHEAD: Cover and refrigerate for up to 1 day.

PER SERVING:

321 calories; 14 g fat (2 g sat, 9 g mono); 0 mg cholesterol; 42 g carbohydrate; 7 g protein; 6 g fiber; 365 mg sodium; 99 mg potassium

NUTRITION BONUS:

Vitamin C (15% daily value)

Cooked Wheat Berries

2	cups hard red winter-wheat berries (*see Note, page 241*)
7	cups cold water
1	teaspoon salt

1. Sort through wheat berries carefully, discarding any stones. Rinse well under cool running water. Place in a large heavy saucepan. Add water and salt.

2. Bring to a boil over high heat, then reduce heat, cover, and simmer gently for 1 hour, stirring occasionally. Drain and rinse. To serve hot, use immediately. Otherwise, follow the make-ahead instructions.

MAKES ABOUT 4½ CUPS.

ACTIVE TIME: 5 minutes

TOTAL TIME: 1¼ hours

TO MAKE AHEAD: Cover and refrigerate for up to 2 days or freeze for up to 1 month.

PER ½ CUP:

151 calories; 1 g fat (0 g sat, 0 g mono); 0 mg cholesterol; 29 g carbohydrate; 6 g protein; 4 g fiber; 265 mg sodium; 2 mg potassium

Braised Broccoli Rabe with Orecchiette

Broccoli rabe (also called rapini) is a pencil-thin cousin to broccoli that has a deliciously bitter taste. Here we mellow its bitterness just a bit by plunging it into boiling water for a minute before adding it to the rest of the dish. For a variation, try adding crumbles of browned Italian turkey sausage.

ACTIVE TIME: 20 minutes

TOTAL TIME: 35 minutes

PER SERVING:

342 calories; 9 g fat (1 g sat, 3 g mono); 0 mg cholesterol; 56 g carbohydrate; 15 g protein; 9 g fiber; 759 mg sodium; 168 mg potassium

NUTRITION BONUS:

Vitamin C (175% daily value)
Vitamin A (173% dv)

H✕W H↑F H♥H

1	pound broccoli rabe, tough stems trimmed
2	teaspoons extra-virgin olive oil
3	cloves garlic, minced
1	teaspoon dried rosemary
¼	teaspoon crushed red pepper
5	cups vegetable broth, reduced-sodium chicken broth *or* water
8	ounces whole-wheat orecchiette
¼	teaspoon salt
	Freshly ground pepper to taste
¼	cup chopped walnuts, toasted (*see Tip, page 239*)

1. Cook broccoli rabe in a large pot of boiling salted water until bright green and still crisp, about 1 minute. Drain and refresh under cold running water. Coarsely chop.

2. Combine oil, garlic, rosemary and crushed red pepper in a large pot; cook, stirring, over medium heat, until fragrant, about 1 minute. Add broth (or water) and bring to a boil. Add pasta and the broccoli rabe. Increase heat to medium-high and cook, uncovered, stirring occasionally, until the pasta is tender and most of the liquid is absorbed, 15 to 18 minutes. Season with salt and pepper.

3. Serve in shallow bowls, sprinkled with walnuts.

MAKES 4 SERVINGS, ABOUT 1 ⅔ CUPS EACH.

Mushrooms are virtually calorie-free and a source of
the B vitamins riboflavin and niacin.

MUSHROOMS

Wild Mushroom & Sage Pizzettas

The smell of sage brings to mind the steamy aroma of Thanksgiving turkey stuffing. But the pungent herb is really quite versatile, pairing well with pork, chicken, citrus and here with wild mushrooms on this earthy-flavored pizza. Dried sage will do, but is not as aromatic as fresh. Try this pizza as a light main course or cut into wedges and serve as an appetizer.

1½	teaspoons extra-virgin olive oil
8	cups sliced wild *and/or* cultivated mushrooms, such as chanterelles, cepes, shiitake, oyster, button (about 1½ pounds)
2	cups sliced onions
¼	teaspoon salt
	Freshly ground pepper to taste
1	pound whole-wheat pizza dough (*see Tip*), thawed if frozen
	Cornmeal for dusting
1	cup shredded part-skim mozzarella cheese (4 ounces)
4	teaspoons chopped fresh sage *or* 1 teaspoon dried, rubbed

1. Heat oil in a large nonstick skillet over medium heat. Add mushrooms and onions and sauté until tender, 3 to 5 minutes. Season with salt and pepper. Let cool.

2. Place a pizza stone or an inverted baking sheet on the lowest rack of the oven; preheat to 500°F or the highest oven setting. Divide dough into 8 pieces. Using your fists, stretch one piece into a 6-inch round. Alternatively, with a rolling pin, roll out on a lightly floured surface. (Keep remaining dough covered with a towel or plastic wrap.) Place on a cornmeal-dusted pizza peel or an inverted baking sheet, using enough cornmeal so that the dough slides easily. Stretch or roll a second piece of dough and place beside the first.

3. Sprinkle 2 tablespoons mozzarella over each round. Arrange ⅓ cup of the mushroom-onion mixture evenly over the cheese. Sprinkle with ½ teaspoon fresh sage (or ⅛ teaspoon dried).

4. Carefully slide the pizzas onto the heated pizza stone or baking sheet and bake until the bottoms are crisp and browned, 10 to 14 minutes. Repeat with the remaining dough and toppings.

MAKES EIGHT 6-INCH PIZZAS.

ACTIVE TIME: 1 hour

TOTAL TIME: 1 hour

PER PIZZA:

170 calories; 2 g fat (0 g sat, 1 g mono); 0 mg cholesterol; 28 g carbohydrate; 8 g protein; 2 g fiber; 242 mg sodium; 282 mg potassium

NUTRITION BONUS:

Selenium (28% daily value)
Folate (27% dv)
Vitamin C (19% dv)

H❋W H♥H

TIP: Look for **whole-wheat pizza-dough** balls at your supermarket. Check the ingredient list to make sure the dough doesn't contain any hydrogenated oils. Or visit *eatingwell.com* for an easy pizza-dough recipe.

Leeks provide sulfur-containing compounds that may benefit your heart and immune system.

LEEKS

Turkey & Leek Shepherd's Pie

The mashed potato–covered shepherd's pie was originally created to use up the leftovers from a festive roast. This version blends peas, leeks and carrots with diced turkey, all in a creamy herb sauce. The dish is a perfect way to create a second meal with the holiday turkey but if you like, use leftover roast chicken, duck or goose.

FILLING

2	teaspoons extra-virgin olive oil
2	large leeks, white and light green parts only, well washed and thinly sliced
1½	cups thinly sliced carrots
3	cloves garlic, minced
⅓	cup dry white wine
3	tablespoons all-purpose flour
2	teaspoons chopped fresh sage *or* ½ teaspoon dried, rubbed
2	cups reduced-sodium chicken broth
2	cups diced cooked turkey *or* chicken (*see Tip*)
1	cup frozen peas
¼	teaspoon salt
	Freshly ground pepper to taste

MASHED POTATOES

2	pounds potatoes, preferably Yukon Gold, peeled and cut into chunks
½-¾	cup nonfat buttermilk (*see Tip, page 239*)
¼	teaspoon salt
	Freshly ground pepper to taste
1	large egg, lightly beaten
1	tablespoon extra-virgin olive oil

1. **To prepare filling:** Preheat oven to 425°F. Heat 2 teaspoons oil in a large skillet or Dutch oven over medium heat. Add leeks and carrots and cook, stirring, until the leeks soften, about 7 minutes. Add garlic and cook, stirring, 1 minute more.

2. Pour in wine and stir until most of the liquid has evaporated. Add flour and sage and cook, stirring constantly, until the flour starts to turn light brown, about 2 minutes. Stir in broth and bring to a simmer, stirring constantly, until the sauce thickens and the carrots are barely tender, about 5 minutes.

3. Add turkey (or chicken) and peas and season to taste with salt and pepper. Transfer the mixture to a deep 10-inch pie pan or other 2-quart baking dish and set aside.

4. **To mash potatoes and bake pie:** Place potatoes in a large saucepan and add cold salted water to cover. Bring to a boil over medium heat. Cook, partially covered, until the potatoes are tender, about 10 minutes. Drain and return the potatoes to the pan. Cover and shake the pan over low heat to dry the potatoes slightly, about 1 minute. Remove from the heat.

5. Mash the potatoes with a potato masher or whip with an electric mixer, adding enough buttermilk to make a smooth puree. Season with salt and pepper. Stir in egg and 1 tablespoon oil.

6. Spread the potatoes on top of the turkey mixture. With the back of a spoon, make decorative swirls. Set the dish on a baking sheet and bake until the potatoes and filling are heated through and the top is golden brown, 25 to 30 minutes.

MAKES 6 SERVINGS.

ACTIVE TIME: 45 minutes

TOTAL TIME: 1¼ hours

EQUIPMENT: 10-inch pie pan or other 2-quart baking dish

PER SERVING:

331 calories; 8 g fat (2 g sat, 4 g mono); 73 mg cholesterol; 42 g carbohydrate; 22 g protein; 5 g fiber; 358 mg sodium; 991 mg potassium

NUTRITION BONUS:

Vitamin A (120% daily value)
Vitamin C (63% dv)
Potassium (29% dv)
Iron (19% dv)

H✳W H↑F H♥H

TIP: Use leftover roasted turkey or chicken. Or **to poach chicken breasts**, place boneless, skinless chicken breasts in a medium skillet or saucepan. Add lightly salted water to cover and bring to a boil. Cover, reduce heat to low and simmer gently until chicken is cooked through and no longer pink in the middle, 10 to 12 minutes.

Chicken with Grapes & Mushrooms

Grapes often symbolize a plentiful harvest so this dish that joins red grapes, mushrooms and fresh tarragon with lean chicken breasts is a lovely way to celebrate the season. To complete the theme, serve with Pear Risotto with Prosciutto & Fried Sage Leaves (page 156).

4	boneless, skinless chicken breasts (1-1¼ pounds total), trimmed
2	cups seedless red grapes, sliced in half
4	ounces mushrooms, trimmed and sliced (2 cups)
1	tablespoon chopped fresh tarragon *or* 1 teaspoon dried
¼	cup brandy
¼	teaspoon salt
¼	teaspoon freshly ground pepper

1. Preheat oven to 400°F. Cut 4 pieces of parchment paper or foil about 12 inches by 16 inches each. Fold each in half to get an 8-by-12-inch rectangle, then cut it into a half-heart shape as you would to make a valentine. This is a *papillote*.

2. Open the papillotes and place a chicken breast on one half of each opened paper (or foil) heart. Distribute grapes, mushrooms and tarragon over the chicken. Spoon a little brandy over the top and season with salt and pepper. Fold the other half of the heart over to cover the food and bring the edges together. Seal the package by crimping the cut edges together in a series of small, neat folds. Place on a baking sheet.

3. Bake until the packages are puffed, 10 to 12 minutes. (You may want to open one package to check that the chicken is no longer pink inside.) Transfer to plates and let diners open their own packages.

MAKES **4** SERVINGS.

ACTIVE TIME: 30 minutes

TOTAL TIME: 40 minutes

EQUIPMENT: Parchment paper or foil

PER SERVING:

216 calories; 2 g fat (0 g sat, 0 g mono); 66 mg cholesterol; 15 g carbohydrate; 28 g protein; 1 g fiber; 222 mg sodium; 531 mg potassium

NUTRITION BONUS:

Selenium (33% daily value)
Vitamin C (18% dv)
Potassium (15% dv)

H✂W L↓C H♥H

Curried Chicken with Fresh & Dried Cranberries

New England cranberries are harvested from September to about November and appear in markets through the new year. Fresh and dried cranberries, tomatoes, mustard seeds and fragrant curry spices brighten this zesty chicken stew. The dish is excellent prepared ahead and reheated, so it is a convenient entree for casual entertaining. Serve with brown basmati rice.

3	teaspoons canola oil, divided
2	pounds boneless, skinless chicken breasts, trimmed and cut crosswise into ½-inch-thick slices
3	tablespoons mild *or* medium-hot curry powder, divided
2	teaspoons butter
1	small onion, chopped
1	tablespoon yellow mustard seeds
	Generous ¼ teaspoon ground cardamom *or* cloves
1	15-ounce can diced tomatoes with mild green chiles
1½	cups reduced-sodium chicken broth
1⅓	cups sweetened dried cranberries
1	cup cranberries, fresh *or* frozen, thawed, coarsely chopped (*see Note*)
1	tablespoon minced fresh ginger
¼	teaspoon salt
	Chopped fresh cilantro for garnish

1. Heat 1½ teaspoons oil in a nonreactive Dutch oven (*see Note*) over medium-high heat. Add half the chicken pieces and sprinkle with a generous ½ teaspoon curry powder. Cook, stirring occasionally, until the chicken is beginning to brown, about 5 minutes. Transfer to a large plate. Heat the remaining 1½ teaspoons oil in the pot. Add the remaining chicken; sprinkle with another generous ½ teaspoon curry powder and cook, stirring occasionally, until beginning to brown, about 5 minutes. Transfer to the plate.

2. Add butter, onion and mustard seeds to the pot; cook, stirring, until the seeds pop and the onion begins to brown, 2 to 4 minutes. Return the chicken and any accumulated juices to the pot, sprinkle with the remaining curry powder and cardamom (or cloves); stir to coat the chicken with the spices. Cook, stirring, for 1 minute. Stir in tomatoes, broth, dried and fresh cranberries, ginger and salt. Bring to a boil, reduce heat to a simmer and cook, uncovered and stirring occasionally, until the mixture reduces slightly and the chicken is cooked through, 10 to 12 minutes more. Serve garnished with cilantro.

MAKES 8 SERVINGS, ¾ CUP EACH.

ACTIVE TIME: 50 minutes

TOTAL TIME: 1 hour

TO MAKE AHEAD: Cool, cover and refrigerate for up to 2 days.

PER SERVING:

246 calories; 6 g fat (2 g sat, 2 g mono); 66 mg cholesterol; 24 g carbohydrate; 25 g protein; 4 g fiber; 224 mg sodium; 267 mg potassium.

NUTRITION BONUS:

Niacin (50% daily value)
Selenium (32% dv)
Fiber (15% dv)

H�саW H♥H

NOTES: To make quick work of chopping **cranberries**, place whole berries in a food processor and pulse a few times until the berries are coarsely chopped.

A **nonreactive pan**—stainless steel, enamel-coated or glass—is necessary when cooking acidic foods, such as cranberries, to prevent the food from reacting with the pan. Reactive pans, such as aluminum and cast-iron, can impart an off color and/or off flavor in acidic foods.

Rigatoni with Beef & Eggplant Ragu

Eggplant, which ripens from midsummer into the fall, gives this sauce a rich meatiness that complements the ground beef. Plus the eggplant allows us to use a little less beef but still have a generous and hearty serving. Try serving this hearty pasta dish with Crunchy Pear & Celery Salad (page 138) for a starter.

8	ounces whole-wheat rigatoni *or* penne
8	ounces 92%-lean ground beef
4	cloves garlic, chopped
½	teaspoon fennel seed
3	cups diced eggplant (about ½ medium)
2	teaspoons extra-virgin olive oil
2	8-ounce cans no-salt-added tomato sauce
1	cup red wine
1	tablespoon chopped fresh oregano *or* 1 teaspoon dried
½	teaspoon salt
½	teaspoon freshly ground pepper
2	teaspoons pine nuts, toasted (*see Tip*)
½	cup crumbled feta (optional)

1. Bring a large pot of water to a boil. Cook pasta until tender, 8 to 10 minutes or according to package directions.

2. Meanwhile, cook beef, garlic and fennel seeds in a large nonstick skillet over medium heat until the beef is browned, about 3 minutes. Add eggplant and oil; cook, stirring occasionally, until the eggplant browns, about 5 minutes. Add tomato sauce and wine; cook, stirring occasionally, until the sauce thickens, about 10 minutes. Stir in oregano, salt and pepper.

3. Drain the pasta; serve topped with the sauce and sprinkled with pine nuts and feta, if using.

MAKES **4** SERVINGS.

ACTIVE TIME: 25 minutes

TOTAL TIME: 35 minutes

TO MAKE AHEAD: Prepare the sauce (Step 2); cover and refrigerate for up to 2 days.

PER SERVING:

399 calories; 7 g fat (1 g sat, 3 g mono); 30 mg cholesterol; 57 g carbohydrate; 22 g protein; 11 g fiber; 345 mg sodium; 788 mg potassium.

NUTRITION BONUS:

Vitamin C (30% daily value)
Zinc (26% dv)
Vitamin A (25% dv)
Potassium (21% dv)
Iron (20% dv)

H↑F H♥H

TIP: To toast **pine nuts**, cook in a small dry skillet over medium-low heat, stirring constantly, until fragrant and lightly browned, 2 to 4 minutes.

Pork Cutlets with Maple-Spiced Apples & Red Cabbage

Pork and apples and red cabbage are meant for each other. Here all three appear together, combining the Japanese tradition of panko-crusted pork chops with the New England tradition of seasoning with maple syrup and cider vinegar. Serve with a wild rice pilaf.

5	teaspoons extra-virgin olive oil, divided
2	tangy-sweet apples, such as Braeburn, chopped
2	cups thinly sliced red cabbage
1	small red onion, thinly sliced
2	teaspoons minced fresh thyme *or* ½ teaspoon dried
2	tablespoons pure maple syrup
1	tablespoon cider vinegar
4	½-inch-thick center-cut boneless pork loin chops (about 1 pound), trimmed
¼	teaspoon salt
¼	teaspoon freshly ground pepper, plus more to taste
⅓	cup all-purpose flour
1	large egg, lightly beaten
2	tablespoons Dijon mustard
1½	cups panko breadcrumbs (*see Note*)

1. Preheat oven to 475°F. Set a wire rack on a foil-lined baking sheet and coat with cooking spray.

2. Heat 2 teaspoons oil in a large nonstick skillet over medium-high heat. Add apples, cabbage, onion and thyme and cook, stirring occasionally, until the mixture begins to soften, 6 to 8 minutes. Stir in maple syrup and vinegar. Reduce heat to low and cook until the cabbage is tender, about 5 minutes more. Remove from heat, cover and keep warm.

3. Meanwhile, place each pork chop between 2 pieces of plastic wrap. Pound with the smooth side of a meat mallet or a heavy saucepan until ¼ inch thick. Season the pork on both sides with salt and pepper. Place flour on a large plate. Whisk egg and mustard in a shallow dish. Mix panko and 1 tablespoon oil in another shallow dish. Dredge the pork in the flour, dip in the egg mixture, then dredge in the panko. Place on the wire rack. Coat both sides with cooking spray.

4. Bake until the pork is cooked through and the breadcrumbs are just beginning to brown, about 10 minutes. Season the cabbage mixture with pepper and serve with the cutlets.

MAKES 4 SERVINGS.

ACTIVE TIME: 40 minutes

TOTAL TIME: 50 minutes

PER SERVING:

517 calories; 15 g fat (4 g sat, 6 g mono); 116 mg cholesterol; 64 g carbohydrate; 37 g protein; 6 g fiber; 764 mg sodium; 543 mg potassium

NUTRITION BONUS:

Selenium (62% daily value)
Vitamin C (30% dv)
Fiber (22% dv)
Potassium (17% dv)

H F

NOTE: **Panko breadcrumbs**, also known as Japanese breadcrumbs or bread flakes, are coarser than other dried breadcrumbs. Found in the Asian section of large supermarkets and in Asian specialty markets, they produce a crispy crust and are less likely to become soggy.

Tunisian Spiced Lamb Chops & Chard

A great complement for lamb, the bold dry rub in this recipe is a typical Tunisian combination of spices that includes cumin, caraway and crushed red pepper. Sautéed chard gets a twist with toasted pine nuts and sweet dates. We loved the sweetness of the dates in this dish, but we also tried it without and thought it was delicious. The choice is yours. Round out the meal with some whole-wheat couscous and a glass of Australian Shiraz.

4	teaspoons ground cumin
2	teaspoons caraway seeds
1	teaspoon kosher salt, divided
¾	teaspoon crushed red pepper
½	teaspoon freshly ground pepper
8	lean lamb loin chops, trimmed (about 2 pounds)
4	teaspoons canola oil
1	small shallot, minced
¼	cup chopped dates (optional)
1	pound chard, stems removed, leaves chopped
¼	cup pine nuts, toasted (*see Tip*)

1. Combine cumin, caraway, ¾ teaspoon salt, crushed red pepper and pepper in a small bowl. Rub both sides of lamb chops with the spice rub. Heat 2 teaspoons oil in a large nonstick skillet over medium-high heat. Add the chops and cook until browned, about 2 minutes per side. Reduce heat to medium and continue cooking to desired doneness, 3 to 5 more minutes per side for medium. Transfer to a plate; tent with foil to keep warm.

2. Add the remaining 2 teaspoons oil to the pan and heat over medium heat. Add shallot and dates (if using); cook, stirring, until softened, about 1 minute. Add chard leaves and cook, stirring, until wilted, 2 to 3 minutes. Stir in pine nuts and the remaining ¼ teaspoon salt. Serve the chard topped with the lamb chops.

MAKES 4 SERVINGS.

ACTIVE TIME: 35 minutes

TOTAL TIME: 35 minutes.

PER SERVING:

345 calories; 21 g fat (4 g sat, 9 g mono); 90 mg cholesterol; 8 g carbohydrate; 33 g protein; 4 g fiber; 568 mg sodium; 1,069 mg potassium

NUTRITION BONUS:

Vitamin A (140% daily value)
Vitamin C (40% dv)
Magnesium (38% dv)
Iron (35% dv)
Zinc (33% dv)
Potassium (31% dv)

L↓C

TIP: To toast **pine nuts**, cook in a small dry skillet over medium-low heat, stirring constantly, until fragrant and lightly browned, 2 to 4 minutes.

Pete's Greens at
Craftsbury Village Farm
Craftsbury, Vermont
(802) 586-2882
petesgreens.com

Growing Greens in Any Weather

In northern Vermont, Pete Johnson has figured out how to work with the seasons

At an age when most toddlers were playing with blocks, Pete Johnson was pushing around earth in his parents' plot in Vermont. "I always picked up soil," he remembers, "and smelled it, felt it, rolled it in my hands." As a teenager, he experimented with hand-made greenhouses, watching most of them blow away or collapse under snow. "By the time I was 14," he says, "I remember thinking that I was going to be a farmer."

Fast-forward two decades—Pete Johnson's hands are still in the dirt. Johnson (*left*), now 36, owns and operates Pete's Greens, a 230-acre farm in rural northern Vermont. He sells organic produce at a seasonal farmstand and through a CSA program to over 250 members. His greens are featured on the menus of acclaimed restaurants from Vermont to Boston to New York City.

"So much," says Johnson, "depends on your soil." He extensively composts his fields to build a base of nutrients. He cover crops—that is, he rotates nutrient-recycling and soil-protecting crops in with his actively producing plants—as a sustainable way to increase and maintain his soil's fertility. Why the emphasis on his soil? Because produce from small organic farms should be more flavorful and more packed with nutrients. "When I eat food that was grown in lively soil—soil with nutrients that really feed the plants—I can taste the difference," he says. Most of all, says Johnson, "I can care for every foot of soil in a way that just isn't possible on a large operation."

Johnson has to maximize his growing seasons. To protect crops, he designed four innovative 7,000-square-foot greenhouses that slide on metal tracks. He can now plant tomatoes in March or April under cover of one of the structures while frost and snow still cover the ground outside. After harvesting tomatoes in August, he'll slide the structure over his signature crops—his greens, such as chard, parsley and kale—which will allow him to harvest into December. Meanwhile, the elements will cleanse the newly uncovered soil he holds so dear, and cool temperatures will rid it of the pests that often plague stationary greenhouses.

While Johnson would probably love to grow year-round, his greenhouses are not heated and he isn't trying to completely defy the northern seasons. "Glory in the limitations of the seasons," he says, "and fully exhaust what each season has to offer." Eat it while it's fresh, and pine for it when it's not. It will taste that much better when it comes around again next year. —*Mark Aiken*

Salmon over Warm Lentil, Apple & Walnut Salad

This restaurant-worthy dish is worth the extra effort. Broiled salmon nestles on top of a warm lentil salad and a simple sauce made with pureed lentils and their cooking liquid. Serve with sautéed spinach or chard.

LENTIL SALAD

6	cups water, divided	3	whole cloves
1	cup French green lentils (*see Note*)	1	bay leaf
		1/4	teaspoon salt
1	cup dry red wine		Freshly ground pepper to taste
1	medium onion, halved	1	tablespoon extra-virgin olive oil
1	carrot, halved	1/2	Granny Smith apple
5	cloves garlic, peeled	2	tablespoons chopped walnuts, toasted (*see Tip, page 239*)
2	sprigs fresh thyme		
3	parsley stems, cut into 2-inch pieces	1	tablespoon finely chopped fresh parsley

SALMON

1½	pounds salmon fillet, skinned (*see photo, page 239*) and cut into 6 portions	1/4	teaspoon salt
		1/4	teaspoon freshly ground pepper
1	teaspoon canola oil	6	sprigs fresh thyme

1. **To prepare lentil salad:** Combine 2 cups water and lentils in a large saucepan; bring to a boil. Cook for 5 minutes. Drain and return the lentils to the pan.

2. Add remaining 4 cups water, wine, onion, carrot and garlic to the pan. Tie thyme sprigs, parsley stems, cloves and bay leaf in a cheesecloth bag and add to the pan. Bring to a boil, reduce heat to medium-low and simmer, uncovered, for 30 minutes. Season with 1/4 teaspoon salt and pepper. Continue cooking until the lentils are tender, about 20 minutes more. Drain, reserving 1 cup liquid. Discard the cheesecloth bag. Cut carrot and onion into 1/4-inch dice.

3. Place the reserved liquid and 1/2 cup of the cooked lentils in a blender or food processor; puree until smooth. (Use caution when pureeing hot liquids.) Place 1/2 cup of the puree in a large bowl; mix in the remaining lentils, diced carrot, onion and olive oil. Scrape the remaining puree into a small saucepan.

4. Peel, core and finely dice apple. Stir apple, walnuts and parsley into the lentil-carrot mixture. Cover and keep warm.

5. **To broil salmon:** Preheat broiler. Coat a baking sheet with cooking spray. Brush both sides of salmon with canola oil and season each side with 1/4 teaspoon salt and pepper. Place on the prepared baking sheet and lay 1 thyme sprig over each fillet. Broil 6 inches from the flame without turning just until opaque in the center, about 6 minutes.

6. Meanwhile, heat the reserved lentil puree. Make a bed of the lentil salad on 6 plates and spoon the lentil puree around the outside. Place the salmon on top. Serve immediately.

MAKES 6 SERVINGS.

ACTIVE TIME: 40 minutes

TOTAL TIME: 1½ hours

PER SERVING:

409 calories; 18 g fat (3 g sat, 7 g mono); 67 mg cholesterol; 25 g carbohydrate; 30 g protein; 6 g fiber; 282 mg sodium; 821 mg potassium

NUTRITION BONUS:

Selenium (60% daily value)
Vitamin A (38% dv)
Potassium (24% dv)
Vitamin C (15% dv)

H↑F H♥H

NOTE: French green lentils are firmer than brown lentils and cook more quickly. They can be found in natural-foods stores and some supermarkets.

Pear Risotto with Prosciutto & Fried Sage Leaves

Sweet ripe pear matched with the delicate saltiness of prosciutto defines this creamy risotto that goes well with any roast meat or poultry. Pungent, crispy fried sage leaves give a special finishing touch to this dish.

ACTIVE TIME: 1 hour

TOTAL TIME: 1 hour

PER SERVING:

267 calories; 10 g fat (4 g sat, 4 g mono); 22 mg cholesterol; 32 g carbohydrate; 10 g protein; 2 g fiber; 405 mg sodium; 122 mg potassium

H✕W

Olive oil *or* canola oil

2 thin slices prosciutto (1 ounce), 1 thinly sliced crosswise and 1 finely chopped, divided

4 fresh sage leaves, plus 1 teaspoon minced fresh sage, divided

6 cups reduced-sodium chicken broth

1 tablespoon extra-virgin olive oil

2 tablespoons minced shallot

1 cup arborio, carnaroli *or* other medium-grain Italian rice

2 cups finely diced peeled ripe Bosc pears (about 2 pears), divided

1/3 cup dry white wine

2 tablespoons grated Parmigiano-Reggiano, plus more for serving if desired

1 tablespoon butter

Freshly ground pepper to taste

1. Set a small strainer over a heatproof bowl. Heat about ½ inch of olive or canola oil in a small saucepan over medium-high heat until shimmering but not smoking. Add the sliced prosciutto and sage leaves and fry just until crisp, 1 to 3 minutes. Drain in the strainer then spread out on a paper towel. Set aside.

2. Bring broth to a simmer in a medium saucepan. Adjust the heat to maintain a steady simmer.

3. Heat 1 tablespoon extra-virgin olive oil in a large high-sided skillet or Dutch oven over medium-low heat. Add the chopped prosciutto and shallot; cook, stirring, until the shallot is just beginning to brown, 1 to 2 minutes. Add the minced sage, rice and 1 cup pears; stir to coat with the oil. Add wine and increase heat to medium-high. Cook, stirring, until the wine is almost absorbed by the rice, 1 to 3 minutes.

4. Add enough of the hot broth to just cover the rice mixture. Adjust the heat to maintain a steady simmer and cook, stirring constantly, until almost all the broth is absorbed. Continue to add the hot broth, about ½ cup at a time, stirring after each addition until all the liquid has been absorbed and adjusting the heat as necessary to maintain a simmer, until the rice begins to get creamy, 10 to 15 minutes. Stir in the remaining 1 cup pears.

5. Continue to add broth, about ½ cup at a time, stirring after each addition until all the liquid has been absorbed and adjusting the heat as necessary to maintain a simmer, until the rice is just tender, 10 to 15 minutes more. (You may not need all of the simmering broth.) Remove from the heat and let stand for 1 minute. Stir in cheese and butter. Season with pepper.

6. Serve the risotto garnished with the fried sage leaves, fried prosciutto and additional cheese, if desired.

MAKES 4 SERVINGS, 1 CUP EACH.

Apple, Onion & Cranberry Stuffing

Chopped fresh cranberries add a unique, tangy twist to this variation on the classic stuffing. Use fresh sage or rubbed sage in this recipe; the ground version is too bitter.

4	cups cubed whole-wheat bread (6 slices)
4	cups cubed white sandwich bread (6 slices)
	Giblets from 1 turkey (*see Tip*), liver discarded
1	cup water
1½	teaspoons canola oil
2	stalks celery, chopped
1	large onion, chopped
4	apples, peeled, cored and chopped
4	teaspoons chopped fresh sage *or* 1½ teaspoons dried, rubbed
2	teaspoons chopped fresh thyme *or* 1 teaspoon dried
½	cup chopped fresh *or* frozen cranberries (*see Tip*)
1	cup reduced-sodium chicken broth
¼	teaspoon salt
	Freshly ground pepper to taste

1. Preheat oven to 350°F. Spread whole-wheat and white bread on a baking sheet and bake until lightly toasted, 15 to 20 minutes.

2. Meanwhile, place giblets and water in a small saucepan and bring to a boil. Reduce heat to low and simmer, covered, for 10 minutes. Drain, reserving the cooking liquid. Finely chop the giblets and set aside.

3. Heat oil in a large nonstick skillet over medium heat. Add celery and onion; cook, stirring occasionally, until softened, about 5 to 7 minutes. Add apples, cook for 3 minutes longer. Add the giblet-cooking liquid, sage and thyme. Reduce heat to low and simmer until the apples are tender and most of the liquid has evaporated, 5 to 7 minutes. Transfer the mixture to a large bowl and add the toasted bread, giblets and cranberries. Drizzle broth over the bread mixture and toss until evenly moistened. Season with salt and pepper.

4. Reduce oven temperature to 325°. Transfer stuffing to a lightly oiled casserole dish and cover with foil. Bake until heated through, 35 to 45 minutes. If you would like a crisp top, uncover for the last 15 minutes of baking.

MAKES 8 SERVINGS, 1 CUP EACH.

ACTIVE TIME: 40 minutes

TOTAL TIME: 50 minutes

PER SERVING:

241 calories; 3 g fat (1 g sat, 1 g mono); 31 mg cholesterol; 43 g carbohydrate; 9 g protein; 5 g fiber; 408 mg sodium; 170 mg potassium

NUTRITION BONUS:

Vitamin A (80% daily value)
Folate (19% dv)

H✕W   H↑F   H♥H

TIPS: If you don't have **turkey giblets**, omit Step 2 and substitute ¾ cup chicken broth for the giblet-cooking liquid in Step 3; omit adding chopped giblets.

To make quick work of chopping **cranberries**, place whole berries in a food processor and pulse a few times until the berries are coarsely chopped.

Kohlrabi & Ham Gratin

Kohlrabi is a bulbous relative of the cabbage. Its bulb is purple, white or green, with leafy spinachlike greens attached. If you haven't tried kohlrabi, which tastes like a mild, sweet turnip, this gratin is an excellent place to start—after all, what doesn't taste good with cheese sauce on it? Kohlrabi that are less than 3 inches in diameter will give you the most tender results.

3	pounds kohlrabi (5-6 medium), trimmed, peeled and thinly sliced
1⅓	cups low-fat milk, divided
3	tablespoons all-purpose flour
2	ounces smoked ham, thinly sliced
¼	cup shredded sharp Cheddar cheese
½	teaspoon salt
¼	teaspoon freshly ground black *or* white pepper
	Pinch of freshly grated nutmeg
⅓	cup fresh breadcrumbs, preferably whole-wheat (*see Tip*)

1. Preheat oven to 400°F. Put a large pot of water on to boil. Coat a 1½-quart gratin dish or other shallow baking dish with cooking spray.

2. Cook kohlrabi in the boiling water until tender, 20 to 25 minutes. Drain.

3. Heat 1 cup milk in a small saucepan over medium heat until steaming. Whisk flour and the remaining ⅓ cup milk in a small bowl to make a smooth paste; stir into the hot milk and cook, whisking constantly, until the sauce bubbles and thickens, 2 to 3 minutes. Remove the pan from the heat and stir in ham and cheese. Season with salt, pepper and nutmeg.

4. Distribute the cooked kohlrabi in the prepared dish. Pour the cheese sauce over the top, spreading evenly. Sprinkle with breadcrumbs.

5. Bake the gratin until bubbling and golden on top, 30 to 40 minutes.

MAKES **6** SERVINGS.

ACTIVE TIME: 25 minutes

TOTAL TIME: 1½ hours

TO MAKE AHEAD: Prepare through Step 4; cover and refrigerate for up to 1 day.

PER SERVING:

140 calories; 3 g fat (1 g sat, 1 g mono); 13 mg cholesterol; 22 g carbohydrate; 10 g protein; 9 g fiber; 391 mg sodium; 814 mg potassium

NUTRITION BONUS:

Vitamin C (230% daily value)
Potassium (23% dv)
Calcium (16% dv)

H✕W   L↓C   H↑F   H♥H

TIP: To make **fresh breadcrumbs**, trim crusts from firm whole-wheat bread. Tear bread into pieces and process in a food processor until coarse crumbs form. One slice of bread makes about ½ cup fresh crumbs.

Cranberry, Cherry & Walnut Marmalade

This year why not try an alternative to the same old cranberry sauce? Fresh cranberries get crunch from walnuts and an infusion of sweetness from dried cherries in this take on a classic marmalade. Leftovers are great on a turkey sandwich. (Photograph: left.)

¾	cup sugar	1	12-ounce package fresh *or* frozen cranberries
1	cup water		
½	cup port *or* other sweet red wine	⅔	cup chopped walnuts, toasted (*see Tip, page 239*)
¼	teaspoon ground cinnamon		
⅛	teaspoon freshly grated nutmeg	½	teaspoon freshly grated orange zest
½	cup dried tart cherries		

1. Combine sugar, water, port (or wine), cinnamon and nutmeg in a medium non-reactive saucepan (*see Note, page 240*); bring to a boil. Add cherries and cook for 1 minute. Stir in cranberries; return to a boil. Reduce heat and simmer until about half the cranberries pop, 10 to 12 minutes. Remove from the heat.

2. Stir in walnuts and orange zest. Let cool completely. (The marmalade will thicken as it cools.) Serve at room temperature or chilled.

MAKES 4 CUPS.

ACTIVE TIME: 10 minutes

TOTAL TIME: 2 hours (including cooling time)

TO MAKE AHEAD: Cover and refrigerate for up to 3 days.

PER ¼-CUP SERVING:

91 calories; 3 g fat (0 g sat, 1 g mono); 0 mg cholesterol; 14 g carbohydrate; 2 g protein; 2 g fiber; 2 mg sodium; 53 mg potassium

H✂W L↓C H♥H

Roasted Sweet Potato Wedges with Balsamic Drizzle

A delicious tangy-sweet balsamic-and-honey reduction looks dramatic over sweet potatoes.

1½	pounds sweet potatoes (about 3 medium), peeled		Freshly ground pepper to taste
1	tablespoon extra-virgin olive oil	1	cup balsamic vinegar
¼	teaspoon salt	2	tablespoons honey
		1	teaspoon butter

1. Preheat oven to 425°F. Line a rimmed baking sheet with foil. Cut sweet potatoes into ½-inch-thick wedges. Place on the prepared baking sheet, drizzle with oil and toss well. Spread out in a single layer. Bake until tender when pierced with a knife, 25 to 30 minutes. Season with salt and pepper.

2. Meanwhile, combine vinegar and honey in a small saucepan. Bring to a boil over medium-high heat and cook until syrupy and reduced to ⅓ cup, 12 to 15 minutes. (Watch the syrup carefully during the last few minutes of reducing to prevent burning.) Swirl in butter. Drizzle the sauce over the sweet potatoes.

MAKES 4 SERVINGS.

SWEET POTATOES

ACTIVE TIME: 10 minutes

TOTAL TIME: 40 minutes

PER SERVING:

212 calories; 5 g fat (1 g sat, 3 g mono); 3 mg cholesterol; 41 g carbohydrate; 2 g protein; 3 g fiber; 197 mg sodium; 359 mg potassium

NUTRITION BONUS:

Vitamin A (420% daily value) Vitamin C (30% dv)

H✂W H♥H

Brussels Sprouts with Chestnuts & Sage

Brussels sprouts are hardy enough to withstand a pretty good frost so you can find them fresh at farmers' markets through the fall and into winter. In this recipe they are matched up with the toasty, rich flavor of chestnuts with delicious results. And for holiday kitchen convenience, the dish can be done on the stovetop, leaving the oven free for a bird or roast.

2	pounds Brussels sprouts, trimmed and halved
1	tablespoon butter
1	tablespoon extra-virgin olive oil
3	tablespoons reduced-sodium chicken broth *or* water
¾	cup coarsely chopped cooked chestnuts (about 4 ounces; *see Tip*)
2	teaspoons chopped fresh sage
½	teaspoon salt
	Freshly ground pepper to taste

1. Bring a large saucepan of water to a boil. Add Brussels sprouts and cook until bright green and just tender, 6 to 8 minutes. Drain well.

2. Melt butter with oil and broth (or water) in a large skillet over medium heat. Add Brussels sprouts, chestnuts and sage and cook, stirring often, until heated through, 2 to 4 minutes. Season with salt and pepper. Serve warm or at room temperature.

MAKES **12** SERVINGS, ABOUT ½ CUP EACH.

ACTIVE TIME: 35 minutes

TOTAL TIME: 35 minutes

TO MAKE AHEAD: Prepare through Step 1, cover and refrigerate for up to 8 hours.

PER SERVING:

68 calories; 3 g fat (1 g sat; 1 g mono); 3 mg cholesterol; 10 g carbohydrate; 2 g protein; 3 g fiber; 117 mg sodium; 308 mg potassium

NUTRITION BONUS:

Vitamin C (90% daily value)
Vitamin A (15% dv)

H❉W L↓C H♥H

TIP: **Cooked and peeled chestnuts** are available in jars at this time of year. Or if you have **fresh chestnuts**, prepare as follows: Using a sharp knife, score a cross on the flat side of each chestnut. Dip chestnuts, 4 or 5 at a time, into a saucepan of boiling water. Using a slotted spoon, remove the chestnuts and peel away shells and inner brown skins. If chestnuts are difficult to peel, return them to boiling water for a few seconds. Place the peeled chestnuts in a large saucepan and add enough boiling water to cover. Simmer, covered, until tender, 30 to 45 minutes. Drain and refresh with cold water.

Bok choy is a rich source of vitamin A: 1/2 cup (cooked) provides 72% of the recommended daily dose for this nutrient essential for a healthy immune system.

BOK CHOY

Sesame-Shiitake Bok Choy

Bok choy, a relative of cabbage, is a crunchy staple in Chinese cooking. Its mellow flavor goes beautifully with earthy shiitake mushrooms in this quick stir-fry. Be sure to use toasted rather than plain sesame oil—it has a superior nutty flavor. For a little heat, add a pinch of crushed red pepper.

1	tablespoon canola oil
3	cloves garlic, chopped
1	2-pound head bok choy, trimmed and thinly sliced
4	cups sliced shiitake mushroom caps (9 ounces with stems)
2	tablespoons oyster-flavored *or* oyster sauce (*see Note, page 240*)
1	tablespoon toasted sesame oil
1/4	teaspoon salt
1	tablespoon toasted sesame seeds (*see Tip, page 239*)

Heat oil in a Dutch oven over medium-high heat. Add garlic and cook, stirring constantly, until fragrant but not browned, 30 seconds. Add bok choy and mushrooms; cook, stirring, until wilted, about 2 minutes. Continue cooking, stirring often, until just tender, 3 to 5 minutes more. Stir in oyster sauce, sesame oil and salt. Garnish with sesame seeds.

MAKES 4 SERVINGS, ABOUT 1 CUP EACH.

ACTIVE TIME: 20 minutes

TOTAL TIME: 20 minutes

PER SERVING:

132 calories; 9 g fat (1 g sat, 4 g mono); 0 mg cholesterol; 10 g carbohydrate; 7 g protein; 3 g fiber; 602 mg sodium; 1,046 mg potassium

NUTRITION BONUS:

Vitamin A (170% daily value)
Vitamin C (90% dv)
Potassium (30% dv)
Folate (24% dv)
Calcium (20% dv)

H✕W L↓C H♥H

Braised Fennel, Carrots & Pearl Onions

Earthy fennel and sweet carrots are the perfect combination in this stew. Fresh pearl onions are great, but to save on time you can substitute frozen pearl onions. If you serve it as a side dish with roast chicken or lamb, stir in a few spoonfuls of pan juices just before serving to further enhance the flavor.

4	fennel bulbs, stalks removed
1	tablespoon butter, divided
1	teaspoon extra-virgin olive oil, divided
2	cups fresh pearl onions, peeled (*see Tip*)
1	teaspoon sugar
4	large carrots, cut into thick matchsticks
1-1½	cups reduced-sodium chicken broth *or* vegetable broth
¾	teaspoon salt
	Freshly ground pepper to taste
2	tablespoons finely chopped fennel fronds *or* fresh parsley

1. Cut each fennel bulb into 8 wedges, but do not remove the core. Bring water to a boil in a large saucepan, add the fennel wedges and cook for 5 minutes. Remove with a slotted spoon and blot with paper towels.

2. Heat ½ tablespoon butter and ½ teaspoon oil in a large cast-iron or nonstick skillet over medium-high heat. Reduce heat to medium, add half the fennel and cook, stirring, until nicely browned on all sides, about 8 minutes. Transfer to a dish. Repeat with the remaining butter, oil and fennel; transfer to the dish. Add onions to the pan, sprinkle with sugar and cook, shaking the pan back and forth, until nicely browned, 4 to 6 minutes.

3. Return the fennel to the pan along with carrots and 1 cup broth. Season with salt and pepper and simmer, covered, until the vegetables are tender, adding more broth as needed to keep the stew moist, 15 to 20 minutes. Garnish with fennel fronds (or parsley).

MAKES 8 SERVINGS, ABOUT 1 CUP EACH.

ACTIVE TIME: 55 minutes

TOTAL TIME: 1 hour 10 minutes

PER SERVING:

90 calories; 2 g fat (1 g sat, 0 g mono); 4 mg cholesterol; 16 g carbohydrate; 3 g protein; 5 g fiber; 323 mg sodium; 662 mg potassium.

NUTRITION BONUS:

Vitamin A (130% daily value)
Vitamin C (35% dv)
Potassium (19% dv)

H✖W L↓C H↑F H♥H

TIP: To peel pearl onions, cook in boiling water for 1 minute. Drain. Peel when cool enough to handle.

Figs are a rich source of pectin, a soluble fiber that may help to lower blood cholesterol.

FIGS

Baked Figs with Raspberries & Yogurt Cream

Fresh figs are in markets through late October but they're quite perishable so grab them and use them quickly if you see them. Baked figs, warm from the oven, make a heavenly trio with cool yogurt cream and juicy late-harvest raspberries.

1	cup nonfat plain yogurt
1/3	cup light whipping cream
3	tablespoons confectioners' sugar
1	teaspoon *eau-de-vie de framboise or* kirsch (optional)
8	ripe fresh figs, quartered lengthwise
1	tablespoon granulated sugar
1	tablespoon lemon juice
1	cup fresh raspberries

1. Line a small strainer with cheesecloth or a paper coffee filter and set it over a bowl. Spoon in yogurt and let it drain in the refrigerator until reduced to ½ cup, about 2 hours.

2. Beat cream to soft peaks in a chilled mixing bowl. Add the drained yogurt, confectioners' sugar and framboise (or kirsch), if using; fold in with a rubber spatula.

3. Preheat oven to 450°F. Arrange figs in a shallow ovenproof baking dish in a single layer, cut-side up. Sprinkle with granulated sugar and lemon juice. Bake until the figs are heated through and the sugar has melted, about 15 minutes.

4. Spoon the yogurt cream into 4 dessert dishes. Top with the warm figs and garnish with raspberries. Serve immediately.

MAKES 4 SERVINGS.

ACTIVE TIME: 30 minutes

TOTAL TIME: 2 hours

TO MAKE AHEAD: The yogurt cream (Steps 1 & 2) may be used immediately or refrigerated, covered, for up to 8 hours.

PER SERVING:

208 calories; 7 g fat (4 g sat, 2 g mono); 23 mg cholesterol; 37 g carbohydrate; 4 g protein; 5 g fiber; 42 mg sodium; 303 mg potassium

NUTRITION BONUS:

Vitamin C (25% daily value)

H✳W H↑F

Caramelized Pear Bread Pudding

Sweet caramelized pears are the highlight of this comforting, custardy, raisin-studded bread pudding. When turned out of its baking dish, the flanlike pudding sits in a pool of intense caramel syrup, making it worthy of any holiday table. Serve warm or chilled.

2½	cups low-fat milk
4	large eggs
½	cup sugar, divided
1	teaspoon vanilla extract
½	teaspoon freshly grated lemon zest
⅛	teaspoon ground nutmeg
4	cups cubed, day-old country-style bread, crusts trimmed (4-6 slices), preferably whole-wheat
2	tablespoons raisins *or* currants
1	teaspoon butter, softened, plus 2 tablespoons, divided
2	ripe pears, peeled, halved and cored
1	tablespoon lemon juice

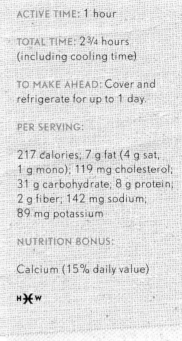

ACTIVE TIME: 1 hour

TOTAL TIME: 2¾ hours (including cooling time)

TO MAKE AHEAD: Cover and refrigerate for up to 1 day.

PER SERVING:

217 calories; 7 g fat (4 g sat, 1 g mono); 119 mg cholesterol; 31 g carbohydrate; 8 g protein; 2 g fiber; 142 mg sodium; 89 mg potassium

NUTRITION BONUS:

Calcium (15% daily value)

H✳W

1. Heat milk in a medium saucepan over medium-low heat, stirring, until steaming, 4 to 6 minutes. Whisk eggs in a large bowl until blended; gradually whisk in ¼ cup sugar. Slowly whisk in the hot milk until blended. Whisk in vanilla, lemon zest and nutmeg.

2. Add bread and raisins (or currants) to the milk mixture; gently fold together. Press down lightly with the back of a large spoon. Cover and set aside at room temperature.

3. Butter the bottom and sides of a round 2-quart baking dish with 1 teaspoon butter. Preheat oven to 350°F. Put a kettle of water on to boil.

4. Cut each pear half lengthwise into 4 slices. Place in a medium bowl and toss with lemon juice.

5. Heat a medium skillet over low heat until hot. Add the remaining 2 tablespoons butter and swirl until just melted and the foam subsides. Sprinkle the remaining ¼ cup sugar over the melted butter. Arrange the pear slices on their sides in the pan in an even layer. Increase the heat to medium-low and, without stirring, let the pears begin to brown and the sauce slowly caramelize, adjusting the heat as needed to prevent burning, about 10 minutes. Remove the pan from the heat and carefully turn each pear slice with a fork. Return to the heat and cook until the sauce is uniformly golden, 2 to 4 minutes more.

6. Carefully transfer the pears one at a time to the prepared baking dish, arranging them decoratively in a circle and slightly overlapping them if necessary. Use a heatproof silicone spatula to scrape any remaining syrup over the pears.

7. Set the baking dish in a shallow baking pan. Spoon the bread and custard mixture into the baking dish. Press down on the bread until it is submerged in the custard. Place the pan in the oven and carefully add the hot water to the shallow baking pan until it is halfway up the sides of the baking dish.

8. Bake until the pudding is browned on top and set in the center, 1 to 1¼ hours. Carefully remove the pan from the oven. Transfer the baking dish to a wire rack and let cool for at least 45 minutes. To serve, run a knife around the edge of the pudding. Place a serving platter over it and invert the pudding onto the platter.

MAKES 8 SERVINGS.

Oatmeal-Nut Crunch Apple Pie

This decadent pie is loaded with juicy apples and adorned with a streusel-lover's crunchy topping. The pie is best served the day it's made. If you're short on time, look for a ready-made whole-wheat pie crust in the freezer section of the store.

ACTIVE TIME: 1 hour

TOTAL TIME: 3½ hours (including cooling time)

EQUIPMENT: 9-inch pie pan

PER SERVING:

340 calories; 13 g fat (6 g sat, 2 g mono); 21 mg cholesterol; 53 g carbohydrate; 4 g protein; 4 g fiber; 110 mg sodium; 199 mg potassium

NUTRITION BONUS:

Vitamin C (18% daily value)

CRUST

1	cup all-purpose flour
½	cup whole-wheat pastry flour
¼	teaspoon salt
4	tablespoons cold unsalted butter, cut into small pieces
2	ounces reduced-fat cream cheese (Neufchâtel)
2	tablespoons canola oil
3	tablespoons ice water

FILLING

3	medium Granny Smith apples, peeled and thinly sliced
3	medium McIntosh apples, peeled and thinly sliced

TOPPING

½	cup whole-wheat pastry flour
⅓	cup old-fashioned rolled oats
¼	cup packed light brown sugar
½	teaspoon ground cinnamon
⅛	teaspoon salt
2	tablespoons cold unsalted butter, cut into small pieces
2	tablespoons frozen orange juice concentrate, thawed
¼	cup coarsely chopped walnuts
½	cup packed light brown sugar
1	tablespoon lemon juice
½	teaspoon ground cinnamon
2	tablespoons all-purpose flour

1. **To prepare crust:** Whisk 1 cup all-purpose flour, ½ cup whole-wheat flour and ¼ teaspoon salt in a medium bowl. Cut in 4 tablespoons butter and cream cheese using a pastry blender or a fork until the mixture is pebbly. Add oil; stir until evenly moistened. Sprinkle water over the mixture; toss with a fork to combine. Knead the dough in the bowl a few times. Gather into a ball, press into a disk and wrap in plastic. Refrigerate for at least 30 minutes or up to 2 days.

2. Roll the dough into a 14-inch circle between 2 large pieces of parchment or wax paper. Peel off the top sheet and invert the dough into a 9-inch pie pan. Peel off the remaining paper. Press the dough firmly into the bottom and up the sides of the pan. Tuck the overhanging dough under, forming a double-thick edge. Crimp the edge with your fingers. Using a fork, prick the dough in several places. Refrigerate the crust for 15 minutes.

3. Position a rack in the lower third of the oven; preheat to 375°F. Bake the crust for 15 minutes. Remove from the oven and let cool, about 30 minutes.

4. **To prepare filling:** Combine apples, ½ cup brown sugar, lemon juice and ½ teaspoon cinnamon in a large bowl. Let stand for 10 minutes. Sprinkle 2 tablespoons all-purpose flour over the apples and toss again; mound the filling into the cooled crust. Coat the crust edges with cooking spray, return the pie to the oven and bake for 30 minutes.

5. **Meanwhile, prepare topping:** Combine ½ cup whole-wheat flour, oats, ¼ cup brown sugar, ½ teaspoon cinnamon and ⅛ teaspoon salt in a medium bowl. Cut in 2 tablespoons butter with a pastry blender or a fork until evenly distributed. Stir in orange juice concentrate and nuts.

6. After the pie has baked for 30 minutes, remove it from the oven and scatter the topping over the apples. Return it to the oven (covering the edges of the crust with foil if they're browning too quickly) and bake until the topping is golden and the juices are bubbling around the edges, 20 minutes more. Cool for at least 1 hour before serving.

MAKES 10 SERVINGS.

Apple-Cranberry Coffee Cake

When September rolls around the apple harvest begins to arrive and the variety is staggering—over 3,000 worldwide—and a good market usually has dozens. This recipe calls for a tart apple, such as a Granny Smith or a Pippin, combined with cranberries and spices to make a beautiful topping for a coffee cake festive enough for any brunch.

ACTIVE TIME: 45 minutes

TOTAL TIME: 1 hour, 50 minutes (including cooling time)

TO MAKE AHEAD: Cover and store at room temperature for up to 2 days.

EQUIPMENT: 9-inch springform pan

PER SERVING:

268 calories; 8 g fat (3 g sat, 3 g mono); 26 mg cholesterol; 47 g carbohydrate; 4 g protein; 3 g fiber; 113 mg sodium; 114 mg potassium

NUTRITION BONUS:

Vitamin C (20% daily value)

TIP: To make quick work of chopping **cranberries**, place whole berries in a food processor and pulse a few times until the berries are coarsely chopped.

TOPPING

1/2	cup packed light brown sugar
1	tablespoon cornstarch
1/4	teaspoon ground cinnamon
1 1/2	cups cranberries, fresh *or* frozen, thawed, chopped (*see Tip*)
1 1/2	cups finely chopped peeled tart apple, such as Granny Smith (about 1 large)
1/2	cup cranberry juice cocktail, orange juice *or* apple juice

CAKE

1	cup all-purpose flour
1/2	cup whole-wheat flour
1	teaspoon baking powder
1/4	teaspoon salt
1/8	teaspoon baking soda
1/4	cup canola oil
3	tablespoons butter, slightly softened
3/4	teaspoon freshly grated lemon zest
3/4	cup granulated sugar, plus 1 tablespoon for sprinkling
1	large egg
3/4	cup low-fat milk
2	teaspoons vanilla extract

1. Preheat oven to 375°F. Coat a 9-inch springform pan with cooking spray.

2. **To prepare topping:** Whisk brown sugar, cornstarch and cinnamon in a medium nonreactive saucepan (*see Note, page 240*) until combined. Stir in cranberries, apple and juice. Bring the mixture to a boil over medium-high heat, stirring. Continue to cook, stirring, until the mixture thickens and the berries soften, about 2 minutes. Remove from the heat and let cool.

3. **To prepare cake:** Whisk all-purpose flour, whole-wheat flour, baking powder, salt and baking soda in a medium bowl. Beat oil, butter and lemon zest in a large mixing bowl with an electric mixer, first on medium speed, then on medium-high, until well combined, about 1 1/2 minutes. Gradually add 3/4 cup sugar, beating until the mixture is light in color and well blended. Add egg and beat until the batter is smooth, about 1 minute longer. With the mixer on low speed, beat in half the flour mixture until just incorporated. Gradually beat in milk and vanilla until just incorporated. Add the remaining flour mixture and beat until a smooth batter forms, about 1 minute, scraping down the sides of the bowl as needed. Scrape the batter into the prepared pan, spreading to the edges. Spread the topping in an even layer over the batter; do not stir.

4. Bake the cake on the middle rack until the top is puffed in places and a toothpick inserted in the center comes out clean (the fruit topping will still be moist), 40 to 50 minutes. Sprinkle the remaining 1 tablespoon sugar over the top. Transfer the pan to a wire rack; let stand until cooled to warm, about 20 minutes. Remove the pan sides and cut the cake into wedges.

MAKES **12** SERVINGS.

Cranberry-Orange Pistachio Bars

Bright red cranberries and toasted green pistachios stud these tart-and-tangy bar cookies and make them a colorful addition to any cookie platter. They hold well in both the refrigerator and the freezer so they're an excellent make-ahead option.

CRUST

3	tablespoons unsalted butter
2	tablespoons granulated sugar
2	tablespoons light brown sugar
2/3	cup whole-wheat pastry flour (*see Note*)
1/3	cup all-purpose flour
	Pinch of salt

TOPPING

3/4	cup granulated sugar
2	tablespoons all-purpose flour
1/2	teaspoon baking powder
	Pinch of salt
1	large egg
1	large egg white
1	teaspoon freshly grated orange zest
1/4	cup orange juice
2	cups cranberries, fresh *or* frozen, thawed, coarsely chopped (*see Tip, page 172*)
1/3	cup pistachios, preferably unsalted, chopped and toasted (*see Tip, page 239*)

1. **To prepare crust:** Position rack in center of oven; preheat to 350°F. Coat an 8-inch-square baking pan with cooking spray.

2. Beat butter, 2 tablespoons granulated sugar and brown sugar in a medium bowl with an electric mixer until creamy. Stir in whole-wheat flour, 1/3 cup all-purpose flour and salt until well combined (the mixture will still be crumbly). Evenly press the mixture into the bottom of the prepared pan. Bake until just barely golden around the edges, 10 to 12 minutes.

3. **To prepare topping:** Combine 3/4 cup granulated sugar, 2 tablespoons all-purpose flour, baking powder and salt in a medium bowl. Add egg, egg white, orange zest and juice; stir until blended and smooth.

4. Sprinkle cranberries over the baked crust. Pour the orange mixture over the cranberries and sprinkle with pistachios.

5. Bake until golden and set, 40 to 45 minutes. Let cool completely on a wire rack; if possible, chill before cutting into squares.

MAKES 16 BARS.

ACTIVE TIME: 20 minutes

TOTAL TIME: 1 1/4 hours (not including cooling time)

TO MAKE AHEAD: Store in an airtight container in the refrigerator for up to 5 days or in the freezer for up to 1 month.

PER SERVING:

126 calories; 4 g fat (2 g sat, 1 g mono); 19 mg cholesterol; 22 g carbohydrate; 2 g protein; 1 g fiber; 44 mg sodium; 58 mg potassium

H✸W   L↓C   H♥H

NOTE: **Whole-wheat pastry flour** is milled from soft wheat. It contains less gluten than regular whole-wheat flour and helps ensure a tender result in delicate baked goods while providing the nutritional benefits of whole grains.

WINTER

> When I picked up rosemary and sage instead of basil, I actually felt a twinge of guilt about turning my back on what I had desired so recently. But this act also made me feel like a human animal, and it felt good. Yes, I was fickle toward summer and all its offerings but true to the promise of winter, the time for rooty stews laced with robust herbs.

—DEBORAH MADISON, FROM
HER BOOK *LOCAL FLAVORS*

Triple Celery Bisque

Celery root (celeriac) is a knobby, ugly thing but it has a lovely flavor that's a cross between celery and parsley. In this pureed bisque, it stars with russet potatoes and more celery flavor in the form of a celery stalk and lovage or celery leaves. Evaporated nonfat milk adds creaminess without adding cream.

ACTIVE TIME: 25 minutes

TOTAL TIME: 1 hour 10 minutes

PER SERVING:

136 calories; 2 g fat (0 g sat, 1 g mono); 1 mg cholesterol; 26 g carbohydrate; 5 g protein; 3 g fiber; 436 mg sodium; 697 mg potassium

NUTRITION BONUS:

Vitamin C (27% daily value)
Potassium (20% dv)

H✖W   H♥H

NOTE: Lovage is related to celery and has a similar taste and appearance. Its leaves are used as a seasoning.

1	tablespoon extra-virgin olive oil
1	large celery root (celeriac; about 2 pounds), peeled and chopped (*see Guide, page 222*)
1	pound russet potatoes, peeled and chopped
1	large onion, chopped
1	stalk celery, chopped
1	large leek, trimmed, washed thoroughly and sliced
4	cups water
1	teaspoon salt
1/4	teaspoon ground white pepper
1/2	cup lovage (*see Note*) *or* celery leaves, plus a few extra for garnish
1/2	cup evaporated nonfat milk

1. Heat oil in a large saucepan or Dutch oven over medium-low heat. Add celery root, potatoes, onion, celery and leek. Reduce heat to low, cover and cook until the vegetables are softened, stirring occasionally, 45 to 50 minutes.

2. Add water, salt and white pepper to the pan. Bring to a simmer and cook for 5 minutes. Remove from the heat and stir in lovage (or celery leaves). Puree in batches in a food processor or blender until smooth. (Use caution when pureeing hot liquids.)

3. Return the soup to the pan, stir in evaporated milk and heat through. Garnish each bowl with a lovage (or celery) leaf.

MAKES 8 SERVINGS, GENEROUS 1 CUP EACH.

Broccoli, Cannellini Bean & Cheddar Soup

Broccoli's great in late fall, right through winter and into spring. White beans pureed into this soup make it extra creamy so you don't need heaps of cheese to do the job. Serve with a crunchy whole-grain roll and a glass of winter ale.

1	14-ounce can reduced-sodium chicken broth *or* vegetable broth
1	cup water
1	pound broccoli crowns, trimmed and chopped (about 6 cups)
1	14-ounce can cannellini beans, rinsed (*see Tip*)
¼	teaspoon salt
¼	teaspoon ground white pepper
1	cup shredded extra-sharp Cheddar cheese

1. Bring broth and water to a boil in a medium saucepan over high heat. Add broccoli, cover and cook until tender, about 8 minutes. Stir in beans, salt and pepper and cook until the beans are heated through, about 1 minute.

2. Transfer half the mixture to a blender with half the cheese and puree. (Use caution when pureeing hot liquids.) Transfer to a bowl. Repeat with the remaining broccoli mixture and cheese. Serve warm.

MAKES 6 SERVINGS, SCANT 1 CUP EACH.

ACTIVE TIME: 20 minutes

TOTAL TIME: 20 minutes

PER SERVING:

153 calories; 7 g fat (4 g sat, 0 g mono); 21 mg cholesterol; 15 g carbohydrate; 11 g protein; 6 g fiber; 437 mg sodium; 435 mg potassium.

NUTRITION BONUS:

Vitamin C (94% daily value)
Vitamin A (25% dv)
Calcium (21% dv)

H�ం✻W   L↓C   H↑F

TIP: While we love the convenience of **canned beans**, they tend to be high in sodium. Give them a good rinse before adding to a recipe to rid them of some of their sodium (up to 35 percent) or opt for low-sodium or no-salt-added varieties. (These recipes are analyzed with rinsed, regular canned beans.) Or, if you have the time, cook your own beans from scratch. You'll find our Bean Cooking Guide at *eatingwell.com/guides*.

Pork, White Bean & Kale Soup

Kale grows best in cool temperatures and can be found at farmers' markets straight into winter. It's matched up here with white beans and chunks of lean pork tenderloin to create a soup that's satisfying and quick to make. Smoked paprika gives the soup a Spanish flair so some warm bread and sliced Manchego cheese would go well on the side.

1	tablespoon extra-virgin olive oil
1	pound pork tenderloin, trimmed and cut into 1-inch pieces
¾	teaspoon salt
1	medium onion, finely chopped
4	cloves garlic, minced
2	teaspoons paprika, preferably smoked
¼	teaspoon crushed red pepper, or to taste (optional)
1	cup white wine
4	plum tomatoes, chopped
4	cups reduced-sodium chicken broth
1	bunch kale, ribs removed, chopped (about 8 cups lightly packed)
1	15-ounce can white beans, rinsed (*see Tip, page 177*)

1. Heat oil in a Dutch oven over medium-high heat. Add pork, sprinkle with salt and cook, stirring once or twice, until no longer pink on the outside, about 2 minutes. Transfer to a plate with tongs, leaving juices in the pot.

2. Add onion to the pot and cook, stirring often, until just beginning to brown, 2 to 3 minutes. Add garlic, paprika and crushed red pepper (if using) and cook, stirring constantly, until fragrant, about 30 seconds. Add wine and tomatoes, increase heat to high and stir to scrape up any browned bits. Add broth and bring to a boil.

3. Add kale and stir just until it wilts. Reduce heat to maintain a lively simmer and cook, stirring occasionally, until the kale is just tender, about 4 minutes. Stir in beans, the reserved pork and any accumulated juices; simmer until the beans and pork are heated through, about 2 minutes.

MAKES **6** SERVINGS, ABOUT 1⅔ CUPS EACH.

ACTIVE TIME: 40 minutes

TOTAL TIME: 40 minutes

PER SERVING:

262 calories; 6 g fat (1 g sat, 3 g mono); 45 mg cholesterol; 26 g carbohydrate; 25 g protein; 7 g fiber; 627 mg sodium; 1,024 mg potassium

NUTRITION BONUS:

Vitamin A (290% daily value)
Vitamin C (190% dv)
Potassium (29% dv)
Iron (20% dv)

H✱W L↓C H↑F H♥H

Tom Yum Soup with Pineapple

Somehow the lack of sun in the winter makes tropical fruits all the more appealing. Pineapple, which hits its peak season in late winter, is added to this variation on sweet-and-sour Thai soup. This soup has intense flavor with a bit of heat that makes a great winter cold remedy.

ACTIVE TIME: 45 minutes

TOTAL TIME: 45 minutes

PER SERVING:

119 calories; 1 g fat (1 g sat, 0 g mono); 62 mg cholesterol; 14 g carbohydrate; 13 g protein; 2 g fiber; 597 mg sodium; 243 mg potassium

NUTRITION BONUS:

Vitamin C (58% daily value)
Vitamin A (19% dv)

H⌘W L↓C H♥H

TIP: Lemongrass, galangal, Thai lime leaves (sometimes called Kaffir or makrut lime leaves) and **fish sauce** lend the signature Thai flavors to this soup. If unavailable at your supermarket, find these ingredients at Asian markets.

1	stalk lemongrass, cut into 1-inch pieces (*see Tip*)
2	¼-inch-thick slices galangal (*see Tip*) *or* ginger
6	cups reduced-sodium chicken broth
2	jalapeño peppers, sliced
4	Thai lime leaves (*see Tip*) *or* 3 2-inch strips lime zest
1½	cups chopped fresh pineapple
1	cup sliced shiitake mushroom caps
1	medium tomato, chopped
½	medium red bell pepper, cut into 1-inch cubes
2	tablespoons fish sauce (*see Tip*)
1	teaspoon sugar
8	ounces raw shrimp (26-30 per pound; *see Note, page 241*), peeled and deveined
¼	cup fresh lime juice
2	scallions, sliced
⅓	cup chopped fresh cilantro

1. Gently smash lemongrass and galangal (or ginger) on a cutting board with the side of a knife. Place in a large saucepan with broth, jalapeños and lime leaves (or zest). Bring to a boil, reduce to a simmer; cover and cook for 15 minutes. Strain into a bowl. Discard solids.

2. Return the broth to the pan. Add pineapple, mushrooms, tomato, bell pepper, fish sauce and sugar. Bring to a simmer and cook, uncovered, for 5 minutes. Add shrimp and cook until they are pink and just cooked through, 2 to 3 minutes. Remove from the heat and stir in lime juice, scallions and cilantro.

MAKES **6** SERVINGS, ABOUT 1⅓ CUPS EACH.

Barley-Root Vegetable Chowder

Even long ago, root vegetables kept well in cellars, but with modern storage facilities they stay even fresher. A trip into the cellar, so to speak, will be called for to prepare this hearty soup, which includes celery root, rutabaga, carrot and parsnip. The chowder is made with beef broth, but vegetable broth can be used instead to make a vegetarian version. This robust-flavored recipe makes 12 first-course portions. Or serve double-size portions along with a salad and crusty bread for dinner.

4	cups reduced-sodium beef broth *or* vegetable broth
4	cups water
½	cup pearl barley
1	celery root (celeriac), peeled and cut into ½-inch pieces
1	turnip, peeled and cut into ½-inch pieces
1	rutabaga, peeled and cut into ½-inch pieces
1	carrot, peeled and cut into ½-inch pieces
1	parsnip, peeled, cored and cut into ½-inch pieces
1	cup chopped green cabbage
1	onion, cut into ½-inch pieces
2	tomatoes, chopped, *or* 1 15-ounce can diced tomatoes, with juice
1	bay leaf
1	teaspoon salt
½	teaspoon dried sage
½	teaspoon dried thyme
	Pinch of freshly ground pepper

1. Bring broth and water to a boil in a Dutch oven. Add barley. Reduce heat, cover and simmer until the barley is tender, about 20 minutes.

2. Add celery root, turnip, rutabaga, carrot, parsnip, cabbage, onion, tomatoes, bay leaf, salt, sage, thyme and pepper and bring to a boil. Reduce heat to low, cover and simmer until all the vegetables are tender, about 30 minutes. Discard the bay leaf before serving.

MAKES **12** SERVINGS.

ACTIVE TIME: 30 minutes

TOTAL TIME: 1½ hours

PER SERVING:

78 calories; 1 g fat (0 g sat, 0 g mono); 0 mg cholesterol; 15 g carbohydrate; 4 g protein; 4 g fiber; 251 mg sodium; 372 mg potassium

NUTRITION BONUS:

Vitamin A (21% daily value)
Vitamin C (28% dv)

H✕W · L↓C · H♥H

NOTE: If you're not familiar with root vegetables, see the Guide to learn how to prepare them: celery root, page 222; turnip, page 232; rutabaga, page 230; parsnip, page 227.

Spinach & Citrus Salad

Grapefruit from Florida and Texas become available right around the holiday season and last through the cold winter months. Spinach and red onion join this citrus fruit in a refreshing salad that would be an excellent starter for, say, a Hanukkah dinner of Braised Brisket & Roots (page 198). If you can't get grapefruit, oranges or even a pomelo would be a fine stand-in. Add sliced chicken breast to turn this salad into a light entree.

ACTIVE TIME: 25 minutes

TOTAL TIME: 25 minutes

PER SERVING:

91 calories; 4 g fat (1 g sat, 3 g mono); 0 mg cholesterol; 13 g carbohydrate; 3 g protein; 3 g fiber; 232 mg sodium; 498 mg potassium

NUTRITION BONUS:

Vitamin A (131% daily value)
Vitamin C (87% dv)
Folate (32% dv)
Magnesium (15% dv)

H✱W L↓C H♥H

- 1/2 small red onion, thinly sliced
- 2 small grapefruit, preferably pink or red, *or* 3 oranges
- 1 tablespoon white-wine vinegar
- 1 tablespoon extra-virgin olive oil
- 1/2 tablespoon coarse-grain mustard
- 1/2 teaspoon honey
- 1 clove garlic, very finely chopped
- 1/4 teaspoon salt
- Freshly ground pepper to taste
- 8 cups torn fresh spinach leaves
- 1 teaspoon poppy seeds

1. Place onion in a small bowl, cover with cold water and soak for 10 minutes. Drain and set aside.
2. Meanwhile, remove skin and white pith from grapefruit (or oranges) with a sharp knife and discard. (*See photos, page 222.*) Working over a small bowl to catch the juice, cut the grapefruit (or orange) segments from their surrounding membrane; reserve the segments in a small bowl. Measure 2 tablespoons of the juice into a salad bowl.
3. Add vinegar, oil, mustard, honey, garlic, salt and pepper to the salad bowl. Add spinach and the reserved onion and fruit sections. Toss and garnish with poppy seeds.

MAKES 4 SERVINGS.

Radicchio is a virtually calorie-free way to add a bit of folate and potassium to salads and other dishes.

RADICCHIO

Bold Winter Greens Salad

Radicchio, escarole and chicory thrive in cooler weather and have hearty, robust flavor. For this cousin of the Caesar salad they are served with a tangy dressing made with anchovies and lemon juice, which tempers the bitterness of the greens. Vary the amount of garlic and anchovy according to your preference.

2-3	cloves garlic, minced
1/4	teaspoon kosher salt
1/4	teaspoon freshly ground pepper, or to taste
2	tablespoons lemon juice
1	tablespoon sherry vinegar
3-4	anchovy fillets, rinsed and chopped
1/3	cup extra-virgin olive oil
12	cups chopped mixed bitter salad greens, such as chicory, radicchio and escarole
3	large hard-boiled eggs (*see Tip*)

1. Place garlic to taste in a large salad bowl and sprinkle with salt and pepper. Add lemon juice and vinegar; let stand for 5 minutes. Stir in anchovies to taste. Whisk in oil in a slow steady stream until well combined.

2. Add salad greens and toss. Shred 3 egg whites and 1 egg yolk through the large holes of a box grater (reserve the remaining yolks for another use or discard). Sprinkle the salad with the grated egg.

MAKES **10** SERVINGS, ABOUT 1¼ CUPS EACH.

ACTIVE TIME: 20 minutes

TOTAL TIME: 20 minutes

TO MAKE AHEAD: Prepare the dressing (Step 1), cover and refrigerate for up to 1 day.

PER SERVING:

92 calories; 8 g fat (1 g sat, 6 g mono); 22 mg cholesterol; 3 g carbohydrate; 2 g protein; 1 g fiber; 102 mg sodium; 168 mg potassium

NUTRITION BONUS:

Vitamin A (120% daily value)
Vitamin C (50% dv)
Folate (34% dv)
Potassium (16% dv)

H✳W L↓C H♥H

TIP: To hard-boil eggs, place eggs in a single layer in a saucepan; cover with water. Bring to a simmer over medium-high heat. Reduce heat to low and cook at the barest simmer for 10 minutes. Remove from heat, pour out hot water and cover the eggs with ice-cold water. Let stand until cool enough to handle before peeling.

Roasted Winter Vegetables with Cheesy Polenta

Creamy polenta laced with sharp Parmigiano-Reggiano makes a savory bed for sweet roasted vegetables. Butternut squash and cauliflower florets are called for, but you could vary the combination of roasted vegetables depending on the season or your cravings at the moment. Complete the meal with a salad of assertive winter greens (page 185).

4	cups cauliflower florets (*see photo, page 221*)
4	cups cubed peeled butternut squash (1½-inch chunks)
1	medium onion, sliced
2	tablespoons extra-virgin olive oil
½	teaspoon garlic powder
¾	teaspoon freshly ground pepper, divided
¼	teaspoon salt
2½	cups vegetable broth *or* reduced-sodium chicken broth
1	cup water
¾	cup cornmeal
1	teaspoon chopped fresh rosemary *or* ½ teaspoon dried
⅔	cup finely shredded Parmesan cheese, preferably Parmigiano-Reggiano

1. Preheat oven to 500°F.

2. Toss cauliflower, squash and onion in a large bowl with oil, garlic powder, ½ teaspoon pepper and salt. Spread on a rimmed baking sheet. Roast, stirring once, until tender and browned in spots, 25 to 30 minutes.

3. Meanwhile, combine broth and water in a small saucepan. Bring to a boil. Slowly whisk in cornmeal, rosemary and the remaining ¼ teaspoon pepper until smooth. Reduce heat to low, cover and cook, stirring occasionally, until very thick and creamy, 10 to 15 minutes. Stir in cheese; remove the polenta from the heat. Serve the vegetables over the polenta.

MAKES 4 SERVINGS.

ACTIVE TIME: 45 minutes

TOTAL TIME: 45 minutes

PER SERVING:

336 calories; 14 g fat (5 g sat, 5 g mono); 20 mg cholesterol; 44 g carbohydrate; 14 g protein; 9 g fiber; 688 mg sodium; 812 mg potassium

NUTRITION BONUS:

Vitamin A (520% daily value)
Vitamin C (160% dv)
Potassium (33% dv)
Calcium (30% dv)
Folate (29% dv)

H✕W H↑F

Sesame-Crusted Tofu with Spicy Pineapple Noodles

The tropical flavors of the hot chile-spiked pineapple noodles that accompany the crispy tofu in this dish will take the chill out of any cold day.

4	ounces udon noodles *or* whole-wheat spaghetti
1/3	cup sesame seeds, preferably a mixture of white and black
1	tablespoon plus 1 teaspoon cornstarch, divided
1/2	teaspoon salt
1	14-ounce package extra-firm water-packed tofu, drained
4	teaspoons canola oil, divided
1	tablespoon minced fresh ginger
2	cloves garlic, minced
1-2	small dried red chiles, such as Thai, cayenne *or* chile de arbol
8	ounces sugar snap peas, trimmed (*see photo, page* 228) and cut in half
1	6-ounce can pineapple juice (3/4 cup)
2	tablespoons plus 2 teaspoons reduced-sodium soy sauce
2	cups diced fresh pineapple
2	teaspoons hot sesame oil

1. Bring a large saucepan of water to a boil. Cook pasta according to package directions, drain and rinse well under cold water.

2. Mix sesame seeds, 1 tablespoon cornstarch and salt in a shallow dish. Cut the block of tofu lengthwise into 8 thin "steaks." Pat dry with a paper towel, and press both sides into the sesame-seed mixture.

3. Heat 2 teaspoons canola oil in a large nonstick skillet over medium-high heat. Add the tofu and cook until golden brown, about 3 minutes per side. Transfer to a plate, cover and keep warm.

4. Wipe out the pan. Heat the remaining 2 teaspoons canola oil. Add ginger, garlic and chiles and cook, stirring, until fragrant, about 30 seconds. Add snap peas and cook, stirring, until beginning to brown, about 2 minutes more. Add pineapple juice, bring to a boil and cook 2 minutes. Whisk the remaining 1 teaspoon cornstarch and soy sauce in a small bowl until smooth. Add to the pan and cook, stirring, until the sauce is thickened, about 1 minute. Reduce heat to low, add pineapple, sesame oil and the noodles; toss to coat with the sauce and cook until heated through, about 1 minute. Remove the chiles. Serve the noodles with the tofu.

MAKES **4** SERVINGS.

ACTIVE TIME: 40 minutes

TOTAL TIME: 40 minutes

PER SERVING:

444 calories; 19 g fat (2 g sat, 6 g mono); 0 mg cholesterol; 51 g carbohydrate; 19 g protein; 6 g fiber; 739 mg sodium; 258 mg potassium

NUTRITION BONUS:

Vitamin C (70% daily value)
Magnesium (28% dv)
Iron (20% dv)
Calcium (17% dv)

H↑F H♥H

| Butternut squash is an excellent source of beta carotene, which your body converts to vitamin A, a nutrient that helps keep your immune system strong.

Squash & Leek Lasagna

Grated butternut squash, pine nuts and sautéed leeks in a creamy white sauce are layered with sheets of whole-wheat pasta for this wintery variation on a vegetable lasagna. Any Parmesan cheese can be used in this casserole, but we recommend Parmigiano-Reggiano for its superior flavor.

ACTIVE TIME: 1 hour

TOTAL TIME: 2¾ hours

TO MAKE AHEAD: Bake, let cool for 1 hour, cover with parchment paper then foil and refrigerate for up to 3 days. Reheat, covered, at 350°F for 1 hour, then uncovered for 30 minutes more.

PER SERVING:

277 calories; 9 g fat (4 g sat, 2 g mono); 19 mg cholesterol; 37 g carbohydrate; 14 g protein; 6 g fiber; 464 mg sodium; 514 mg potassium

NUTRITION BONUS:

Vitamin A (150% daily value) Calcium & Vitamin C (30% dv) Iron (15% dv)

H✳W H↑F

TIP: To toast pine nuts, cook in a small dry skillet over medium-low heat, stirring constantly, until fragrant and lightly browned, 2 to 4 minutes.

10	ounces lasagna noodles, preferably whole-wheat
2	tablespoons unsalted butter
4	large *or* 5 medium leeks, pale green and white parts only, thinly sliced and washed thoroughly (about 6 cups)
½	cup all-purpose flour
4	cups nonfat milk
1	teaspoon dried thyme
1	teaspoon salt
¾	teaspoon freshly grated nutmeg
½	teaspoon freshly ground pepper
1	2-pound butternut squash, peeled, halved, seeded and grated using the large-hole side of a box grater
6	ounces Parmigiano-Reggiano, grated using the large-hole side of a box grater
¼	cup toasted pine nuts (*see Tip*)

1. Preheat oven to 350°F. Coat a 9-by-13-inch baking dish with cooking spray.

2. Bring a large pot of water to a boil. Cook noodles until not quite al dente, about 2 minutes less than the package directions. Drain; return the noodles to the pot and cover with cool water.

3. Melt butter in a Dutch oven over medium heat. Add leeks; cook, stirring often, until softened, about 6 minutes. Sprinkle flour over the leeks; stir well. Cook, stirring constantly, for 2 minutes. Whisk in milk in a slow stream and cook, whisking constantly, until thick and bubbling, 8 to 10 minutes. Whisk in thyme, salt, nutmeg and pepper. Remove from the heat.

4. Assemble lasagna in the prepared baking dish by layering one-third of the noodles, one-third of the sauce, half the squash, one-third of the cheese, half the remaining noodles, half the remaining sauce, all the pine nuts, all the remaining squash, half the remaining cheese, all the remaining noodles, all the remaining sauce and all the remaining cheese. Cover with parchment paper then foil.

5. Bake the lasagna for 50 minutes. Uncover and bake until bubbling and lightly browned, 30 to 45 minutes more. Let stand for 10 minutes before serving (or follow make-ahead instructions).

MAKES **12** SERVINGS.

Braised Chicken Thighs with Broccoli & Olives

Black olives and lemon juice join steamed broccoli to make a rich-tasting sauce to spoon over sautéed chicken thighs and garlic cloves. Serve this stew over brown rice or barley.

16	large cloves garlic, unpeeled
1	bunch broccoli (1¼ pounds), trimmed into florets
¼	cup all-purpose flour
¼	teaspoon salt
¼	teaspoon freshly ground pepper
1½	pounds bone-in chicken thighs, skin and fat removed
1	tablespoon extra-virgin olive oil
½	cup dry white wine
1	cup reduced-sodium chicken broth
4	sprigs fresh thyme *or* ½ teaspoon dried
1	teaspoon cornstarch *or* arrowroot
1	tablespoon water
8	black olives, pitted
1	tablespoon lemon juice
2	tablespoons chopped fresh parsley

1. Place garlic cloves in a small saucepan and cover with water. Bring to a boil. Cook for 5 minutes. Drain, slip off skins. Set aside.

2. Bring 1 inch of water to a boil in a medium saucepan fitted with a steamer basket. Steam broccoli until tender-crisp, 4 to 5 minutes. Remove from the steamer. Set aside. (*Alternatively, microwave broccoli with ¼ cup water, covered, on High for 3 to 5 minutes. Drain.*)

3. Combine flour, salt and pepper in a shallow dish. Dredge chicken in the flour mixture, shaking off excess.

4. Heat oil in a large skillet over medium-high heat. Add the chicken and cook, turning, until browned on all sides, 4 to 5 minutes total. Transfer the chicken to a plate.

5. Pour wine into the pan and bring to a boil, stirring to scrape up any browned bits. Boil for several minutes until reduced to ¼ cup. Add broth, thyme and the reserved garlic cloves; bring to a boil. Reduce heat to low and add the reserved chicken. Cover and simmer until the chicken is cooked through, about 20 minutes. With a slotted spoon or tongs, transfer the chicken and garlic to a platter and keep warm.

6. Dissolve cornstarch (or arrowroot) in water in a small bowl. Stir into the pan and simmer, stirring, for 30 seconds to 1 minute, or until slightly thickened. Add the reserved broccoli and heat through. Add olives and lemon juice. Spoon the broccoli sauce over the chicken and garlic. Garnish with parsley.

MAKES **4** SERVINGS.

ACTIVE TIME: 55 minutes

TOTAL TIME: 1¼ hours

PER SERVING:

352 calories; 15 g fat (4 g sat, 7 g mono); 87 mg cholesterol; 20 g carbohydrate; 30 g protein; 5 g fiber; 380 mg sodium; 769 mg potassium

NUTRITION BONUS:

Vitamin C (234% daily value)
Vitamin A (90% dv)
Selenium (50% dv)
Folate (34% dv)
Potassium (22% dv)
Zinc (21% dv)
Iron (20% dv)
Magnesium (17% dv)

L↓ C H↑ F

Southwestern Stuffed Acorn Squash

Cumin and chili powder season an aromatic stuffing made with turkey sausage, tomatoes, black beans and Swiss cheese. The mixture, which also has some heat from hot red pepper sauce, does a delicious job of balancing the sweet creaminess of the golden acorn squash. Serve this stuffed squash with warmed corn tortillas for wrapping up bites of all the tasty ingredients.

3	acorn squash (¾-1 pound each)
5	ounces bulk turkey sausage
1	small onion, chopped
½	medium red bell pepper, chopped
1	clove garlic, minced
1	tablespoon chili powder
1	teaspoon ground cumin
2	cups chopped cherry tomatoes
1	15-ounce can black beans, rinsed (*see Tip, page 239*)
½	teaspoon salt
	Several dashes hot red pepper sauce, to taste
1	cup shredded Swiss cheese

1. Preheat oven to 375°F. Lightly coat a large baking sheet with cooking spray.

2. Cut squash in half horizontally. Scoop out and discard seeds. Place the squash cut-side down on the prepared baking sheet. Bake until tender, about 45 minutes.

3. Meanwhile, lightly coat a large skillet with cooking spray; heat over medium heat. Add sausage and cook, stirring and breaking up with a wooden spoon, until lightly browned, 3 to 5 minutes. Add onion and bell pepper; cook, stirring often, until softened, 3 to 5 minutes. Stir in garlic, chili powder and cumin; cook for 30 seconds. Stir in tomatoes, beans, salt and hot sauce, scraping up any browned bits. Cover, reduce heat, and simmer until the tomatoes are broken down, 10 to 12 minutes.

4. When the squash are tender, reduce oven temperature to 325°. Fill the squash halves with the turkey mixture. Top with cheese. Place on the baking sheet and bake until the filling is heated through and the cheese is melted, 8 to 10 minutes.

MAKES **6** SERVINGS.

ACTIVE TIME: 45 minutes

TOTAL TIME: 1½ hours

PER SERVING:

259 calories; 7 g fat (4 g sat, 1 g mono); 29 mg cholesterol; 38 g carbohydrate; 15 g protein; 7 g fiber; 482 mg sodium; 884 mg potassium

NUTRITION BONUS:

Vitamin C (80% daily value)
Vitamin A (45% dv)
Calcium (20% dv)
Iron (15% dv)

H✳W   H↑F

Pan-Seared Chicken with Orange & Grapefruit Sauce

There are never too many recipes for quick-cooking boneless chicken breast sautés. This variation on the theme celebrates the citrus season using whole, fresh fruit and marmalade to make a thicker and sweeter pan sauce than it would be with just the juice.

1	small pink grapefruit
1	medium orange
1/4	cup all-purpose flour
1/2	teaspoon salt
1/2	teaspoon freshly ground pepper
4	boneless, skinless chicken breasts, trimmed (1 pound)
1	tablespoon canola oil, divided
1	leek, trimmed, washed thoroughly and sliced
1/4	cup dry vermouth
2	tablespoons orange marmalade
2	tablespoons chopped fresh mint *or* 1/2 teaspoon dried

1. Remove skin and white pith from grapefruit and orange with a sharp knife and discard. (*See photos, page 222.*) Cut the segments away from their surrounding membranes into a bowl (discard seeds). Squeeze any remaining juice from the membranes into the bowl. Drain the segments and measure the juice. Add enough water, if necessary, to make 1/2 cup and set the juice and fruit aside.

2. Combine flour, salt and pepper in a shallow dish. Dredge chicken lightly in the flour mixture.

3. Heat 2 teaspoons oil in a nonstick skillet over medium-high heat. Add the chicken and cook until golden on the outside and no longer pink inside, 3 to 4 minutes per side. (Reduce heat to medium if the chicken is browning too quickly.) Remove to a plate, cover and keep warm.

4. Add the remaining 1 teaspoon oil to the pan. Add leek and cook, stirring, until softened, about 3 minutes. Add the reserved fruit juices and vermouth and bring to a boil. Boil until reduced by half, about 3 minutes. Reduce heat to low and add marmalade, the reserved fruit, mint and pepper to taste. Return chicken to the pan and reheat gently.

MAKES **4** SERVINGS.

Pork Roast with Walnut-Pomegranate Filling

Pomegranates become available in late fall just in time to grace holiday tables—all too often as decorations. For this festive roast the fruit is used in three forms: as a thick, sweet molasses for the filling plus whole seeds and juice for the sauce. Slicing through the roast reveals a colorful pinwheel of crushed walnuts mixed with the pomegranate molasses.

PORK & FILLING

½	cup shelled walnuts
4	tablespoons pomegranate molasses (*see Note, page 240*), divided
3	tablespoons extra-virgin olive oil
2	cloves garlic, minced
¼	teaspoon salt, divided
	Freshly ground pepper to taste
1	2-pound boneless center-cut pork loin roast, trimmed

SAUCE

1½	cups pomegranate juice
1½	cups reduced-sodium chicken broth
2	tablespoons honey
¼	teaspoon salt
1½	teaspoons cornstarch
1	tablespoon water
1	cup pomegranate seeds (1 large fruit; *see Guide, page 229*) for garnish

ACTIVE TIME: 50 minutes

TOTAL TIME: 2 hours 10 minutes

TO MAKE AHEAD: Prepare through Step 4. Wrap in plastic wrap and refrigerate for up to 8 hours. The sauce (Step 6) can be made ahead: cover and refrigerate for up to 2 days; reheat before serving.

EQUIPMENT: Kitchen string

PER SERVING:

298 calories; 14 g fat (3 g sat, 7 g mono); 72 mg cholesterol; 16 g carbohydrate; 26 g protein; 0 g fiber; 238 mg sodium; 534 mg potassium

H✕W L↓C H♥H

1. Preheat oven to 350°F. Line a roasting pan with foil. Coat a rack with cooking spray.

2. **To prepare pork & filling:** Toast walnuts in a small dry skillet over medium-low heat, stirring constantly, until fragrant, 2 to 3 minutes. Transfer to a small bowl and let cool. Place the walnuts in a sealable plastic bag and crush with a rolling pin. Transfer to a medium bowl and mix in 2 tablespoons pomegranate molasses, oil, garlic, ⅛ teaspoon salt and pepper.

3. Using a sharp knife, make a vertical cut two-thirds of the way to the bottom of the pork. From there, slice outward horizontally to about ¾ inch from the sides. Unfold the pork.

4. Place the pork between 2 sheets of plastic wrap. Using a meat mallet or heavy skillet, pound the pork to an even ½-inch thickness. Remove the plastic wrap. Using a spatula, spread the filling over the surface, leaving a 1-inch border. Starting at the short edge, roll the roast up fairly tightly, completely enclosing the filling. Tie the roast at 1½-inch intervals with kitchen string.

5. Season the roast with the remaining ⅛ teaspoon salt and pepper and coat with the remaining 2 tablespoons pomegranate molasses. Set the roast seam-side down on the prepared rack. Roast until an instant-read thermometer inserted in the center registers 155°F (it will increase to 160°F as it rests), about 1 hour 10 minutes. Transfer the pork to a clean cutting board; tent with foil and let rest for 10 minutes.

6. **Meanwhile, prepare sauce:** Combine pomegranate juice, broth, honey and ¼ teaspoon salt in a medium saucepan; bring to a boil over medium-high heat. Boil until the sauce has reduced to 1 cup, 15 to 25 minutes. Mix cornstarch and water in a small bowl; add to the sauce and cook, whisking, until slightly thickened, about 1 minute.

7. Remove the string and carve the roast into ¾-inch-thick slices. Serve with the sauce and garnish each serving with pomegranate seeds.

MAKES 8 SERVINGS.

Spaghetti Squash & Pork Stir-Fry

The spaghetti squash with its silky threads of golden flesh is one of the more unusual winter squashes. So here's an unusual but delicious way to use it—in an Asian-inspired pork stir-fry. The flavors of toasted sesame oil, fresh ginger, garlic and a hit of spicy red chile sauce cling to the beautiful strands. Serve with jasmine rice.

1	3-pound spaghetti squash
1	pound pork tenderloin, trimmed
2	teaspoons toasted sesame oil
5	medium scallions, thinly sliced
2	cloves garlic, minced
1	tablespoon minced fresh ginger
1/2	teaspoon salt
2	tablespoons reduced-sodium soy sauce
2	tablespoons rice vinegar
1	teaspoon Asian red chile sauce, such as sriracha, *or* chile oil

1. Preheat oven to 350°F.

2. Cut squash in half. Scoop out and discard seeds. Place each half, cut-side down, on a baking sheet. Bake until the squash is tender, about 1 hour. Let cool for 10 minutes then shred the flesh with a fork into a bowl. Discard the shell.

3. Slice pork into thin rounds; cut each round into matchsticks.

4. Heat a large wok over medium-high heat. Swirl in oil, then add scallions, garlic, ginger and salt; cook, stirring, until fragrant, 30 seconds. Add the pork; cook, stirring constantly, until just cooked through, 2 to 3 minutes. Add the squash threads and cook, stirring, for 1 minute. Add soy sauce, rice vinegar and chile sauce (or chile oil); cook, stirring constantly, until aromatic, about 30 seconds.

MAKES 4 SERVINGS, ABOUT 1 1/2 CUPS EACH.

ACTIVE TIME: 30 minutes

TOTAL TIME: 1 1/2 hours

TO MAKE AHEAD: Prepare the squash (Steps 1 & 2), cover and refrigerate for up to 2 days.

PER SERVING:

236 calories; 6 g fat (1 g sat, 2 g mono); 74 mg cholesterol; 22 g carbohydrate; 27 g protein; 5 g fiber; 707 mg sodium; 878 mg potassium

NUTRITION BONUS:

Vitamin C (25% daily value)
Potassium (24% dv)
Iron (17% dv)

H✄W L↓C H↑F H♥H

Braised Brisket & Roots

While a barbecued brisket served with corn on the cob is perfect for backyard entertaining, this braised brisket has a decidedly wintery feel. A root vegetable trio of carrots, parsnips and rutabaga imparts sweet and earthy flavors to the brisket.

ACTIVE TIME: 1¼ hours

TOTAL TIME: 3 to 5½ hours

PER SERVING:

385 calories; 11 g fat (3 g sat, 5 g mono); 78 mg cholesterol; 22 g carbohydrate; 41 g protein; 5 g fiber; 279 mg sodium, 850 mg potassium

NUTRITION BONUS:

Vitamin A (110% daily value)
Zinc (64% dv)
Selenium 57% dv)
Vitamin C (35% dv)
Iron (25% dv)
Potassium (21% dv)

L↓C H↑F H♥H

NOTE: **Briskets** are notoriously fatty. But the flat, first-cut section is a far better choice for healthy eating than the fattier point cut. Don't worry about a first-cut brisket being tough—there's enough juice in this mélange of root vegetables to keep the meat moist, no matter how lean it is.

1	tablespoon canola oil	1	cup dry vermouth *or* dry white wine
2	pounds flat, first-cut brisket (*see Note*), trimmed	3	cups reduced-sodium beef broth
3	medium onions, sliced	4	medium carrots, peeled
6	allspice berries *or* pinch of ground allspice	3	medium parsnips, peeled and cored (*see Guide, page 227*)
2	teaspoons chopped fresh thyme *or* ¾ teaspoon dried	1	medium rutabaga (about ¾ pound), peeled (*see Guide, page 230*)
1	teaspoon sweet paprika	1	teaspoon Dijon mustard
½	teaspoon salt	2	teaspoons arrowroot *or* 1 tablespoon cornstarch
½	teaspoon freshly ground pepper	1-2	tablespoons water
2	bay leaves		

1. Preheat oven to 325°F. Heat oil in a Dutch oven over medium-high heat. Add brisket and cook until browned, 3 to 5 minutes per side. Transfer to a large plate and set aside.

2. Add onions to the pot; cook, stirring frequently, until softened, about 2 minutes. Stir in allspice, thyme, paprika, salt, pepper and bay leaves, then pour in vermouth (or wine). Bring to a boil. Cook for 3 minutes.

3. Stir in broth and return the brisket to the pot along with any accumulated juices. Bring to a simmer. Cover, place in the oven and bake for 1½ hours. Meanwhile, cut carrots, parsnips and rutabaga into 2-by-½-inch sticks.

4. Transfer the brisket to a plate. Discard the bay leaves and allspice berries (if using). Stir mustard into the sauce. Add the carrots, parsnips and rutabaga. Return the brisket to the pot; cover and bake for 1 hour more.

5. Test the vegetables and brisket for tenderness by piercing with the tip of a sharp knife. As they get done, transfer to a cutting board or platter, cover with foil and set aside. If necessary, continue to cook, testing for doneness every 20 minutes. Total cooking time for the brisket may range from 2½ to 5 hours, depending on the particular piece of meat.

6. Skim fat from the sauce. Bring the sauce to a boil over high heat. Cook for 5 minutes, stirring occasionally, to reduce and intensify flavors. Dissolve arrowroot in 1 tablespoon water (or cornstarch in 2 tablespoons water); add to the sauce and cook, stirring constantly, just until thickened, about 10 seconds.

7. Slice the brisket thinly against the grain and arrange slices on a serving platter. Using a slotted spoon, mound the vegetables around the brisket. Spoon half the sauce over the meat and vegetables; pass remaining sauce separately.

MAKES 8 SERVINGS: 3 OUNCES MEAT, 1 CUP VEGETABLES, ¼ CUP SAUCE EACH.

Lina's Pasta & Broccoli

We all know that broccoli sometimes gets a bad rap for its assertive flavor, but if you like it, then celebrate it. For this pasta, the vegetable in question meets its match with the bold and salty taste of anchovies. Golden raisins add sweet notes to this unusual—but tasty—combination.

1	pound broccoli
2	quarts water
1½	teaspoons extra-virgin olive oil
1	onion, thinly sliced
1	clove garlic, peeled and crushed
4	anchovy fillets, rinsed and minced
¼	cup dry white wine
1	tablespoon chopped fresh basil
⅛	teaspoon cayenne pepper
¾	cup canned tomato sauce
2	tablespoons golden raisins, soaked in warm water
2	tablespoons pine nuts
¼	teaspoon salt
	Freshly ground pepper to taste
6	ounces whole-wheat penne *or* ziti
3	tablespoons freshly grated pecorino cheese

1. Cut the tops off the broccoli and separate into small florets. Trim the tough ends from stalks. Peel the stalks down to the pale green center and dice.

2. Bring water to a boil in a large saucepan; add the broccoli florets and stalks. Cook until tender, about 5 minutes. Transfer the broccoli to a bowl with a slotted spoon and set aside. Reserve the cooking water.

3. Heat oil in a large skillet over medium heat. Add onions and garlic and cook, stirring, until softened, about 2 minutes. Add anchovies and cook, stirring, for about 1 minute. Add wine, basil and cayenne and cook, stirring, for about 30 seconds. Add tomato sauce and cook, stirring, for 2 minutes. Add the broccoli and mash with a wooden spoon. Reduce heat and simmer for about 10 minutes, stirring occasionally. The sauce should have the consistency of a lumpy pea soup. Thin with a little of the reserved cooking water, if necessary.

4. Drain the raisins and add them to the sauce, along with pine nuts. Remove the garlic clove. Season the sauce with salt and pepper and keep warm over low heat.

5. Return the broccoli-cooking water to a boil and add pasta. Cook until just tender, 8 to 10 minutes or according to package directions. Drain and stir the pasta into the sauce. Cook together for 1 or 2 minutes. Serve with a sprinkling of cheese.

MAKES **4** SERVINGS.

ACTIVE TIME: 40 minutes

TOTAL TIME: 50 minutes

PER SERVING:

292 calories; 7 g fat (1 g sat, 3 g mono); 7 mg cholesterol; 48 g carbohydrate; 12 g protein; 9 g fiber; 635 mg sodium; 670 mg potassium

NUTRITION BONUS:

Vitamin C (190% daily value)
Vitamin A (70% dv)
Folate (22% dv)
Potassium (19% dv)
Iron (15% dv)

H❉W L↓C H↑F H♥H

Bananas are rich in vitamin B_6, which is needed to form healthy red blood cells.

BANANAS

Roasted Halibut with Banana-Orange Relish

Sweet bananas combined with oranges, cilantro and lime juice create a fresh relish that has the effect of transporting you to an island in the tropics—well, at least it feels that way. The exotic condiment is served here with mild, white-fleshed fish but would perform the same magic with chicken or pork.

FISH

1	pound halibut, Pacific cod *or* other white-fleshed fish
1/2	teaspoon ground coriander
1/4	teaspoon kosher salt

BANANA-ORANGE RELISH

2	ripe bananas, diced
1/2	teaspoon freshly grated orange zest
2	oranges, peeled, segmented (*see photos, page 222*) and chopped
1/4	cup chopped fresh cilantro
2	tablespoons lime juice
1/2	teaspoon ground coriander
1/4	teaspoon kosher salt

1. **To prepare fish:** Preheat oven to 450°F. Lightly coat a baking sheet with cooking spray.

2. Cut fish into 4 portions. Mix coriander and salt in a small bowl and sprinkle evenly on both sides of the fish. Place on the prepared baking sheet.

3. Bake the fish until it is juicy and almost flakes when pressed with a knife, 8 to 12 minutes, depending on thickness.

4. **To prepare relish:** Meanwhile, stir together bananas, orange zest, chopped oranges, cilantro, lime juice, coriander and salt in a medium bowl. To serve, spoon the relish over the roasted fish.

MAKES **4** SERVINGS.

ACTIVE TIME: 15 minutes

TOTAL TIME: 25 minutes

TO MAKE AHEAD: Cover the relish and refrigerate for up to 2 hours.

PER SERVING:

210 calories; 3 g fat (0 g sat, 1 g mono); 36 mg cholesterol; 22 g carbohydrate; 25 g protein; 3 g fiber; 203 mg sodium; 855 mg potassium

NUTRITION BONUS:

Vitamin C (70% daily value)
Selenium (60% dv)
Potassium (24% dv)

H� W L↓C H♥H

Eating pomegranates (or drinking the juice) has been linked with cardiovascular health and relief from rheumatoid arthritis.

POMEGRANATE

Barley & Wild Rice Pilaf with Pomegranate Seeds

Wild rice, a staple of Native Americans in Minnesota, has traditionally been harvested in the fall and made up an important part of the winter coffers. This pilaf melds the chewy texture of barley and wild rice with the richness of toasted pine nuts and the sweet-sour crunch of pomegranate seeds. The elegant dish is perfect for entertaining.

2	teaspoons extra-virgin olive oil
1	medium onion, finely chopped
1/2	cup wild rice, rinsed
1/2	cup pearl barley
3	cups reduced-sodium chicken broth *or* vegetable broth
1/3	cup pine nuts
1	cup pomegranate seeds (1 large fruit; *see Tip*)
2	teaspoons freshly grated lemon zest
2	tablespoons chopped flat-leaf parsley

1. Heat oil in a large saucepan over medium heat. Add onion and cook, stirring often, until softened. Add wild rice and barley; stir for a few seconds. Add broth and bring to a simmer. Reduce heat to low, cover and simmer until the wild rice and barley are tender and most of the liquid has been absorbed, 45 to 50 minutes.

2. Meanwhile, toast pine nuts in a small, dry skillet over medium-low heat, stirring constantly, until light golden and fragrant, 2 to 3 minutes. Transfer to a small bowl to cool.

3. Add pomegranate seeds, lemon zest, parsley and the toasted pine nuts to the pilaf; fluff with a fork. Serve hot.

MAKES **6** SERVINGS, 3/4 CUP EACH.

ACTIVE TIME: 20 minutes

TOTAL TIME: 1 hour

TO MAKE AHEAD: Prepare through Step 2. Cover and refrigerate for up to 2 days. To reheat, place in a baking dish, add 1/4 cup water and cover. Microwave on High for 10 to 15 minutes or bake at 350°F for 25 to 30 minutes.

PER SERVING:

209 calories; 7 g fat (1 g sat, 3 g mono); 3 mg cholesterol; 31 g carbohydrate; 7 g protein; 4 g fiber; 75 mg sodium; 250 mg potassium

NUTRITION BONUS:

Magnesium (15% dv)

H✖W H♥H

TIP: To seed a pomegranate and avoid the enduring stains of pomegranate juice, work under water. Fill a large bowl with water. Hold the pomegranate in the water and slice off the crown. Lightly score the fruit into quarters, from crown to stem end. Keeping the fruit under water, break it apart, gently separating the plump seeds from the outer skin and white pith. The seeds will drop to the bottom of the bowl and the pith will float to the surface. Discard the pith. Pour the seeds into a colander. Rinse and pat dry. The seeds can be frozen in an airtight container or sealable bag for up to 3 months.

Mashed Roots with Buttermilk & Chives

Plain mashed potatoes may seem a bit tame after you've tried this flavorful version. A trio of roots from the winter cellar—celery root, rutabaga and Yukon Gold potatoes—are cooked and then mashed with sweet garlic and tangy buttermilk. Finish the dish with a handful of snipped fresh chives.

2	pounds celery root (celeriac), peeled (*see Guide, page 222*) and cut into 1-inch pieces
1	pound rutabaga, peeled (*see Guide, page 230*) and cut into 1-inch pieces
1	pound Yukon Gold potatoes, peeled and cut into 1-inch pieces
5	cloves garlic, peeled
4	tablespoons unsalted butter, divided
¾	cup nonfat buttermilk (*see Tip, page 239*)
½	teaspoon salt
¼	teaspoon freshly ground pepper
¼	teaspoon ground nutmeg
⅓	cup snipped fresh chives

1. Bring 1 inch of water to a simmer in a large pan or Dutch oven. Place celery root, rutabaga and potatoes in a large steamer basket over the water, cover and steam over medium-low heat for 20 minutes. Add garlic and continue steaming—checking the water level and replenishing as necessary—until the vegetables are fall-apart tender, 20 minutes more.

2. Remove the vegetables, drain the cooking liquid and return the vegetables to the pan. Add 2 tablespoons butter and mash until chunky-smooth. Gradually stir in buttermilk, salt, pepper and nutmeg.

3. Just before serving, stir in the remaining 2 tablespoons butter and chives.

MAKES 8 SERVINGS, ¾ CUP EACH.

ACTIVE TIME: 20 minutes

TOTAL TIME: 1 hour

TO MAKE AHEAD: Prepare through Step 2 and refrigerate for up to 2 days. Reheat in a double boiler and stir in the remaining butter and chives (Step 3) just before serving.

PER SERVING:

173 calories; 6 g fat (4 g sat, 0 g mono); 15 mg cholesterol; 26 g carbohydrate; 4 g protein; 4 g fiber; 289 mg sodium; 826 mg potassium

NUTRITION BONUS:

Vitamin C (35% daily value)
Potassium (22% dv)

H✳W

Wilted Winter Greens & Black-Eyed Peas

Cool-weather greens, such a collards, kale and escarole, although delicious, can be somewhat bitter. For this sauté, soft, smooth black-eyed peas make a mellow match for those assertive flavors. Country ham or Italian prosciutto makes a nice change from the salt pork or ham hocks that greens are traditionally cooked with.

8	ounces dried black-eyed peas (1¹⁄₃ cups)
¼	teaspoon salt
2	pounds greens, such as collards, kale *and/or* escarole, trimmed, washed and sliced crosswise into ¼-inch-wide strips
1	tablespoon canola oil
2	ounces country ham (*see Note, page 240*) *or* prosciutto, diced (about ½ cup)
2	tablespoons red-wine vinegar, or to taste
	Freshly ground pepper to taste

1. Soak peas overnight in cold water. (*Alternatively, place peas in a large saucepan, cover with water and bring to a simmer. Cook for 2 minutes. Remove from the heat and let stand for 1 hour.*) Drain the peas, rinse well and place in a large saucepan. Add water to cover and bring to a boil. Reduce heat to medium; cook, stirring occasionally, until tender, about 45 minutes. Add salt. Let sit, covered, for ½ hour, then drain and rinse.

2. Heat oil in a large skillet over high heat. Add ham (or prosciutto) and cook, stirring, until lightly browned, about 2 minutes. Add the greens and cook, stirring constantly, until wilted, 5 to 10 minutes, adding more water if necessary. Add the reserved black-eyed peas and heat through.

3. Season with vinegar, salt and pepper and serve.

MAKES **10** SERVINGS.

ACTIVE TIME: 20 minutes

TOTAL TIME: 2 hours (plus overnight soaking)

TO MAKE AHEAD: Prepare through Step 2; cover and refrigerate up to 2 days. Reheat on the stovetop or in the microwave.

PER SERVING:

124 calories; 3 g fat (0 g sat, 1 g mono); 4 mg cholesterol; 18 g carbohydrate; 9 g protein; 7 g fiber; 232 mg sodium; 358 mg potassium

NUTRITION BONUS:

Vitamin A (128% daily value)
Vitamin C (66% dv)
Folate (41% dv)
Calcium (15% dv)

H W L C H F H H

Southern Kale

Kale is a hale and hearty green that thrives in cool weather and along with these characteristics come robust flavor and a toothsome bite. The lengthy cooking time makes the kale melt-in-your-mouth tender in this recipe. Assertive garlic and salty country ham stand up to kale's bold flavor.

2	teaspoons extra-virgin olive oil
2	teaspoons minced garlic
2	ounces country ham (*see Note, page 240*), pancetta *or* prosciutto, diced (about ½ cup)
15	cups stemmed, torn and rinsed kale (1-2 bunches)
2	cups water
¼	teaspoon crushed red pepper

Heat oil in a large high-sided skillet over medium-high heat. Add garlic, stir, and immediately add ham (or pancetta or prosciutto). Add kale by the handful, stirring to make room for more leaves. When all the kale has been added, add water and crushed red pepper; stir to combine. Bring to a simmer, cover and cook, stirring occasionally, for 15 minutes. Uncover and continue to simmer, stirring occasionally, until most of the water has evaporated and the kale is tender, 10 to 15 minutes more. Serve warm.

MAKES 4 SERVINGS.

ACTIVE TIME: 50 minutes

TOTAL TIME: 50 minutes

PER SERVING:

93 calories; 4 g fat (1 g sat, 2 g mono); 10 mg cholesterol; 8 g carbohydrate; 6 g protein; 3 g fiber; 412 mg sodium; 371 mg potassium

NUTRITION BONUS:

Vitamin A (360% daily value)
Vitamin C (90% dv)

H✖W L↓C H♥H

Ginger Broccoli

A Southeast-Asian treatment is an exotic way to get out of a steamed broccoli rut. For this dish, it is chopped and quickly sautéed with fresh ginger, mellow rice vinegar and rich, salty fish sauce. Serve alongside any Asian noodle or fried rice dish.

1	tablespoon canola oil
2	tablespoons minced garlic
4	teaspoons minced fresh ginger
1	pound broccoli crowns, trimmed and chopped (about 6 cups)
3	tablespoons water
1	tablespoon fish sauce (*see Note, page 240*)
1	tablespoon rice vinegar

Heat oil in a large skillet over medium-high heat. Add garlic and ginger and cook until fragrant but not browned, 30 seconds to 1 minute. Add broccoli and cook, stirring, until the broccoli is bright green, 2 minutes. Drizzle water and fish sauce over the broccoli; reduce heat to medium, cover and cook until the broccoli is just tender, about 3 minutes. Stir in vinegar just before serving.

MAKES 4 SERVINGS, 1 CUP EACH.

ACTIVE TIME: 20 minutes

TOTAL TIME: 20 minutes

PER SERVING:

74 calories; 4 g fat (0 g sat, 2 g mono); 0 mg cholesterol; 8 g carbohydrate; 4 g protein; 3 g fiber; 328 mg sodium; 372 mg potassium

NUTRITION BONUS:

Vitamin C (170% daily value)
Vitamin A (60% dv)
Folate (19% dv)

H✖W L↓C H♥H

Balsamic & Parmesan Roasted Cauliflower

Roasting isn't usually the first cooking method you think of for cauliflower but the results are quite delicious. The florets are cut into thick slices and tossed with extra-virgin olive oil and herbs. Wherever the flat surfaces come into contact with the hot roasting pan, a deep browning occurs that results in a sweet, nutty flavor.

ACTIVE TIME: 10 minutes

TOTAL TIME: 35 minutes

PER SERVING:

149 calories; 10 g fat (3 g sat, 6 g mono); 7 mg cholesterol; 10 g carbohydrate; 7 g protein; 4 g fiber; 364 mg sodium; 490 mg potassium

NUTRITION BONUS:

Vitamin C (120% daily value)
Folate (22% dv)
Fiber (16% dv)
Calcium (15% dv)

H✸W L↓C

8	cups 1-inch-thick slices cauliflower florets (about 1 large head; *see photo, page 221*)
2	tablespoons extra-virgin olive oil
1	teaspoon dried marjoram
1/4	teaspoon salt
	Freshly ground pepper to taste
2	tablespoons balsamic vinegar
1/2	cup finely shredded Parmesan cheese

1. Preheat oven to 450°F.

2. Toss cauliflower, oil, marjoram, salt and pepper in a large bowl. Spread on a large rimmed baking sheet and roast until starting to soften and brown on the bottom, 15 to 20 minutes. Toss the cauliflower with vinegar and sprinkle with cheese. Return to the oven and roast until the cheese is melted and any moisture has evaporated, 5 to 10 minutes more.

MAKES 4 SERVINGS, ABOUT 1 CUP EACH.

For the Love of Pineapple

Ken Love cultivates his passion for pineapple on Hawaii's Big Island

At Love Family Farms, on the Big Island of Hawaii, Ken Love has been growing pineapple and other tropical fruit for nearly 30 years. Middle-aged, tall, with thinning hair, he wears big aloha shirts and an even bigger grin.

"At one time, Hawaii supplied nearly 75 percent of the world's commercial pineapple," says Love (*left*). "Dole Hawaii began when James Drummond Dole started a pineapple plantation in 1900. Today, much of the mainland pineapple comes from Central and South America, Mexico and other places." Most often, the fruit you will find in the supermarket is the gold pineapple. Highly aromatic, it has a gorgeous golden hue and is consistently sweet and juicy. It's also loaded with vitamin C. "It's got all the desirable qualities of an ideal fruit," says Love. But his favorite is the white pineapple, which he and other Hawaiians still grow in spiky sweet-scented fields that rim the islands' shores.

According to Love, pineapple, a member of the bromeliad family, which also includes Spanish moss, is easy to cultivate. "If the soil stays above 68°F, it grows anywhere, even in a pot," he says. Pineapple does best in the tropics, where it takes about one and a half to two years to bear fruit. "First a flower forms, then a baby pineapple. It's a composite fruit, made of hundreds of tiny fruitlets that merge into one."

When working the fields, he often cuts up a ripe pineapple for a quick energy boost. "I've been known to substitute thick pineapple slices for bread," he admits. "Warm brie between two slices of pineapple is hard to beat." Sometimes Love dons his other hat (culinary instructor and trained chef) with his wife, Margy, to make pineapple jams, jellies, fudge and sauces.

Standing on his porch, Love can see pineapple plants growing just 50 feet away. "You can always tell when a pineapple needs picking," he says. "It smells so sweet." He likes to pick them when they are nearly overripe. "They melt in your mouth." —*Janice Wald Henderson*

Love Family Farms
Captain Cook, Hawaii
(808) 323-2417
hawaiifruit.net
(fruit orders: in-state only)

Pineapple-Coconut Layer Cake

For everyone who loves the flavors of the Caribbean, this festive cake has it all. Two layers of coconut-flavored cake are filled with sweet pineapple curd and topped with creamy coconut frosting, chunks of fresh pineapple and toasted coconut.

CAKE

1½	cups cake flour
1	cup whole-wheat flour, preferably white whole-wheat (*see Note, page 241*)
2	teaspoons baking powder
¼	teaspoon salt
¾	cup granulated sugar
½	cup honey
⅓	cup canola oil
3	tablespoons butter, melted
¾	cup nonfat buttermilk *or* milk
2	tablespoons coconut rum *or* dark rum
2	teaspoons coconut extract
3	large eggs, separated (reserve 2 yolks for pineapple curd)

PINEAPPLE CURD

2	large egg yolks
1	6-ounce can pineapple juice (¾ cup)
¼	cup granulated sugar
5	teaspoons cornstarch

FROSTING & GARNISH

12	ounces reduced-fat cream cheese (Neufchâtel), at room temperature
⅓	cup confectioners' sugar, sifted
1	teaspoon coconut extract *or* rum
	Pinch of salt
1½	cups finely diced fresh pineapple, divided
2	tablespoons toasted coconut (*see Tip, page 239*)

ACTIVE TIME: 1¼ hours

TOTAL TIME: 2½ hours

EQUIPMENT: Two 9-inch round cake pans

PER SERVING:

317 calories; 13 g fat (5 g sat, 4 g mono); 48 mg cholesterol; 45 g carbohydrate; 6 g protein; 1 g fiber; 205 mg sodium; 101 mg potassium

1. **To prepare cake:** Preheat oven to 350°F. Coat two 9-inch cake pans with cooking spray.

2. Sift cake flour, whole-wheat flour, baking powder and ¼ teaspoon salt into a medium bowl. Beat ¾ cup sugar, honey, oil and melted butter in a large bowl with an electric mixer on medium speed until well blended. Whisk buttermilk (or milk), rum and coconut extract in a small bowl. With the mixer on low speed, alternately mix the dry ingredients and the wet ingredients into the sugar mixture, starting and ending with dry ingredients and scraping the sides of the bowl as needed, until just combined.

3. Clean and dry the beaters. Beat 3 egg whites in a medium bowl with the electric mixer on medium-high until soft peaks form. Gently fold the whites into the batter in two additions until just combined. Divide the batter between the prepared pans, spreading to the edges.

4. Bake the cake until a toothpick inserted in the center comes out clean, 26 to 30 minutes. Cool in the pans on a wire rack for 10 minutes. Turn out and let cool to room temperature, about 1 hour.

5. **To prepare curd:** Whisk 2 egg yolks, pineapple juice, ¼ cup sugar and cornstarch in a small saucepan. Cook over medium-low heat, whisking constantly, until thick and beginning to bubble, 3 to 5 minutes. Let cool completely.

6. **To prepare frosting & assemble cake:** Beat cream cheese, confectioners' sugar, extract (or rum) and a pinch of salt in a medium bowl with an electric mixer until smooth and creamy.

7. Place one cake layer, top-side down, on a cake stand or plate. Spread evenly with the pineapple curd, stopping just short of the edge. Scatter ½ cup diced pineapple over the curd. Place the remaining layer, top-side up, on top. Spread the frosting over the top and sides. Decorate the top with the remaining 1 cup pineapple and toasted coconut.

MAKES **16** SERVINGS.

Citrus Ginger Cake with Spiced Orange Compote

Just as peaches and strawberries make the perfect summer desserts, citrus fruits are well suited to the winter months. This festive olive-oil cake can be made with orange juice or Meyer lemon juice and gets an extra hit of citrus from the spiced orange compote that accompanies it. The cake tastes even better if made a day in advance, as the flavors get a chance to intensify.

¹/₂	cup honey
¹/₄	cup mild-flavored extra-virgin olive oil
2	large eggs, at room temperature, separated (*see Tip*)
2	tablespoons freshly grated orange *or* Meyer lemon zest
¹/₃	cup fresh orange *or* Meyer lemon juice
5	tablespoons chopped crystallized ginger, divided
1	cup whole-wheat pastry flour
²/₃	cup all-purpose flour
1	teaspoon baking powder
¹/₂	teaspoon salt
2	teaspoons confectioners' sugar
	Spiced Orange Compote (*page 214*)

1. Preheat oven to 350°F. Oil an 8-inch round cake pan (*see Variation*), line with parchment paper and oil the parchment.

2. Stir together honey, oil, egg yolks, zest, juice and 3 tablespoons crystallized ginger in a medium bowl. Sift whole-wheat pastry flour, all-purpose flour, baking powder and salt into a large bowl. Beat egg whites with an electric mixer on high in another medium bowl until soft peaks form, 1 to 2 minutes.

3. Stir the honey mixture into the flour mixture with a wooden spoon. Gently fold in the egg whites with a rubber spatula until they are well combined. Pour the batter into the prepared pan.

4. Bake the cake until a toothpick inserted into the center comes out clean, about 35 minutes. Transfer the pan to a wire rack to cool for 10 minutes. Run a knife around the edges of the pan to loosen the cake and turn it out onto the rack. Let cool completely.

5. Just before serving, sift sugar evenly over the top of the cake and garnish with the remaining 2 tablespoons ginger. Serve with Spiced Orange Compote on the side.

MAKES **10** SERVINGS.

ACTIVE TIME: 35 minutes

TOTAL TIME: 1 hour 35 minutes

TO MAKE AHEAD: Prepare through Step 4, tightly wrap in plastic wrap and hold at room temperature for up to 1 day.

EQUIPMENT: 8-inch cake pan (*see Variation*), parchment paper

PER SERVING:

280 calories; 7 g fat (1 g sat, 5 g mono); 42 mg cholesterol; 52 g carbohydrate; 4 g protein; 3 g fiber; 175 mg sodium; 189 mg potassium

NUTRITION BONUS:

Vitamin C (80% daily value)

H ♥ H

VARIATION: You can use a 9-inch cake pan for this recipe, but you will get a thinner cake. Reduce the baking time to 25 to 30 minutes. You can find 8-inch cake pans at well-stocked kitchenware stores or online at *surlatable.com*.

TIP: To bring an egg to room temperature, set it out on the counter for 15 minutes or submerge it (in the shell) in a bowl of lukewarm (not hot) water for 5 minutes.

Spiced Orange Compote

These juicy spiced oranges go beautifully with Citrus Ginger Cake (page 213) or serve them on their own. The flavor of this compote improves with time so make it a day ahead or the morning of your party. Serve chilled in a clear bowl so the colors show through.

8	small oranges, preferably seedless
2	cups water
5	tablespoons sugar
1	vanilla bean
1	cinnamon stick
2	whole cloves
1	star anise

1. Use a 5-hole zester to remove zest from oranges into long, thin, spindly strips (*see Variation*). Bring water to a boil in a small saucepan. Add the zest to the boiling water and cook for 3 minutes. Remove with a slotted spoon to a small strainer (reserve the cooking liquid). Rinse with cold water; separate and drain on a paper towel.

2. Stir sugar into the reserved cooking liquid; bring to a simmer. Cut vanilla bean in half lengthwise; scrape the seeds into the sugar water and add the pod along with cinnamon stick, cloves and star anise. Continue to simmer until the sauce reduces to ½ cup and thickens slightly, 20 to 30 minutes. Remove from the heat.

3. Meanwhile, slice off an end of each orange so they stand upright steadily. In careful sculpting slices, remove all the remaining peel and white pith from the oranges with a very sharp knife. Slice the peeled oranges into ¼-inch-thick rounds. Remove any extraneous pith or rind and any stray seeds.

4. Discard the vanilla pod and whole spices. Stir the zest into the sauce. Layer the orange slices in a serving bowl, spooning the sauce between layers to distribute the zest evenly throughout.

MAKES **10** SERVINGS, ABOUT ½ CUP EACH.

ACTIVE TIME: 50 minutes

TOTAL TIME: 50 minutes

TO MAKE AHEAD: Cover and refrigerate for up to 2 days.

PER SERVING:

61 calories; 0 g fat (0 g sat, 0 g mono); 0 mg cholesterol; 15 g carbohydrate; 1 g protein; 2 g fiber; 1 mg sodium; 140 mg potassium.

NUTRITION BONUS:

Vitamin C (70% daily value).

H✂W L↓C H♥H

VARIATION: If you don't have a 5-hole zester, use a vegetable peeler to remove long strips of the outer skin (zest) of the orange. Cut the zest into thin slivers.

Creamy Lemon Mousse

The tangy essence of fresh lemon juice and lemon zest in this light and fluffy mousse will brighten up even the darkest days of the season. Add to the inherent cheeriness of this dessert by serving it with sauce made with frozen summer blueberries, blackberries or raspberries. (See page 221 for a quick Chunky Blueberry Sauce recipe.)

⅔	cup plus ¼ cup sugar, divided	2	large eggs
3	large egg whites	1	tablespoon freshly grated
½	teaspoon cream of tartar		lemon zest
6	tablespoons water, divided	½	cup lemon juice
	Yellow food coloring (optional)	¼	cup whipping cream
1	teaspoon unflavored gelatin		Lemon slices for garnish

1. Bring about 1 inch of water to a simmer in a saucepan. Combine ⅔ cup sugar, egg whites, cream of tartar and 3 tablespoons water in a heatproof mixing bowl large enough to fit over the saucepan. Set the bowl over the barely simmering water and beat with an electric mixer at low speed, moving the beaters around the bowl constantly, until an instant-read thermometer registers 140°F, 3 to 5 minutes. Increase the mixer speed to high and continue beating over the heat a full 3½ minutes. Remove the bowl from the heat and beat the meringue until cool, about 4 minutes. Set aside.

2. Place the remaining 3 tablespoons cold water in a small bowl. If using food coloring, add about 3 drops to the water. Sprinkle gelatin over the water and let stand for 2 minutes to soften. Microwave on High, uncovered, until the gelatin has completely dissolved but the liquid is not boiling, 10 to 20 seconds. (*Alternatively, bring ½ inch water to a gentle simmer in a small skillet. Set the bowl with the gelatin mixture in the simmering water until the gelatin has dissolved completely.*) Stir the mixture until smooth.

3. Combine whole eggs, lemon zest, lemon juice and the remaining ¼ cup sugar in another heatproof bowl large enough to fit over the saucepan of simmering water. Set the bowl over the barely simmering water and whisk slowly and constantly until the mixture thickens and reaches a temperature of 160°F. Remove the bowl from the heat and whisk in the melted gelatin. Let cool for 20 minutes.

4. Beat the cream in a chilled bowl until soft peaks form.

5. Whisk about one-fourth of the beaten egg whites into the cooled lemon mixture to lighten it. Add the remaining whites and use a whisk to incorporate them with a folding motion. Fold in the whipped cream with a rubber spatula.

6. Divide the mousse among 6 dessert dishes or stemmed glasses. Cover loosely and refrigerate until set, about 3 hours. Garnish with lemon slices before serving.

MAKES **6** SERVINGS.

ACTIVE TIME: 45 minutes

TOTAL TIME: 3¾ hours
(including chilling time)

TO MAKE AHEAD: Cover and
refrigerate for up to 2 days.

PER SERVING:

187 calories, 5 g fat (2 g sat,
2 g mono); 82 mg cholesterol;
33 g carbohydrate; 5 g protein;
0 g fiber; 56 mg sodium;
128 mg potassium

NUTRITION BONUS:

Vitamin C (18% daily value)

H✂W   H♥H

Pomegranate Poached Pears

Here's a twist on the traditional pears poached in red wine. Firm Boscs are simmered in a blend of tart pomegranate juice and sweet dessert wine with gorgeous garnet-red results. The pears are served with the reduced poaching liquid and a sprinkling of pomegranate seeds and toasted almonds. A touch of tangy reduced-fat sour cream adds both flavor and visual contrast. A striking finale to any festive meal.

4	ripe, firm Bosc pears
1½	cups pomegranate juice
1	cup sweet dessert wine, such as Muscatel *or* Riesling
2	tablespoons sliced almonds
½	cup pomegranate seeds (½ large fruit; *see Guide, page 229*)
4	tablespoons reduced-fat sour cream *or* low-fat plain yogurt
4	fresh *or* dried bay leaves for garnish

1. Peel pears, leaving them whole and stems intact. Slice off the bases so the pears will stand upright. Use an apple corer to remove cores, if desired, working from the base up.

2. Place the pears on their sides in a large saucepan or small Dutch oven. Pour pomegranate juice and wine over the pears. Bring to a simmer over medium-high heat. Cover, reduce heat to low and simmer gently until the pears are tender when pierced with the tip of a sharp knife, 30 to 45 minutes. Turn very gently once or twice as they cook so they color evenly. Using a slotted spoon, transfer the pears to a shallow bowl and set aside.

3. Boil the poaching liquid over high heat until the sauce is reduced to ½ cup, 15 to 20 minutes.

4. Meanwhile, toast almonds in a small dry skillet over medium-low heat, stirring constantly, until light golden and fragrant, 2 to 3 minutes. Transfer to a small bowl to cool.

5. To serve, spoon 1 tablespoon sauce onto each of 4 dessert plates. Place a pear upright on each plate. Drizzle remaining sauce over each pear. Sprinkle pomegranate seeds around the pears and top with the almonds. Garnish each serving with a dollop of sour cream (or yogurt) and a bay leaf.

MAKES **4** SERVINGS.

ACTIVE TIME: 30 minutes

TOTAL TIME: 1¼ hours

TO MAKE AHEAD: Prepare through Step 4. Cover and refrigerate pears in sauce for up to 2 days. Serve at room temperature.

PER SERVING:

304 calories; 3 g fat (1 g sat, 2 g mono); 6 mg cholesterol; 54 g carbohydrate; 2 g protein; 6 g fiber; 17 mg sodium; 517 mg potassium

H↑F H♥H

Guide to Fruits & Vegetables

Tips for selecting, prepping and storing over 60 fruits and vegetables, plus quick, easy ways to prepare them

It's a joy to see the beautiful array of fruits and vegetables on display at farmers' markets, farmstands, co-ops or even local supermarkets. Part of the fun is trying fruits and vegetables you may not be familiar with or varieties you haven't seen before. This guide will help you get some of our favorite fruits and vegetables from the market to the table quickly and easily. We've included information to help you select the best produce, store it properly, then prepare and cook it. We've also included great simple, quick recipes. For more recipes for specific produce turn to the index on page 244.

Apples

Peak Season: Fall
Look for: Firm, smooth apples that do not appear bruised.
Store: Refrigerate apples for up to 4 months. Unrefrigerated apples tend to become mealy.

Varieties for baking: For pies and crisps, choose a combination of saucy and shapely apples.

- **Saucy apples** cook down to a saucelike consistency. Varieties to look for include Cortland, Empire, Macoun, McIntosh, Mutsu (Crispin) and Paula Red.
- **Shapely apples** hold their shape after baking. Granny Smith, Golden Delicious, Idared, Jonagold, Jonathan and Northern Spy fall into the shapely apple category.

QUICK RECIPE:

Apple Confit: Peel 3 pounds shapely apples *(see above)*, and slice ¼ inch thick. (You should have about 9 cups.) Place the apples in a 4-quart or larger slow cooker. Add ¼ cup sugar and ¼ to ½ teaspoon ground cinnamon, and toss to coat well. Cover and cook until the apples are very tender and almost translucent, but not pureed, 2 to 2½ hours on high or 4 to 4½ hours on low. Stir in 1 teaspoon vanilla extract. Transfer to a bowl and let cool slightly. Cover and refrigerate until chilled (or for up to 4 days).
Makes 8 servings, about ½ cup each.

Artichoke

Peak Season: Spring
Look for: Tight heads with no bruising.
Store: Refrigerate in a plastic bag for up to 1 week.

TO STUFF LARGE ARTICHOKES *(see recipe, page 39):*
Trim the top 1 inch of leaves (**Photo 1**). Remove the outer small, tough leaves. Snip remaining spiky tips from the outer leaves (**Photo 2**). Cut off stem to make a flat bottom (discard stem). Starting at the outer layers, pull the leaves apart to loosen. Pull open the leaves at the center until you see the spiky, lighter leaves around the heart (**Photo 3**). Pull out the lighter leaves to expose the fuzzy choke. Scoop out the choke with a melon baller or grapefruit spoon and discard (**Photo 4**). Spoon ½ cup stuffing into the center (**Photo 5**). Stuff additional stuffing between the outer leaves, toward the base, using a small spoon (**Photo 6**).

Prep 1 pound baby artichokes (*see Photos 1 & 2, page 219*) for 4 servings.

Braise: Heat 2 teaspoons extra-virgin olive oil in a large skillet; add artichokes and cook for 1 minute, stirring constantly. Add 1 cup each white wine (or dry vermouth) and water, 1/2 teaspoon salt and 1 teaspoon dried thyme (or rosemary or tarragon). Bring to a simmer; cover, reduce heat and cook until tender, about 15 minutes.

Steam: Place artichokes in a steamer basket over 1 inch of boiling water in a large pot set over high heat. Cover and steam until tender, about 15 minutes.

Asparagus

Peak Season: Spring

Look for: Sturdy spears with tight, clean heads; the cut ends should not look dried out, wrinkled or woody. Fresh asparagus should snap when bent.

Store: Trim the ends of spears and stand them upright in about an inch of water, cover with plastic and store in the refrigerator for up to 3 days. Or wrap ends with a damp paper towel and store in a plastic bag for up to 3 days.

Prep: Trim or snap off stem ends; peel more woody, mature stalk ends with a vegetable peeler, if desired.

QUICK RECIPES: Prep 1 pound asparagus for 4 servings.

Grill: Preheat grill to medium; lightly oil rack *(see photo, page 239)*. Grill asparagus until browned, turning occasionally, about 6 minutes.

Pan-steam: Place a large skillet over high heat. Add asparagus, 1/2 cup water and a slice of lemon. Cover, bring to a simmer, and cook until tender, about 5 minutes.

Roast: Preheat oven to 500°F. Spread asparagus on a baking sheet or in a pan large enough to hold it in a single layer. Coat with 2 teaspoons extra-virgin olive oil and sprinkle with 1/2 teaspoon salt. Roast, turning once halfway through cooking, until wilted and browned, about 10 minutes.

Beets

Peak Season: Spring, Summer, Fall

Look for: Firm beets. The most common are dark red, but other types, such as golden and 'Chioggia'—an heirloom variety with concentric rings of red and white flesh—are also available and have a similar sweet, earthy flavor. They are sold with or without their greens attached.

Store: Refrigerate for up to 1 month. If the greens are attached, trim and store them separately in a plastic bag.

Prep: Cut off greens and reserve *(see page 224 for recipe ideas)*, trim the ends. Peel.

QUICK RECIPES: Prep 1 pound beets for 4 servings.

Roast: Preheat oven to 500°F. Cut beets into 1 1/2-inch chunks. Spread on a baking sheet or in a pan large enough to hold them in a single layer. Coat with 2 teaspoons extra-virgin olive oil and sprinkle with 1/2 teaspoon salt. Roast, turning once halfway through cooking, until tender, about 30 minutes.

Sauté: Grate beets using the large-hole side of a box grater. Heat 1 tablespoon extra-virgin olive oil in a large skillet over medium heat. Add beets and 1 minced garlic clove and cook, stirring constantly, for 1 minute. Add 1/3 cup water and bring to a simmer. Cover, reduce heat to low and cook until tender, about 8 minutes.

Steam: Cut beets into quarters. Place in a steamer basket over 1 inch of water in a large pot set over high heat. Cover and steam until tender, about 15 minutes.

Blueberries

Peak Season: Summer

Look for: Firm, plump berries. Moisture causes berries to mold, so fruit should be dry. Reddish berries are not ripe but are fine for baking.

Store: Cover and refrigerate for up to 5 days.

Prep: Do not wash blueberries until just prior to use.

Baking: When fresh berries are not in season, frozen are a good alternative. If using frozen berries, do not thaw. Simply rinse off ice crystals, then pat dry completely on paper towels.

QUICK RECIPES:

Blueberry-Lime Yogurt: Line a large sieve with cheesecloth or coffee filters and set it over a bowl; spoon in 3 cups low-fat vanilla yogurt. Place in the refrigerator to drain for about 30 minutes. Meanwhile, combine 2 cups fresh blueberries, 1 1/2 teaspoons freshly grated lime zest, 3 tablespoons lime juice and 2 tablespoons sugar in a medium saucepan. Stir over medium heat

until the berries are just beginning to break down and release their juices, 2 to 3 minutes. Transfer to a bowl and refrigerate. Just before serving, add the drained yogurt to the cooled berries and stir to combine. Garnish with additional strips of lime zest.
Makes 4 servings.

Chunky Blueberry Sauce: Stir 2 cups fresh *or* frozen (*not* thawed) blueberries, 1/4 cup honey, 1 teaspoon freshly grated lemon zest and 2 tablespoons lemon juice in a medium saucepan. Bring to a boil; reduce heat and simmer, stirring occasionally, until thickened, about 15 minutes. Serve warm.
Makes about 1 1/3 cups.

Broccoli

Peak Season: Spring, Fall, Winter
Look for: Sturdy, dark-green spears with tight buds and a high floret-to-stem ratio; there should be no yellowing.
Store: Refrigerate in a plastic bag for up to 3 days.
Prep: Cut off florets; cut stalks in half lengthwise and then into 1-inch-thick half-moons.

QUICK RECIPES: Prep 1 pound broccoli for 4 servings.
   Microwave: Place stems and florets in a large glass baking dish. Cover tightly and microwave on High until tender, about 4 minutes.
   Roast: Preheat oven to 500°F. Spread stems and florets on a baking sheet or in a pan large enough to hold them in a single layer. Coat with 1 tablespoon extra-virgin olive oil and sprinkle with 1/2 teaspoon salt. Roast, turning once halfway through cooking, until tender and browned in places, about 10 minutes.

Brussels Sprouts

Peak Season: Fall & Winter
Look for: Tight, firm, small deep-green heads without brown or yellow leaves or insect holes.
Store: Refrigerate sprouts in a plastic bag for up to 1 week.
Prep: Peel off outer leaves; trim stem. If not cutting down further, score an X into the base with a paring knife to speed up cooking.

QUICK RECIPES: Prep 1 pound sprouts for 4 servings.
   Pan-steam: Place sprouts and 1 cup dry white wine (or dry vermouth) in a large skillet over medium-high heat. Cover and cook until tender, about 7 minutes.

Remove the sprouts with a slotted spoon; increase heat to high, add 1 teaspoon butter and reduce liquid to a glaze. Pour over the sprouts.
   Roast: Preheat oven to 500°F. Cut sprouts in half. Spread on a baking sheet or in a pan large enough to hold them in a single layer. Coat with 1 tablespoon extra-virgin olive oil and sprinkle with 1/2 teaspoon salt. Roast, turning once halfway through cooking, until browned and tender, about 20 minutes.

Carrots

Peak Season: All seasons.
Look for: Brightly colored, firm carrots without any gray or shriveled spots on the skin. The greens should preferably still be attached.
Store: Trim greens and refrigerate carrots in a plastic bag for up to 3 weeks.
Prep: Peel; cut off greens. Cut into 1/8-inch-thick rounds.

QUICK RECIPES: Prep 1 pound carrots for 4 servings.
   Microwave: Place sliced carrots in a large glass baking dish or pie pan. Add 1/4 cup broth (or dry white wine). Cover tightly and microwave on High until tender, about 3 minutes.
   Sauté: Melt 1 tablespoon butter in a large skillet over medium-low heat. Add carrots; stir and cook until tender, about 4 minutes. Add 1 teaspoon sugar; stir until glazed.

Cauliflower

Peak Season: Spring, Fall & Winter
Look for: Tight white or purple heads without black, brown or yellow spots; the green leaves at the stem should still be attached firmly to the head, not limp or withered.
Store: Refrigerate in a plastic bag for up to 5 days.
Prep: To prepare florets from a whole head of cauliflower, remove outer leaves. Slice off the thick stem. With the head upside down and holding a knife at a 45° angle, slice into the smaller stems with a circular motion—removing a "plug" from the center of the head. Break or cut florets into the desired size.

QUICK RECIPES: Prep 1 pound cauliflower for 4 servings.
Pan-steam: Place florets, ½ cup dry white wine (or dry vermouth) and ½ teaspoon caraway seeds in a large skillet. Bring to a simmer, reduce heat, cover and cook until tender, about 4 minutes.

Roast: Preheat oven to 500°F. Spread florets on a baking sheet or in a pan large enough to hold them in a single layer. Coat with 1 tablespoon extra-virgin olive oil and sprinkle with ½ teaspoon salt. Roast, turning once halfway through cooking, until tender and beginning to brown, about 15 minutes.

Celery Root (Celeriac)

Peak Season: Fall & Winter
Look for: The gnarled celery root, also known as celeriac, is a root vegetable with a subtle celery-like flavor. Select firm bulbs free of soft spots.
Store: Refrigerate for 1 to 2 weeks.
Prep: To peel a celery root, cut off one end to create a flat surface to keep it steady. Cut off the skin with your knife, following the contour of the root. Or use a vegetable peeler and peel around the root at least three times to ensure all the fibrous skin has been removed.

Cherries

Peak Season: Spring & Summer
Look for: Unblemished, shiny, large, deeply colored fruit.
Store: Refrigerate in a plastic bag for up to 3 days.
Prep: Halve sweet cherries with a paring knife, then pry out the pit with the tip of the knife or use a cherry pitter (*see Tool Smarts, page 237*). To pit sour cherries, squeeze them gently until the pit pops out.
Varieties: There are two basic types of cherries—sweet and sour.

- **Sweet cherry** varieties include Bing, Rainier and Lambert. Sweet cherries can be found in the produce section of most markets during cherry season.
- **Sour cherries**, which are too tart to eat out of hand, are most often used as pie filling. Varieties include Early Richmond, Montmorency and Morello. Find them frozen, canned and dried in most supermarkets; they are more difficult to find fresh. Find them at King Orchards, (877) 937-5464, *kingorchards.com*, and The Cherry Stop, (800) 286-7209, *cherrystop.net*.

Using frozen cherries: Be sure to measure frozen cherries while still frozen, then thaw. (Drain juice before using.)

Citrus (Grapefruit, Lemons, Limes, Oranges)

Peak Season: Winter
Look for: Choose fruits that yield only slightly to firm hand pressure.
Store: Citrus fruits can be stored at room temperature for 2 to 4 weeks or in the refrigerator for 6 to 8 weeks.
To zest: Wash and dry the fruit. Set a microplane (*see page 238*) or box grater on a piece of wax paper to catch the zest; rub the fruit over the small holes with quick strokes. Avoid using too much pressure when grating because the white pith below the zest is bitter. Use a pastry brush to sweep off any zest left clinging to the grater.
To julienne citrus zest: Use a vegetable peeler to easily remove strips of the outer skin (zest), leaving the bitter white pith behind. Stack the pieces on top of each other and slice into ⅛-inch-wide strips.

To juice: Citrus fruits at room temperature give the most juice. Before juicing, roll the fruit on the counter, pressing down with your hand. If the recipe calls for both zest and juice, grate the zest before squeezing the juice.

To segment (or suprême):

1. Slice both ends off the fruit.
2. With a sharp knife, remove the peel and white pith; discard.
3. Cut the segments from the surrounding membranes.

Grapefruit Brûlée: Position oven rack about 5 inches from broiler; preheat broiler. Cut the rind and pith off 3 large pink or ruby-red grapefruits with a sharp knife, making sure to remove all the white pith. **(See Photos 1 & 2, page 222.)** Cut each fruit into 4 rounds, about 1/2 inch thick. Place the slices in a large baking pan in a single layer. Top each slice with 1 1/2 teaspoons brown sugar, dot with 1/2 teaspoon butter and sprinkle with a pinch of cinnamon and nutmeg. Broil the grapefruit until bubbling and starting to brown, 6 to 8 minutes. Drizzle pan juices over each serving.
Makes 6 servings, 2 slices each.

Corn

Peak Season: Summer
Look for: Pale to dark green husks with moist silks. The cob should fill the husk, and the cut at the stem should look fresh.
Store: Refrigerate, with the husks left on, in a plastic bag, for up to 2 days.
Prep: Husk corn.
To remove corn from the cob: Stand an uncooked ear of corn on its stem end in a shallow bowl and slice the kernels

off with a sharp, thin-bladed knife. This technique produces whole kernels that are good for adding to salads and salsas. If you want to use the corn kernels for soups, fritters or puddings, you can add another step to the process. After cutting the kernels off, reverse the knife and, using the dull side, press it down the length of the ear to push out the rest of the corn and its milk.

QUICK RECIPES: Start with 1 pound husked corn for 4 servings.
Grill: Preheat grill to medium-high. Grill corn, turning occasionally, until marked and tender, 8 to 12 minutes.
Sauté: Cut kernels from cobs *(see above)*. Melt 2 teaspoons butter in a large skillet over medium heat. Add corn kernels; cook, stirring constantly, until tender, about 3 minutes. Stir in 1/2 teaspoon white-wine vinegar before serving.

Cranberries

Peak Season: Fall
Look for: Shiny, unblemished fruit.
Store: Fresh cranberries store well. Leave in their original packaging and refrigerate for up to 2 weeks or freeze for up to 6 months.
To chop cranberries: Place whole berries in a food processor and pulse a few times until coarsely chopped.

Eggplant

Peak Season: Summer & Fall
Look for: Smooth, glossy skins without wrinkles or spongy spots.
Store: Refrigerate for up to 1 week.
Prep: Slice into 1/2-inch-thick rounds (peeling is optional).

QUICK RECIPES: Prep 1 pound eggplant.
Grill: Preheat grill to medium-high. Brush both sides of eggplant slices lightly with 2 teaspoons extra-virgin olive oil and sprinkle with 1/2 teaspoon salt. Grill, turning once, until browned, about 8 minutes.
Roast: Preheat oven to 500°F. Brush both sides of eggplant slices with 2 teaspoons extra-virgin olive oil and arrange on a baking sheet or in a pan large enough to hold them in a single layer. Sprinkle with 1/2 teaspoon salt. Roast, turning once halfway through cooking, until tender, about 15 minutes.

Fennel

Peak Season: Spring, Fall, Winter
Look for: Small, white, unbruised bulbs with bright green stalks and feathery fronds.
Store: Refrigerate in a plastic bag for 3 to 5 days.
Prep: Cut off the stalks and fronds where they meet the bulb, remove any damaged outer layers, cut 1/4 inch off the bottom and remove the core. The edible fronds are a delicious garnish for any fennel dish containing the bulb.

QUICK RECIPES: Prep 1 pound fennel for 4 servings.
Braise: Cut bulb into 1-inch pieces. Heat 1 tablespoon extra-virgin olive oil in a large skillet over medium heat. Add fennel, 1/2 teaspoon salt and 2 teaspoons dried rosemary, crushed. Cook 1 minute, stirring constantly. Add 1/2 cup dry white wine (or dry vermouth). Cover, reduce heat and cook until tender, about 15 minutes.
Roast: Preheat oven to 500°F. Cut bulb into 1/4-inch slices. Spread on a baking sheet or in a pan large

enough to hold them in a single layer. Coat with 2 teaspoons extra-virgin olive oil and sprinkle with ½ teaspoon salt. Roast, turning once halfway through cooking, until tender and beginning to brown, 18 to 20 minutes.

Green Beans

Peak Season: Summer
Look for: Small, thin, firm beans.
Store: Refrigerate in a plastic bag for 3 to 5 days.
Prep: Trim stem ends.

QUICK RECIPES: Prep 1 pound green beans for 4 servings.
Microwave: Place beans in a large glass baking dish or pie pan. Add ¼ cup broth (or water). Cover tightly and microwave on High until tender, about 4 minutes.
Sauté: Heat 2 teaspoons walnut oil (or canola oil) in a large skillet over medium-high heat. Add beans; cook, stirring often, until seared, about 2 minutes. Add ½ cup water, cover, reduce heat to medium and cook until tender, 3 to 6 minutes.

Greens, Dark Leafy

Peak Season: Spring, Fall & Winter
Look for: Crisp, brightly colored greens; avoid those that are wilted or blemished. Bunches of smaller-sized leaves are often sweeter.
Store: Store unwashed; wrap stem ends in damp paper towels and refrigerate in a plastic bag for up to 10 days.
Prep: Wash well and coarsely chop. Though all of the stems are edible, we prefer to use only chard and beet stems, discarding the tough stems of collards, kale and mustard greens. If you do choose to use the stems, keep them separate when prepping and cook them for 3 to 5 minutes longer than the leaves. One pound of greens cooks down to 1-2 cups.

Varieties:

- Find **beet greens** still attached to the beets or separate in bunches. Common varieties include red, gold and 'Chioggia.' The greens have a rich, earthy flavor, similar to beets.
- Look for **chard's** shiny ribbed leaves and the multicolored stems of the rainbow variety, the red-speckled leaves of red (or ruby) chard, or white chard's white stems and veins. White chard has the most mild taste, similar to spinach, and red chard has a stronger, earthier flavor, like that of beets.
- You can spot **collard greens** by their flat, broad leaves. While many other greens wilt down when cooked, collards keep most of their volume. Perhaps the most neutral in taste, they benefit from other big flavors in a dish.
- Popular varieties of **kale** include red Russian, lacinato (or dinosaur) and curly kale, the most bitter variety, which can range from green to deep purple. Kale's sharp, peppery flavor is best balanced by a touch of acidity or sweetness.
- Pungent, peppery **mustard greens** are identified by their frilly edges. Their flavor is bold so you may want to combine them with more mild dark leafy greens, like chard, to balance their strong flavor.
- For **spinach**, see page 230.

QUICK RECIPE: Prep 1 pound greens for 4 servings.
Sauté: Heat 1 tablespoon extra-virgin olive oil in a Dutch oven over medium heat. Add greens and cook, tossing with two large spoons, until bright green. Add ½ cup water, reduce heat to medium-low, cover and cook, stirring occasionally, until the greens are tender, 12 to 15 minutes. Push greens to one side, add 1 teaspoon oil to the empty side and cook 2 cloves minced garlic and ¼ teaspoon crushed red pepper in it until fragrant. Remove from the heat. Stir in 2-3 teaspoons sherry vinegar (or red-wine vinegar) and ¼ teaspoon salt.
Makes 4 servings.

Greens, Salad

Peak Season: Spring, Summer & Fall

Look for: Salad greens should look fresh, crisp and green. Avoid greens that are brown, yellow, wilted, blemished, bruised or slimy. If stems are still attached they should be undamaged.

Store: Moisture encourages decay, so don't wash greens until ready to use. If greens are damp when you buy them, dry on kitchen towels, wrap in dry towels and refrigerate in a plastic bag. Most greens keep in the refrigerator crisper for 3 to 5 days.

Prep: Gently swirl greens in a large bowl of water to loosen any sand or dirt; lift greens from the water to a colander or salad spinner; repeat up to 2 more times for particularly gritty greens. A salad spinner (*see Tool Smarts, page 238*) is a worthwhile investment, as dressings adhere best to dry greens.

Varieties: Common salad greens to look for include:

- Also called "rocket," **arugula** is an aromatic green that lends a peppery mustard flavor to salads. Find it in bags or bunches near other salad greens in the supermarket. Watercress is a good substitute.
- **Belgian endive** has compact, slender, elongated heads with cream-colored leaves that have yellow or pink tips.
- **Butterhead** lettuces (**Boston** and **Bibb**) are soft, buttery-textured lettuces with mild flavor. Lettuce heads are medium-large and the leaves are very tender, with dark green outer leaves.
- A type of chicory (whose botanical name, *cichorium intybus*, means "January plant"), **escarole** has tender, broad, pale green leaves that can be eaten raw in salads or lightly cooked in soups, pasta or as a side dish.
- **Mâche** ("mosh"), also known as lamb's lettuce or corn salad, is a tangy green that resembles watercress. Popular in Europe, it is enjoyed in the first salads of spring. Look for it in specialty stores, large supermarkets and farmers' markets.
- Heads of **radicchio** are comprised of thick purple-red leaves streaked with white veins. Its firm texture stands up well to dressing. Try it along with other salad greens to add color and to balance its bitter flavor or throw it on the grill for something different.
- The lettuce of choice for Caesar salad, **romaine** grows in tall, cylindrical heads of narrow, crisp leaves.
- For **spinach**, see page 230.
- A member of the mustard family, **watercress** has a peppery flavor and is used in salads and sautés. For the best flavor, look for supple, thin stems (not woody stalks) with small, heart-shaped, dark green leaves that have no yellow blemishes.

Leeks

Peak Season: Spring, Fall & Winter

Look for: Long, thin stalks that do not bend and are not bruised; the outer layers should not be wrinkly or dried out.

Store: Leeks can be refrigerated in a plastic bag for up to 1 week.

Prep: Trim off the thick green leaves, leaving only the pale green and white parts; pull off damaged outer layers and trim off the root end. Cut leek in half lengthwise. Submerge in cold water and shake, fanning out the inner layers to rinse out grit and sand.

QUICK RECIPES: Prep 1 pound leeks for 4 servings.

Roast: Preheat oven to 500°F. Slice the leeks in half crosswise and then into ¼-inch-thick slices lengthwise. Spread on a baking sheet or in a pan large enough to hold them in a single layer. Coat with 2 teaspoons extra-virgin olive oil and sprinkle with ½ teaspoon salt. Roast, stirring once halfway through cooking, until browned and tender, 10 to 15 minutes.

Sauté: Thinly slice leeks into half-moons. Heat 1 tablespoon butter in a large skillet over medium heat. Add leeks; cook, stirring often, until softened and very aromatic, about 5 minutes.

Mango

Peak Season: Spring & Summer

Look for: Fruit without dark spots or blemishes. Ripe when very fragrant and yields to gentle pressure.

Store: Store ripe mangoes in the refrigerator for up to 5 days.

To peel and dice a mango:

1. Slice both ends off the mango, revealing the long, slender seed inside.
2. Set the fruit upright on a work surface and remove the skin with a sharp knife.

3. With the seed perpendicular to you, slice the fruit from both sides of the seed, yielding two large pieces.

4. Turn the seed parallel to you and slice the two smaller pieces of fruit from each side. Cut the fruit into the desired shape.

Melons

Peak Season: Summer

Look for: Melons that yield when pressed on the end opposite the stem: if it yields, it's ripe. Leave hard ones behind; most melons won't ripen more after they're picked. **Honeydew** is one of the few melons that continues to ripen after it's harvested, so firm with a bit of softness at the stem is fine. Look for symmetrical unblemished **watermelons**, without flat sides, that have a creamy yellow spot on the bottom indicating ripeness. At 92% water, this fruit should feel heavy when you heft it. Precut melon flesh should be dense, firm and appear moist.

Store: Refrigerate whole ripe melons for up to 3 days, watermelon for up to 1 week. Cut melon should be refrigerated immediately either in an airtight container or covered with plastic wrap to prevent it from becoming mushy.

Prep: Using a sharp knife slice through center of melon, remove seeds (not necessary for watermelon) and cut into desired shape.

QUICK RECIPES:

Melon Balls in Port: Stir 1/3 cup tawny port, 1 tablespoon honey, 1/2 teaspoon freshly grated lime zest, 1 tablespoon lime juice and 5 crushed mint leaves in a bowl until the honey is dissolved. Add 1 1/2 cups each cantaloupe and honeydew melon balls and stir gently to coat them. Cover with plastic wrap and chill in the refrig-

erator for 30 minutes, stirring every 10 minutes or so. Serve garnished with fresh mint leaves.
Makes 4 servings.

Watermelon Salsa: Place 3 cups finely diced seedless watermelon, 2 seeded and minced jalapeño peppers, 1/3 cup chopped fresh cilantro, 1/4 cup minced red onion and 1/4 cup lime juice in a medium bowl; stir well to combine. Season with 1/4 teaspoon salt. Serve at room temperature or chilled.
Makes 8 servings, 1/2 cup each.

Mushrooms

Peak Season: All seasons (depending on region and mushroom variety).

Look for: Firm mushrooms with a fresh, smooth appearance. They should appear dry, but not dried out.

Store: Refrigerate in their original container up to 1 week. Once opened, store in a paper bag. Do not store fresh mushrooms in airtight containers, which will cause condensation and speed up spoilage.

Prep: Wipe off any dirt with a damp paper towel.

Onions

Peak Season: Spring, Summer & Fall

Look for: Firm, heavy onions without cuts, bruises or sprouting. Scallions should have a firm white base and bright, fresh-looking greens.

Store: Keep in a cool, dry, dark, well-ventilated place away from potatoes, which give off moisture and gas that can cause onions to spoil quickly. Refrigerate scallions and chives for up to 5 days.

To crisp raw onion: Soak sliced onion in ice water for 10 minutes or more to render it less pungent and more crisp.

To chop without tears: Onions contain a volatile compound called lachrymator that reacts with the fluid in your eyes and makes them water. Try wearing goggles (*see Tool Smarts, page 238*), burning a candle nearby or cutting them under cold water.

To peel pearl onions: Cook in boiling water for 1 minute. Drain. Peel when cool enough to handle.

Parsnips

Peak Season: Fall & Winter
Look for: Sturdy, firm parsnips, free of soft spots.
Store: Refrigerate in a plastic bag for up to 3 weeks.
Prep: Peel and remove the fibrous, woody core.

QUICK RECIPE: Prep 1 pound parsnips for 4 servings.

Roast: Preheat oven to 500°F. Cut parsnips in half lengthwise then cut into 1½-inch-long pieces. Spread on a baking sheet or in a pan large enough to hold them in a single layer. Coat with 2 teaspoons extra-virgin olive oil and sprinkle with ½ teaspoon salt. Roast, turning once halfway through cooking, until tender and beginning to brown, about 15 minutes.

Peaches

Peak Season: Summer
Look for: A "peachy" scent, slightly sweet and flowery. Ripe peaches will give a little when gently pressed. The red or blush color on the skin is a characteristic of variety, not ripeness. To ripen, set them in a single layer on the counter, not stacked, for a day or so at room temperature.

Store: Refrigerate ripe peaches for up to 1 week.

To peel peaches: Dip peaches in boiling water for about 1 minute to loosen their skins. Let cool slightly, then remove the skins with a paring knife.

Baking with peaches: Ripe peaches that are still firm bake up perfectly tender while continuing to hold their shape.

QUICK RECIPES:

Roasted Peach Sundaes: Preheat oven to 425°F. Coat a baking sheet with cooking spray. Halve and pit 3 ripe peaches. Toss peach halves with 1 tablespoon brown sugar and 2 teaspoons lemon juice; place cut-side up on the prepared baking sheet. Roast until tender, 20 to 30 minutes. If the juice on the pan begins to burn, add a little water and loosely cover the fruit with foil. Top each peach half with a ½-cup scoop of nonfat vanilla frozen yogurt and a sprinkle of crumbled gingersnaps, if desired.
Makes 6 servings.

Peach-Bourbon Frozen Yogurt: Peel, pit and dice 2 peaches. Combine with 3 tablespoons bourbon and 1 tablespoon brown sugar in a mixing bowl. Let stand for 10 minutes. Add 1 pint softened nonfat vanilla frozen yogurt to the bowl. Use a potato masher to mix in the fruit mixture. Cover and freeze for 15 minutes, or until ready to serve. Top each serving with 1 tablespoon chopped toasted pecans, if desired.
Makes 4 servings, ½ cup each.

Pears

Peak Season: Fall & Winter
Look for: Unblemished fruit with taut skin. Pears are ripe when they are soft near the stem.
Store: Let pears sit at room temperature, near other ripening fruit or in a brown bag with a ripe banana (which stimulates ripening). Refrigerate ripe pears for up to 3 days.
Varieties:
- **Anjous** have a spicy taste and smooth, white flesh. Enjoy fresh.
- The spicy taste and smooth flesh of a **Red Anjou** is great fresh or baked.
- **Bartletts** have smooth, juicy flesh, excellent for canning, poaching or eating plain. Skin turns bright yellow when ripe.
- A **Red Bartlett** is similar to the regular Bartlett, but it turns bright red when ripe. Adds color to salads, also great cooked.
- Distinguished by a long, tapered neck, slim stem and golden brown skin, **Bosc** pears have dense, aromatic flesh with a buttery texture. Great for poaching, roasting, broiling and grilling.

Peas

Peak Season: Spring & Summer
Look for: Firm, vibrant green pods without blotches and with the stem end still attached.
Varieties:
- **English peas** need to be popped from their pods before cooking.
- Flat-podded **snow peas** are common in Asian cooking and equally delicious raw or cooked. Both the peas and pods are tender and edible.

- **Sugar snap peas** have a woody stem on one end of the pod that needs to be trimmed before eating and fibrous strings along the sides.

Store: Refrigerate in a plastic bag for 2 to 3 days

Prep: To shell English peas, open the hull, using the stem end as a tab, and run your finger along the inside to remove the peas. To remove the stem and strings at the same time from sugar snap peas (*below*), hold the stem between your thumb and index finger, snap and pull down.

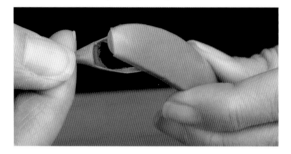

QUICK RECIPES: Prep 1 pound of peas for 4 servings.

Sauté: Heat 2 teaspoons butter in a large skillet over medium heat. Add peas; cook, stirring often, until bright green, about 3 minutes.

Steam: Place snow or sugar snap peas in a steamer basket over 1 inch of boiling water in a large pot set over high heat. Cover and steam until tender, 3 to 5 minutes.

Peppers, Hot & Sweet

Peak Season: Summer & Fall

Look for: Brightly colored, shiny skin free of blemishes and soft spots.

Store: Refrigerate in a plastic bag for up to 1 week.

Hot tip: The compound that makes chiles hot, capsaicin, is found in the inner membrane and, by association, in the seeds. Smaller varieties are generally hotter. To increase the heat in a recipe, use some or all of the seeds along with the flesh of the pepper. (Taste as you go along.) Fresh and dried chiles vary widely in spiciness depending on variety and time of the year. You may want to wear gloves to protect your hands when you're working with hot peppers.

Three methods for roasting peppers:

Oven-roasting (Photo 1): Preheat oven to 450°F. Roast peppers on a baking sheet in the center of the oven, turning occasionally with tongs, until the peppers are soft, wrinkled and blackened in spots, 20 to 30 minutes.

Gas burner-roasting (Photo 2): Turn a gas burner to high. Using long-handled tongs, hold pepper directly in the flame, turning often, until the skin is blistered on all sides and blackened in spots, 10 to 15 minutes. (Use caution and be sure to have proper ventilation. This method doesn't work on an electric stove.)

Grill-roasting (Photo 3): Preheat grill to high or prepare a hot charcoal fire. Grill peppers, turning frequently, until the skin is blistered on all sides and blackened in spots, about 10 minutes.

Peeling & storing roasted peppers:

Loosen the skins (Photo 4): Transfer the peppers to a large bowl and cover with plastic wrap. Let steam for 10 minutes. Uncover and let cool.

Remove the skins (Photo 5): Working over a bowl, peel off the skin with your hands or a paring knife. Remove the stems and seeds. If you're working with hot peppers, you may want to wear gloves to protect your skin from burning.

Storage (Photo 6): Store peppers, whole or sliced, in airtight containers in the refrigerator for up to 2 weeks or in the freezer for up to 6 months. Separating peppers with layers of wax paper or parchment paper before freezing makes it easier to remove one at a time from the freezer. Previously frozen roasted peppers will be softer in texture than peppers that have been stored in the refrigerator.

Pineapple

Peak Season: Spring & Winter

Look for: Bright yellow-gold color on the skin and eyes around the base of the fruit. It should have a pleasant, mild pineapple scent at the base with a firm and gently yielding surface.

Store: Refrigerate the whole pineapple for 2 to 4 days. Refrigerate cut pineapple in an airtight container for 2 to 3 days.

To cut a pineapple:

1. Cut off the top and bottom of the pineapple with a sharp knife, making a stable flat base.
2. Stand the pineapple upright and cut off the skin.
3. Use a paring knife to remove any remaining eyes.
4. Slice the fruit away from the core. Discard core.

QUICK RECIPE:

Roasted Pineapple: Preheat broiler. Trim leaves and bud end from a 2½- to 3-pound pineapple. Cut into ½-inch-thick slices with a sharp, serrated knife. Set slices in a single layer on a baking sheet. Sprinkle with 2 tablespoons brown sugar. (Cover the pineapple slices only; any sugar on the sheet may burn.) Broil, rearranging slices as needed for even cooking, for 10 to 15 minutes. Turn the slices over and continue broiling on the other side until the pineapple is tender and golden brown, 5 to 10 minutes. **Makes 6 servings.**

Pomegranate

Peak Season: Fall & Winter

Look for: Soft, leathery skin that gives lightly when pressed. Some markings do not affect the flavor, but avoid fruit with shriveled skin.

Store: Refrigerate whole fruit for up to 3 months. Freeze seeds in an airtight container or sealable bag for up to 3 months.

To remove seeds: To avoid the stains of pomegranate juice, fill a large bowl with water. Hold the pomegranate in the water and slice off the crown. Lightly score the fruit into quarters, from crown to stem end. Keeping the fruit under water, break it apart, gently separating the plump seeds from the outer skin and white pith. The seeds will drop to the bottom of the bowl and the pith will float to the surface. Discard the pith. Pour the seeds into a colander. Rinse and pat dry.

Potatoes

For sweet potatoes, see page 231.

Peak Season: All seasons.

Look for: Small potatoes with firm skins that are not loose, papery or bruised.

Store: Keep in a cool, dark place with good air circulation, to discourage softening, sprouting and spoiling. Properly stored, potatoes will keep 10 to 12 weeks.

Prep: Scrub off any dirt (peeling is optional; the skin is fiber-rich and the nutrients are clustered in the ½ inch below the skin).

QUICK RECIPES: Prep 1 pound potatoes for 4 servings.

Roast: Preheat oven to 500°F. Halve potatoes then cut into ½-inch wedges. Spread on a baking sheet or in a pan large enough to hold them in a single layer. Coat with 2 teaspoons extra-virgin olive oil and sprinkle with ½ teaspoon salt. Roast, stirring once halfway through cooking, until crispy and browned on the outside and tender on the inside, 20 to 25 minutes.

Sauté: Shred potatoes using the large-hole side of a box grater. Heat 1 tablespoon canola oil in a large skillet over medium heat. Add potatoes; reduce heat. Cook for 6 minutes. Flip the cake over and continue cooking until browned, about 5 minutes more.

Raspberries

Peak Season: Summer

Look for: Juicy-looking, brightly colored fruit. If the hulls are still attached, don't buy them—they were picked too early and will be sour. As with all berries, check for signs of mold or spoilage.

Store: Refrigerate for up to 2 days.

Prep: Gently spray with a fine mist just before using—the weight of water pouring from a faucet may crush them.

Raspberry-Chocolate Chip Frozen Yogurt: Place 3 cups fresh *or* frozen *(not* thawed) raspberries, 2 cups low-fat plain yogurt, 1/3 cup sugar and 1 1/2 teaspoons vanilla extract in a food processor and process until smooth. Transfer the mixture to an ice cream maker. *(If you don't have an ice cream maker, see Step 2 on page 123.)* Freeze according to manufacturer's directions, or until desired consistency. Add 1/2 cup mini chocolate chips during the last 5 minutes of freezing. Transfer to an airtight container and freeze until ready to serve. **Makes 8 servings, 1/2 cup each (1 quart).**

Rutabaga

Peak Season: Fall & Winter
Look for: Firm, unblemished bulbs. They're often thinly coated with wax to prolong storage. They have an earthy, buttery flavor.
Store: Keep in a cool, dark place for up to 2 weeks or refrigerate for up to 1 month.
Prep: To peel a rutabaga, cut off one end to create a flat surface to keep it steady. Cut off the skin with your knife, following the contour of the bulb. Or use a vegetable peeler and peel around the bulb at least three times to ensure all the fibrous skin has been removed.

Spinach

Peak Season: Spring, Fall & Winter
Look for: Supple, deeply colored leaves without mushy spots.
Store: If spinach is damp, dry on kitchen towels, wrap in dry towels and refrigerate in a plastic bag for 3 to 5 days.
Prep: Trim stems. Wash leaves in several changes of water. Cut into 1-inch pieces.

QUICK RECIPE: Prep 1 pound spinach for 4 servings.

Braise: Heat 2 teaspoons walnut oil (or canola oil) in a large skillet over medium heat. Add spinach and toss until wilted. Add 1/2 cup dry white wine (or dry vermouth). Cover, reduce heat and cook until tender, about 5 minutes. Uncover and cook until liquid is reduced to a glaze. Stir in 2 teaspoons balsamic vinegar (or rice vinegar).

Squash, Summer & Zucchini

Peak Season: Summer
Look for: No breaks, gashes or soft spots; smaller squash (under 8 inches) are sweeter and have fewer seeds; do not peel, but scrub gently under running water.
Store: Refrigerate in a plastic bag for 4 to 5 days.
Prep: Cut off stem ends.

QUICK RECIPES: Prep 1 pound squash for 4 servings.

Grill: Cut squash lengthwise into 1/2-inch slices. Preheat grill to medium; brush slices lightly with 1 tablespoon extra-virgin olive oil and sprinkle with 1/2 teaspoon salt. Grill, turning once, until marked and lightly browned, 3 to 4 minutes.

Sauté: Cut squash into 1/4-inch-thick rounds. Heat 1 tablespoon extra-virgin olive oil in a large skillet over medium heat. Add 1 minced garlic clove and squash; cook, stirring frequently, until tender, about 7 minutes.

Squash, Winter

Peak Season: Fall & Winter
Look for: Hard squash that does not look shiny and has a remnant of the dried-out stem still attached. Look for vivid colors during harvest season. Later in the year, after the squash has been stored, the skin color may fade as the flesh becomes sweeter.
Store: Store in a cool spot with good air circulation for up to 1 month.
To cut a squash: Winter squash can be difficult to peel and cut. Soften the skin slightly by piercing the squash in several places with a fork; microwave on High for 45 to 60 seconds, heating it just long enough to slightly steam the skin without actually cooking the flesh. But no need to remove the skin if you're planning to bake it and scoop out the flesh when it's done. Once opened, clean out the seeds and stringy fibers with a spoon.
Varieties:

- **Acorn squash** are a moderately sized variety almost always available in supermarket bins even in the summer. The flesh can be watery; prolonged cooking concentrates the flavor.
- An old-fashioned squash, **buttercup** has a characteristic little cap at the stem; full of natural sugars and fiber, a delectable treat in midwinter.
- Perhaps the most versatile winter

squash, **butternut** is sweet and light when cooked but also substantial—thus able to stand up to both long cooking and quick sautés.

- **Delicata** are small, firm squash with bright yellow or orange skin that has green veins branching like lightning through it. Taste is similar to sweet potatoes.
- **Hubbard squash** are available in blue or gold varieties with somewhat warty skins. Ranges in size from 5 to 40 pounds; perfect cubed and roasted or for purees.
- Actually a name for a set of squash varietals from Japan, **kabocha** has consistently deep, honey-scented flavors.
- Look for smaller-size **pie pumpkins**, which have more tender and flavorful flesh than the larger ones. And for food-safety concerns, don't use carved jack-o'-lanterns.
- Now sometimes called "red curry," **red kuri** is a relative of the kabocha with many seeds, less meat and with a deep, pear-scented flavor.
- **Spaghetti squash** are oblong and mild in flavor. When cooked its flesh yields myriad threads, sort of like little spaghetti strands, best removed with a fork.

QUICK RECIPES: Start with a 2-3 pound squash for 4 servings.

Microwave: Pierce spaghetti squash all over with a sharp small knife. Microwave on High for 8 minutes, then turn over and Microwave on High until squash gives when pressed gently, 8 to 10 minutes more. Cool for 5 minutes. Cut in half, scoop out and discard seeds then shred the flesh with a fork into a bowl.

Roast: Preheat oven to 400°F. Brush a rimmed baking sheet with oil. Cut acorn squash, buttercup, butternut, hubbard, kabocha or red kuri in half and scrape out seeds and membranes. Place the squash, cut-side down, on the prepared baking sheet. Bake until soft, 35 to 45 minutes for acorn squash or buttercup, 40 to 50

minutes for the other varieties.

Puree: Roast squash (*see above*) and let cool slightly. Scoop the squash flesh into a food processor. Pulse until smooth. For a chunkier texture, mash squash with a potato masher.

Sauté: Cut delicata squash in half lengthwise, scoop out the seeds and slice into thin half-moons (peeling is optional). Melt 4 teaspoons butter in a large skillet over medium heat. Add squash slices; cook, stirring frequently, until tender, 10 to 15 minutes. Stir in a pinch of grated nutmeg before serving.

Strawberries

Peak Season: Spring & Summer

Look for: Look for plump, bright red and fully ripe berries (strawberries do not ripen after they have been harvested) with no mold or bruises. Caps should be attached, green and look fresh.

Store: Refrigerate for up to 4 days. Mold on berries spreads quickly so immediately discard any that show signs of mold.

QUICK RECIPES:

Strawberry-Orange Pops: Hull 1 pint strawberries and place in a food processor or blender. Add 2 tablespoons frozen orange juice concentrate and 2-4 tablespoons sugar (depending on the sweetness of the berries) and puree until smooth. Pour into popsicle forms, add sticks and freeze until firm. **Makes 6 pops.**

Strawberry Fool: Chill a small bowl and the beaters of an electric mixer. Whip ¼ cup whipping cream with the chilled beaters in the chilled bowl until soft peaks form. Add 2 teaspoons confectioners' sugar and ⅛ teaspoon vanilla extract and continue beating until the peaks are firm but not stiff. (Do not overbeat.) Fold in 1 quart finely chopped strawberries. **Makes 8 servings, about ½ cup each.**

Sweet Potatoes

Peak Season: Fall & Winter

Look for: Taut, smooth and papery skins with tapered ends and no bruises or soft spots.

Store: Sweet potatoes will keep for 6 to 10 months in a cool, dark place.
Prep: Scrub with a brush.

QUICK RECIPES: Prep 1 pound sweet potatoes for 4 servings.

Pan-steam: Cut sweet potatoes into 1-inch dice. Place in a large skillet with 1 cup broth, 1 teaspoon honey and 1/2 teaspoon dried thyme. Bring to a simmer over high heat; reduce heat, cover and cook until almost tender, about 15 minutes. Uncover, increase heat and cook until the liquid is reduced to a glaze, about 2 minutes more.

Roast: Preheat oven to 500°F. Halve sweet potatoes, then cut into 1/2-inch wedges. Spread on a baking sheet or in a pan large enough to hold them in a single layer. Coat with 2 teaspoons extra-virgin olive oil and sprinkle with 1/2 teaspoon salt. Roast, turning once halfway through cooking, until browned and tender, 20 to 25 minutes.

Tomatillos

Peak Season: Summer
Look for: Tart, plum-size green fruit that look like small, husk-covered green tomatoes. Husks should be brightly colored, not brown, and the tomatillo should be fully encased in the husk.
Store: Refrigerate in their husks in a plastic bag for up to 2 weeks.
Prep: Remove outer husks and rinse well before using.

Tomatoes

Peak Season: Summer & Fall
Look for: Plump, shiny tomatoes that give slightly when pressed. Smell the stem end for that distinctive aroma.
Store: Tomatoes continue to ripen after they are picked. Refrigeration destroys their flavor; store at room temperature, away from sunlight.
See page 233 to learn how to peel and seed tomatoes and make Fresh Tomato Sauce.

Turnips

Peak Season: Fall & Winter
Look for: Smaller turnips with firm skins that are not bruised, soft or shriveled.
Store: Trim greens and refrigerate for up to 1 week.
Prep: Cut off greens and trim

the ends. To peel a turnip, cut off one end to create a flat surface to keep it steady. Cut off the skin with your knife, following the contour of the root. Or use a vegetable peeler and peel around the root at least three times to ensure all the fibrous skin has been removed. Then thinly slice.

QUICK RECIPES: Prep 1 pound turnips for 4 servings.

Grill: Steam turnip slices (*see below*) for 5 minutes; meanwhile, preheat grill to medium-high. Grill steamed turnip slices, turning once, until lightly browned and tender, about 8 minutes.

Sauté: Cut turnip slices into matchsticks. Heat 1 teaspoon each butter and extra-virgin olive oil in a large skillet over medium heat; add turnips and cook, stirring frequently, until tender, about 12 minutes.

Steam: Place in a steamer basket over 1 inch of boiling water in a large pot set over high heat. Cover and cook until tender when pierced with a fork, about 12 minutes.

Fresh Tomato Sauce

ACTIVE TIME: 1 hour | **TOTAL TIME:** 1½ hours | **TO MAKE AHEAD:** Cover and refrigerate for up to 5 days or freeze for up to 6 months.

A basic tomato sauce can be at the heart of so many great meals: pizza, pasta dishes, sautéed vegetables and soups, just to name a few. Take advantage of the summer harvest to stock your freezer with this sauce and you'll be one step closer to a garden-fresh meal.

4½	pounds plum tomatoes		¼	cup tomato paste
¼	cup extra-virgin olive oil		1	teaspoon dried oregano
¾	cup chopped garlic (about 2 heads)		½	cup red wine
4	cups diced onions (3-4 medium)		2	tablespoons red-wine vinegar
1½	teaspoons salt		½	cup chopped fresh basil
				Freshly ground pepper to taste

1. Bring a large pot of water to a boil. Place a large bowl of ice water next to the stove. Using a sharp paring knife, core the tomatoes and score a small X into the flesh on the bottom. **(Photo 1)**

2. Place the tomatoes in the boiling water, in batches, until the skins are slightly loosened, 30 seconds to 2 minutes. **(Photo 2)**

3. Using a slotted spoon, transfer the tomatoes to the ice water and let sit in the water for 1 minute before removing. **(Photo 3)**

4. Place a sieve over a bowl; working over it, peel the tomatoes using a paring knife, and let the skins fall into the sieve. **(Photo 4)**

5. Halve the tomatoes crosswise and scoop out the seeds with a hooked finger, letting the sieve catch the seeds. **(Photo 5)** Press on the seeds and skins to extract any extra juice. Coarsely chop the peeled tomatoes and set aside.

6. Heat oil in a Dutch oven over medium heat. Add garlic and cook, stirring constantly, until fragrant and just beginning to color, 2 to 3 minutes. Add onions and salt, stir to coat, cover and cook, stirring often and adjusting heat as necessary to prevent burning, until soft and turning golden, 10 to 15 minutes. Stir in tomato paste and oregano and cook, stirring often, until the tomato paste is beginning to brown on the bottom of the pan, 2 to 4 minutes.

7. Pour in wine and vinegar; bring to a simmer, scraping up any browned bits with a spoon. Cook until reduced slightly, about 2 minutes. Add the tomatoes and any juice; return to a simmer, stirring often. Reduce heat to maintain a gentle simmer and cook, stirring occasionally, until the tomatoes are mostly broken down, about 25 minutes.

8. Remove from the heat; stir in basil and pepper. Transfer the sauce, in batches, to a blender or food processor. (Use caution when pureeing hot liquids.) Process until desired consistency. For a smooth sauce, puree it all; for a chunky sauce, puree just half and mix it back into the rest of the sauce.

MAKES 2 QUARTS (8 CUPS).

PER ½-CUP SERVING: 89 calories; 4 g fat (1 g sat, 3 g mono); 0 mg cholesterol; 12 g carbohydrate; 2 g protein; 2 g fiber; 223 mg sodium; 417 mg potassium

Guide to Freezing Fresh Produce

Freezing produce is one of the easiest ways to preserve the abundance.
Follow our easy guide to enjoy your harvest throughout the year.

VEGETABLE PREP

The best vegetables to freeze are fresh from the garden or farmers' market and at their peak ripeness. Start by trimming and washing your vegetables under cold water. Remove any stems and wash under cold water. Peel if necessary. Cut to desired size, if necessary, according to their intended use (for example, carrots can be left whole or dice them for an easy soup addition).

It is very important to blanch vegetables before freezing them. It stops the enzymes that keep vegetables ripening, helps get rid of dirt and bacteria, brightens color, slows vitamin and mineral loss, and wilts and softens the vegetables so they are easier to pack.

To blanch vegetables, bring a large pot of water to a boil (use at least 1 gallon of water per pound of vegetables). Add the vegetables to the water. Once the water returns to a boil, cook the vegetables 1 to 2 minutes. Remove the vegetables from the boiling water with a slotted spoon and transfer them immediately to a bowl of ice water until they are completely chilled. Drain the vegetables well.

Tomatoes do not need to be blanched before freezing. Just wash, peel (if desired) and remove the core. For techniques for peeling tomatoes and making tomato sauce, see page 233.

FRUIT PREP

Freeze fruit that is at its peak ripeness. Fruit like raspberries and cherries will be best just after harvesting, while peaches and plums might need to ripen before freezing. Also, only prepare enough fruit for a few containers at a time if the fruit is prone to browning.

Wash and dry the fruit thoroughly. Remove and discard any pieces that are green or rotting. Remove cores, pits and stones as necessary. Cut to desired size, if necessary, according to intended use.

CHOOSING CONTAINERS

Frozen food can develop rancid flavors as a result of contact with air. Prevent this by choosing containers that are moisture- and vapor-proof. Opt for glass jars, metal containers, freezer bags or other plastic containers that are designed for storing frozen foods. If using plastic bags, be sure to remove as much air as possible before sealing. A vacuum sealer is also useful for removing air and preserving quality. (*For more on vacuum sealers, see page 238.*)

PACKING

There are two kinds of packing: solid-pack and loose-pack. To solid-pack produce, place prepared food in the desired container and freeze. Solid-packing conserves space and is useful when planning to use large batches of frozen vegetables or fruit at one time. To loose-pack, freeze one layer of fruit or vegetables on a cookie sheet. Once the produce is frozen, transfer it to the storage container. Loose-packing takes up more space, but it is easier to remove just the amount desired, such as a handful of peas or a cup of raspberries.

Be sure to leave head space (open space at the top of the freezer container) when solid packing produce, as foods expand as they freeze. When loose-packing frozen foods, headspace is not necessary as the foods are already frozen. Moisture or food on the sealing edges of the container will prevent proper sealing, so wipe all edges clean before sealing. Label each container with the name and date packaged. Most frozen produce will keep for 8 to 12 months.

FREEZING FRESH HERBS

Tender herbs, such as basil, chives, cilantro, dill, mint and parsley, are best suited to freezing. Blanching them first helps capture their fresh flavor. Drop into boiling water for several seconds, then with a slotted spoon or tongs, transfer to a bowl of ice water to chill for several seconds more. Blot dry with paper towels. Spread a single layer of the blanched herbs on a wax paper-lined baking sheet, cover loosely with plastic and freeze until solid, about 1 hour. Transfer to plastic storage bags. Blanched herbs can be frozen for up to 4 months and can be chopped while still frozen before using in soups, stews and sauces.

Peach Freezer Jam

ACTIVE TIME: 30 minutes | **TOTAL TIME:** 1 day | **TO MAKE AHEAD:** Refrigerate for up to 3 weeks or freeze for up to 1 year. Defrost frozen jam in the refrigerator. | **EQUIPMENT:** Six 8-ounce wide-mouth glass or plastic canning jars

This fruit spread-style peach jam can be made with no sugar at all, but we use 1 cup sugar for just a touch of sweetness (up to 3 cups sugar can be used for a sweeter jam). If you want to use glass canning jars, be sure to choose wide-mouth dual-purpose jars made for freezing and canning. These jars have been tempered to withstand temperature extremes.

2	pounds ripe peaches, pitted and quartered (5-6 peaches)
1¾	cups unsweetened white grape *or* apple juice
½	teaspoon freshly grated lemon zest
1	tablespoon lemon juice
1	1.75-ounce package "no sugar needed" fruit pectin (*see Tip*)
1-3	cups sugar

1. Coarsely chop peaches in a food processor. Measure out 3 cups. (Reserve the rest for another use, such as a smoothie.)

TIP: "No sugar needed" **pectin** cannot be used interchangeably with regular pectin.

2. Place white grape (or apple) juice, lemon zest and juice in a large saucepan. Gradually stir in pectin; continue stirring until completely dissolved. Place over medium-high heat and bring to a full rolling boil (a boil that cannot be "stirred down"), stirring frequently. Boil hard for 1 minute. Remove from the heat.

3. Immediately stir in the chopped peaches. Stir vigorously for 1 minute. Stir in sugar to taste until dissolved.

4. Divide the jam among six 8-ounce canning jars, leaving at least ½ inch of space between the top of the jam and the top of the jar (this space allows the jam to expand as it freezes). Cover with lids and let the jam stand at room temperature until set, about 24 hours. Store in refrigerator or freezer until ready to use.

MAKES SIX **8-OUNCE JARS.**

PER TABLESPOON: 13 calories; 0 g fat (0 g sat, 0 g mono); 0 mg cholesterol; 3 g carbohydrate; 0 g protein; 0 g fiber; 1 mg sodium; 20 mg potassium

VARIATIONS: This recipe can be adapted to make other fruit jams. Substitute 3 cups chopped or crushed fruit of your choice for the peaches and follow Steps 2 through 4. Cranberry-raspberry juice can be used instead of apple or white grape juice. Omit lemon zest and lemon juice if desired. Here's the amount of fruit you'll need to start with to get 3 cups chopped or crushed:

BLUEBERRIES: about 2 pounds or 2½ pints; remove any stems, crush with a potato masher
CHERRIES, SWEET OR SOUR: about 2¼ pounds; remove stems and pits, finely chop
RASPBERRIES: about 2 pounds or five 6-ounce containers; crush with a potato masher
STRAWBERRIES: about 3 pounds; hull and crush with a potato masher

Variations provided by Jarden Home Brands. For more information on preserving and more jam recipes visit *freshpreserving.com.*

Guide to Fresh Herbs

Basil: No other herb epitomizes the taste of summer like basil. Available in a number of varieties, this tender annual gives cooks attractive options to strew generously over tomato salads—try opal basil with maroon leaves, for instance. Thai basil's anise tones enhance Thai and Vietnamese dishes. Dessert chefs will appreciate cinnamon basil and lemon basil, especially with peaches.

Cilantro: The pungent flavor and aroma of cilantro is popular in many ethnic cuisines, including Mexican and Vietnamese. The entire plant is edible: the dried seeds are sold whole or ground as coriander, the stems are as flavorful as the leaves and some Asian recipes even call for the roots. Heat can temper fresh cilantro's flavor, so add it to a dish right before serving.

Lavender: Fresh or dried blossoms impart a delicate perfume to herb mixtures, such as *herbes de Provence* (for lamb, chicken and vegetables), or can infuse the milk destined for a custard or ice cream. Easy does it when using lavender—you want a subtle fragrance, not the memory of your grandmother's attic. Dried lavender can be found in specialty and natural-foods stores.

Lemon Verbena: This herb captures the tangy scent of lemon without the tart flavor. Unfortunately, it is not commonly available at supermarkets, so look for it at farmers' markets or grow your own. It imparts an exquisite flavor to custards, cream toppings or yogurt; add a finely chopped tablespoon to whipped cream and serve with sliced strawberries. Lemon verbena also makes a beautiful and fragrant garnish for white-wine spritzers or iced tea.

Marjoram: Similar in flavor and appearance to oregano, marjoram is popular in many Mediterranean cuisines. Its slightly sweet flavor goes particularly well with meats and vegetables.

Oregano: A member of the mint family, oregano is related to both marjoram and thyme. Mediterranean oregano has a more mild flavor than its Mexican counterpart. Use it to season spaghetti and pizza sauces, or add a pinch to your favorite chili recipe for another flavor dimension.

Rosemary (*right*): With a distinctive piney aroma and a hint of lemon, this sturdy herb is highly appreciated in Italian cooking to flavor grilled and roasted pork, lamb and chicken, hearty pasta sauces and soups. Infuse a syrup for lemonade or lemon sorbet with sprigs of rosemary.

Sage: The distinctive flavor of sage has long been popular in the Mediterranean for both culinary and medicinal purposes. The long, oval, silver-green leaves have a slightly bitter, musty flavor. It's commonly used to flavor meats and dishes that accompany meat, like stuffing.

Spearmint & Peppermint: These hardy perennials have a reputation for taking over gardens, but considering their culinary uses, maybe that's not such a bad thing. The herb you buy in the supermarket is most likely spearmint. Also known as common mint or garden mint, this is the most practical variety for both sweet and savory dishes. Peppermint contains more menthol and is used primarily in candies, teas and sweets. Numerous varietals include gems like apple mint, orange mint, pineapple mint and chocolate mint. All make delightful flavorings and garnishes for desserts.

Tarragon: Long flat tender leaves identify tarragon. The French have perhaps most heartily embraced its bright licorice-like flavor, making it a star ingredient, along with chervil, parsley and chives, in the seasoning mixture *fines herbes*, as well as in traditional sauces, such as *sauce béarnaise*. To make the most of its particular flavor, add tarragon near the end of cooking.

Thyme: Best known as a background flavoring for stews and soups, thyme is one of the most versatile herbs. Although typically paired with savory robust flavors, such as red meat, poultry and root vegetables, it is also good with apples and pears. Try infusing hot apple cider with thyme sprigs. In summer, lemon thyme is excellent with fish, zucchini and corn and is delicious with raspberries, blackberries and blueberries.

Tool Smarts

When you bring home fresh fruit and vegetables from the farmers' market, you're going to need a few good tools to get them on the table. Besides the basics like cutting boards, good knives and pots and pans, it's helpful to have a few special tools for prepping and storing fruits, vegetables and herbs. Here are a few of our favorites:

Apple Corer: Remove apple cores easily with an apple corer—a hollow cylindrical tool that is inserted down the center of the apple to remove the core without cutting up the apple. Choose a stainless-steel model that is dishwasher-safe for easy cleaning.

Apple Slicer: An apple slicer, which cuts a whole apple into slices while removing the core, is perfect for preparing apples for pies, cobblers or just snacking. Many are dishwasher safe.

Canning Jars: If you want to use glass canning jars, be sure to choose wide-mouth dual-purpose jars made for freezing and canning. These jars have been tempered to withstand temperature extremes.

Cherry Pitter: If you pit lots of fresh cherries every summer, consider purchasing a cherry pitter. Small hand-held pitters don't cost much, but may take more time to use than larger models, as they require inserting each cherry individually. Larger pitters have a hopper and manual feed, making faster work of the project. Find them at *surlatable.com*, *chefscatalog.com* or *amazon.com*.

Citrus Juicer or Reamer or Squeezer: Juice citrus fruits easily with a citrus juicer or reamer. The styles vary as widely as prices, from small hand-held models at around $5 to large electric counter-top machines for hundreds of dollars.

Herb Saver: Fresh herbs—and even asparagus—will stay fresher longer with the Herb-Savor from Prepara. Its sturdy plastic exterior keeps herbs protected from the harsh environment of the fridge, while a small water well at the bottom keeps them hydrated. Herbs stay fresh for up to 3 weeks. The Herb-Savor is available online at *prepara.com* and some kitchen stores.

Ice Cream Maker: With automatic ice cream makers like the one pictured here, from Cuisinart ($49.95), there is no need to add salt and ice—just fill the frozen bowl with your favorite creamy mixture, turn on the motor and in about 30 minutes, you'll have a custom-made frozen treat ready to enjoy. It's worth noting that models like these tend to be a little noisy when in use and only make about 1½ quarts of ice cream at a time. Plus, the freezing bowl needs to be completely frozen before preparing a recipe. It's a good idea to make room in the freezer for storing the bowl so it's always ready to use.

Kitchen Shears: We reach for shears when we open packages of rice and pasta, snip fresh herbs or prepare artichokes, and we really give them a workout when cutting up chicken. When shopping for shears, look for sturdy construction and stainless-steel blades, a pair that feels comfortable in your hand and, maybe most important, that can be taken apart for thorough cleaning.

Mandoline: Slice fruit and vegetables into thin, even slices quickly with a mandoline—a small slicing machine with adjustable blades so you can slice produce to different thicknesses and even julienne. Look for a sturdy model and consider one with a food-safety holder to help prevent cutting yourself on its very sharp blades.

Melon Baller: Use a melon baller for its obvious use, making cute little balls of melon, or get creative and use it to remove strawberry stems, pear cores and artichoke chokes.

Microplane: The original microplane is a fine grater that has only recently been introduced to the culinary world (it was originally a woodworking tool). Use it for citrus zest, Parmesan cheese, nutmeg or anything else you want finely grated. With its increasing popularity, there are also various kinds of microplanes with different grating sizes and shaving options, although just having the fine grater is perfect for most kitchens.

Onion Goggles: If crying while cutting onions is a constant struggle, protect your eyes from tearing up with swim goggles or specially-designed Onion Goggles from RSVP International, Inc. Breathable foam lining fits snugly to prevent fog ups and keeps onion vapors at bay. These goggles not only make chopping onions comfortable, but safer—it's easier to concentrate and avoid cutting yourself when you're not fighting back tears. The unisex glasses come in three colors—white, black and pink—and are available online at *cheftools.com* and *cooking.com*.

Produce Bags: Keep produce from decomposing in your refrigerator before you get to it with produce bags. Some varieties absorb the natural gases emitted by fruits and vegetables that cause them to continue to ripen, and thus go bad, so your produce will stay fresher longer. Other bags regulate moisture inside and out to keep produce from becoming too wet or too dry.

Salad Spinner: The secret to flavorful salads and pestos is clean, dry greens and herbs. Excess water will lead to bruised cut herbs and poorly dressed salad greens. A salad spinner spins greens dry and ready for use in minutes.

Vacuum Sealer: Vacuum sealers remove the air from a package and seal it shut, making it a great way to store food while conserving space. Since air is the enemy of frozen foods (air contact can lead to off flavors), freezing in a vacuum-sealed package helps maintain quality. This also applies to other foods: meats and leftovers are great candidates for vacuum sealing, whether you're planning to freeze them for a few months or just want to refrigerate them for a few days. Vacuum sealer attachments include canisters for dry goods (cereal, coffee beans) and containers for quick-marinating meats.

Vegetable Peeler: Get a good sharp vegetable peeler to easily peel fruit and vegetables, remove strips of zest from citrus fruit and even cut thin slices of vegetables like potatoes and zucchini.

Tips & Notes

Kitchen Tips:

To make **fresh breadcrumbs**, trim crusts from whole-wheat bread. Tear bread into pieces and process in a food processor until coarse crumbs form. One slice of bread makes about 1/2 cup fresh crumbs.

We like Ian's brand of **whole-wheat dry breadcrumbs** labeled "Panko breadcrumbs." Find them in the natural-foods section of large supermarkets. To make your own, trim crusts from whole-wheat bread. Tear bread into pieces and process in a food processor until coarse crumbs form. Spread on a baking sheet and bake at 250°F until crispy, about 15 minutes. One slice of fresh bread makes about 1/3 cup dry crumbs.

No **buttermilk**? You can use buttermilk powder prepared according to package directions. Or make "sour milk": mix 1 tablespoon lemon juice or vinegar to 1 cup milk.

While we love the convenience of **canned beans**, they tend to be high in sodium. Give them a good rinse before adding to a recipe to rid them of some of their sodium (up to 35 percent) or opt for low-sodium or no-salt-added varieties. (Our recipes are analyzed with rinsed, regular canned beans.) Or, if you have the time, cook your own beans from scratch. You'll find our Bean Cooking Guide at *eatingwell.com/guides*.

Portioning **chicken breast**: It's difficult to find an individual breast small enough for one portion. Removing the thin strip of meat from the underside of a 5-ounce breast—the "tender"—removes about 1 ounce of meat and yields a perfect 4-ounce portion. Wrap and freeze the tenders and when you have gathered enough, use them in a stir-fry or for oven-baked chicken fingers.

To **hard-boil eggs**: Place eggs in a single layer in a saucepan; cover with water. Bring to a simmer over medium-high heat. Reduce heat to low and cook at the barest simmer for 10 minutes. Remove from heat, drain and cover the eggs with cold water. Let stand until cool enough to handle before peeling.

To **heat tortillas**: Wrap in foil and bake at 300°F until steaming, about 10 minutes or wrap tortillas in barely damp paper towels and microwave on High for 30 to 45 seconds.

To **clean mussels**, scrub with a stiff brush under cold running water. Scrape off any barnacles using the shell of another mussel. Pull off the fuzzy "beard" from each one (some mussels may not have a beard).

To **oil the grill rack,** oil a folded paper towel, hold it with tongs and rub it over the rack. (Do not use cooking spray on a hot grill.) When grilling delicate foods like tofu and fish, it is helpful to spray the food with cooking spray before placing it on the grill.

How to **skin a salmon fillet**: Place salmon fillet on a clean cutting board, skin-side down. Starting at the tail end, slip the blade of a long knife between the fish flesh and the skin, holding down firmly with your other hand. Gently push the blade along at a 30° angle, separating the fillet from the skin without cutting through either.

To **toast chopped nuts, pine nuts or seeds**, cook in a small dry skillet over medium-low heat, stirring constantly, until fragrant and lightly browned, 2 to 4 minutes. **Sesame seeds** can also be purchased already toasted. Look for them near other Asian ingredients.

Toast coconut in a small dry skillet over medium-low heat until golden, stirring often, about 5 minutes.

To make "ribbon-thin" **zucchini**, slice lengthwise with a vegetable peeler or a mandoline slicer.

Ingredient Notes:

Capicola is rolled pork shoulder cured like ham. It can be found in the deli section of most large supermarkets or Italian markets.

Chipotle chiles in adobo sauce are smoked jalapeños packed in a flavorful sauce. Look for the small cans with the Mexican foods in large supermarkets. Once opened, they'll keep up to 2 weeks in the refrigerator or 6 months in the freezer.

Dry, salt-cured and aged between 90 and 180 days, **country ham** is potent, salty and delicious; a little goes a long way. You can find it online at *country-ham.com* and at *countryham.org*.

Crème fraîche is a tangy, thick, rich cultured cream commonly used in French cooking. Find it in the dairy section of large supermarkets, usually near other specialty cheeses. Sour cream can be used as a substitute, or you can make your own lower-fat version by combining equal portions of reduced-fat sour cream and nonfat plain yogurt.

Daikon is a long, white radish; it can be found in Asian groceries and most natural-foods stores.

Fish sauce is a pungent Southeast Asian condiment made from salted, fermented fish. Find it in the Asian section of large supermarkets and in Asian specialty markets. We use Thai Kitchen fish sauce, lower in sodium than other brands (1,190 mg per tablespoon), in our recipe testing and nutritional analyses.

French green lentils are firmer than brown lentils and cook more quickly. They can be found in natural-foods stores and some supermarkets.

Garam masala is a blend of spices used in Indian cooking, usually including cardamom, black pepper, cloves, nutmeg, fennel, cumin and coriander. It is available in the spice section of most supermarkets.

Garlic oil is oil that has been infused with fresh garlic. We like to use it for salad dressings, as dipping oil with crusty bread, in marinades or to simply drizzle over steamed vegetables. Find it at well-stocked supermarkets, at *boyajianinc.com* or see page 78 for a recipe to make your own.

To avoid trans fats, look for **graham crackers** without partially hydrogenated vegetable oil. To make **graham cracker crumbs**, pulse graham crackers in a food processor or place in a large sealable plastic bag and crush with a rolling pin. (You'll need about 14 whole-wheat graham cracker squares to make 1 cup of crumbs.)

A **nonreactive pan**—stainless steel, enamel-coated or glass—is necessary when cooking acidic foods, such as tomato or lemon, to prevent the food from reacting with the pan. Reactive pans, such as aluminum and cast-iron, can impart an off color and/or off flavor in acidic foods.

Oyster sauce is a richly flavored condiment made from oysters and brine. Vegetarian oyster sauces substitute mushrooms for the oysters. Both can be found in large supermarkets or at Asian specialty markets.

Hulled pumpkin seeds, also known as **pepitas**, are dusky green and have a delicate nutty flavor. They can be found in the natural-food or bulk sections of many supermarkets.

Pomegranate molasses has a bright, tangy flavor. (Don't confuse it with sweet grenadine syrup, which contains little or no pomegranate juice.) Find it in Middle Eastern markets and some large supermarkets near the vinegar or molasses. To buy: Adriana's Caravan, (800) 316-0820, *adrianascaravan.com*; Kalustyan's, (212) 685-3451, *kalustyans.com*.
• **To make your own:** Simmer 4 cups pomegranate juice, uncovered, in a medium nonreactive saucepan over medium heat until thick enough to coat the back of a spoon, 45 to 50 minutes. (Do not let the syrup reduce too much or it will darken and become very sticky.) Makes about 1/2 cup (25 calories per tablespoon). Refrigerate the molasses in an airtight container for up to 3 months.

Red curry paste is a blend of chile peppers, garlic, lemongrass and galangal (a root with a flavor similar to ginger). Look for it in jars or cans in the Asian section of the supermarket or specialty stores.

Look for **wild-caught salmon** from Alaska. It is considered a best choice by Monterey Bay Aquarium Seafood Watch (*mbayaq.org/cr/seafoodwatch.asp*) and is a certified sustainable fish according to Marine Stewardship Council. Find frozen wild Alaskan salmon at *ecofish.com*, (877) 214-FISH.

Serrano ham is full-flavored, savory dry-cured ham made from specific breeds of white pigs. It is traditionally enjoyed very thinly sliced, like its Italian cousin prosciutto. Find it in well-stocked supermarkets, specialty stores or online at *tienda.com*.

Shrimp is usually sold by the number needed to make one pound. For example, "21-25 count" means there will be 21 to 25 shrimp in a pound. Size names, such as "large" or "extra large," are not standardized, so to be sure you're getting the size you want, order by the count (or number) per pound.

Both wild-caught and farm-raised shrimp can damage the surrounding ecosystems when not managed properly. Fortunately, it is possible to buy shrimp that have been raised or caught with sound environmental practices. Look for fresh or frozen shrimp certified by an independent agency, such as Wild American Shrimp or Marine Stewardship Council. If you can't find certified shrimp, choose wild-caught shrimp from North America—it's more likely to be sustainably caught.

• **To peel shrimp**, grasp the legs and hold onto the tail while you twist off the shell. Save the shells to make a tasty stock: Simmer, in enough water to cover, for 10 minutes, then strain. The "vein" running along a shrimp's back (technically the dorsal surface, opposite the legs) under a thin layer of flesh is really its digestive tract.

• **To devein**, use a paring knife to make a slit along the length of the shrimp. Under running water, remove the tract with the knife tip.

The tart berries of a particular variety of **sumac** bush add a distinctive element to many Middle Eastern dishes. Find them whole or ground in Middle Eastern markets or online at *kalustyans.com*, (212) 685-3451, or *lebaneseproducts.com* (no U.S. phone).

Tahini is a thick paste of ground sesame seeds. Look for it in large supermarkets in the Middle Eastern section or near other nut butters.

Wheat berries can be found in natural-foods markets and online at King Arthur Flour, (800) 827-6836, *bakerscatalogue.com*, and Bob's Red Mill, (800) 349-2173, *bobsredmill.com*.

White whole-wheat flour, made from a special variety of white wheat, is light in color and flavor but has the same nutritional properties as regular whole wheat. Whole-wheat pastry flour can sometimes be used as a substitute. Find it in the baking section of the supermarket or online at King Arthur Flour, (800) 827-6836, *bakerscatalogue.com*.

Whole-wheat pastry flour is milled from soft wheat. It contains less gluten than regular whole-wheat flour and helps ensure a tender result in delicate baked goods while providing the nutritional benefits of whole grains. Find it in the baking section of the supermarket or online at King Arthur Flour, (800) 827-6836, *bakerscatalogue.com*.

Look for balls of **whole-wheat pizza dough**, refrigerated or frozen, at your supermarket. Check the ingredient list to make sure the dough doesn't contain any hydrogenated oils. For an easy pizza-dough recipe, go to *eatingwell.com*.

Seasonal Produce Chart

A key to the fruits and vegetables highlighted in each chapter

The recipes in this book are organized by season. In each chapter you'll find recipes highlighting produce that peaks in that particular season. So, for example, tomato recipes are in the Summer chapter while asparagus recipes are in the Spring chapter. Below is a cheat sheet to show which fruits and vegetables we have chosen to highlight in this book and which chapters they're included in. There are of course plenty of fruits and vegetables that span seasons. Eggplant, for example, loves the heat of summer, but it keeps on producing into the fall in many places, so we've included eggplant recipes in both the Summer and Fall chapters. Keep in mind that any seasonal organization is not one-size-fits-all. Seasonality always depends on location. So think of our chart as more of a reminder to you of what's in season when and a way for us to organize the recipes. As always, choose the produce that's best near you at the moment and enjoy it to its fullest.

Spring

apricots	mango	rhubarb
artichoke	new potatoes	spinach
asparagus	onions	strawberries
dandelion greens	peas	sugar snap peas
escarole	radishes	watercress

Summer

blackberries	eggplant	peaches	tomatoes
blueberries	garlic	peppers	watermelon
cantaloupe	green beans	raspberries	zucchini
cherries	honeydew melon	sour cherries	
corn	nectarines	summer squash	
cucumber	okra	tomatillos	

Fall

apples	carrots	figs	pears
beets	chard	grapes	pumpkin
bok choy	cranberries	kohlrabi	red cabbage
broccoli rabe	eggplant	leeks	sweet potatoes
Brussels sprouts	fennel	mushrooms	

Winter

acorn squash	celery root	oranges	rutabaga
bananas	collard greens	parsnips	spaghetti squash
broccoli	grapefruit	pineapple	turnips
butternut squash	kale	pomegranate	
cauliflower	lemons	radicchio	

Recipe Guidelines & Nutrient Analyses

NUTRITION ICONS:

Our nutritionists have highlighted recipes likely to be of interest to those following various dietary plans. Recipes that meet specific guidelines are marked with these icons:

H✖W To qualify for the **Healthy Weight** icon, an entree has reduced calories, fats and saturated fats, as follows:
calories ≤ **350** total fat ≤ **20g** sat fat ≤ **5g**

For soups, salads and side dishes, the limits are:
calories ≤ **250** total fat ≤ **10g** sat fat ≤ **5g**

For muffins, breads and desserts, the limits are:
calories ≤ **230** total fat ≤ **10g** sat fat ≤ **5g**

L⬇C The **Lower Carbs** icon means a recipe has 22 grams or less of carbohydrate per serving.

H⬆F The **High Fiber** icon means a recipe provides 5 grams or more of fiber per serving.

H♥H For the **Healthy Heart** icon, entrees have 3 grams or less of saturated fat, except for fish entrees, which have 5 grams or less of saturated fat. All other recipes have 2 grams or less of saturated fat.

Note: Recipes with small serving sizes (e.g., sauces) don't qualify for icons.

NUTRITION BONUSES:

Nutrition bonuses are indicated for recipes that provide 15% or more of the Daily Value (dv) of specific nutrients. The daily values are the average daily recommended nutrient intakes for most adults. In addition to the nutrients listed on food labels (vitamins A and C, calcium, iron and fiber), we have included bonus information for other nutrients, such as folate, magnesium, potassium, selenium and zinc, when a recipe is particularly high in one or more of these.

We have chosen to highlight these nutrients because of their importance to good health and the fact that many Americans may have inadequate intakes of them.

ANALYSIS NOTES:

Each recipe is analyzed for calories, total fat, saturated (sat) and monounsaturated (mono) fat, cholesterol, carbohydrate, protein, fiber, sodium and potassium. (Numbers less than 0.5 are rounded down to 0; 0.5 to 0.9 are rounded up to 1.) We use Food Processor SQL software (ESHA Research) for analyses.

Recipes are tested with iodized table salt unless otherwise indicated. Kosher or sea salt is called for when the recipe will benefit from the unique texture or flavor. We assume that rinsing with water reduces the sodium in canned foods by 35%. (Readers on sodium-restricted diets can reduce or eliminate the salt in a recipe.)

When a recipe gives a measurement range of an ingredient, we analyze the first amount. When alternative ingredients are listed, we analyze the first one suggested. Optional ingredients and garnishes are not analyzed. We do not include trimmings or marinade that is not absorbed in analyses. Portion sizes are consistent with healthy-eating guidelines.

OTHER DEFINITIONS:

Testers in the EATINGWELL Test Kitchen keep track of the time needed for each recipe.

Active Time includes prep time (the time it takes to chop, dice, puree, mix, combine, etc. before cooking begins), but it also includes the time spent tending something on the stovetop, in the oven or on the grill—and getting it to the table. If you can't walk away from it for more than 10 minutes, we consider it active time.

Total Time includes both active and inactive time and indicates the entire amount of time required for each recipe, start to finish.

Recipes ready to eat in **45 minutes or less** are marked with this icon.

To Make Ahead gives storage instructions for dishes that taste good made in advance. If special **Equipment** is needed to prepare a recipe, we tell you that too.

RECIPE INDEX

(Page numbers in italics indicate photographs.)

ACKNOWLEDGMENTS

A huge thanks to our EATINGWELL *team, who created this beautiful book. Thank you for all the creativity, hard work, attention to detail and passion that went into this project.*

Art Director & Illustrator: Michael J. Balzano
Production Designer: Scuola Group
Production Assistance: Amanda McAllister
Principal Photographer: Ken Burris

Associate Editor: Carolyn Malcoun
Test Kitchen Manager: Stacy Fraser
Test Kitchen: Hilary Meyer (Assistant Editor), Katie Webster (recipe developer, food stylist), Carolyn Casner (recipe tester), Patsy Jamieson (food stylist), Susan Herr (food stylist)
Dietitian & Nutrition Advisor: Sylvia Geiger, M.S., R.D.
Nutrition Intern: Jenna B. Damareck

Managing Editor: Wendy S. Ruopp
Assistant Managing Editor: Alesia Depot
Production Manager: Jennifer B. Brown
Research Editor: Anne C. Treadwell
Indexer: Amy Novick, BackSpace Indexing

Additional Photography: Johnny Miller, 1, 11; Jeb Wallace-Brodeur 2, 21, 154; Harmony Valley Farm, 10; Amy Ouellette Photography, 14; The Center for Urban Education about Sustainable Agriculture (CUESA), 17; Nell Carroll/Austin American-Statesman/WPN, 18; Robin Coleburn, 22; Michael & Anna Costa, 37; Chris Hornaday Photography, 93; Marge Love, 210; Melissas.com, 230-231 (squash)

Contributing Writers: Mark Aiken, James Cox, Lisa Gosselin, Janice Wald Henderson, Patsy Jamieson, Peter Jaret, Roz Kooker, Marissa Lippert, Nicci Micco, Jim Romanoff, Mark Scarbrough, Bruce Weinstein, Virginia Willis, Brierley Wright

CONTRIBUTORS

Our thanks to the fine food writers whose work was previously published in EATINGWELL *Magazine.*

Baggett, Nancy: Grilled Chicken with Cherry-Chipotle Barbecue Sauce, 98; Sour Cherry-Fruit Slump, 119; Curried Chicken with Fresh & Dried Cranberries, 147; Apple-Cranberry Coffee Cake, 172
Cherkasky, Lisa: Rhubarb Waffles with Rhubarb Sauce, 71
Fritschner, Sarah: Southern Kale, 207
Harris, Jessica B.: Stewed Okra & Tomatoes, 115
Hendley, Joyce: Green Salad with Asparagus & Peas, 33
Herr, Susan: Strawberry Cream, 68; Roasted Sweet Potato Wedges with Balsamic Drizzle, 161
Hill, Laban Carrick: Tomatillo Sauce (Salsa Verde), 115
Iyer, Raghavan: Mango Salad with Ginger-Raisin Vinaigrette, 34
Jamison, Cheryl & Bill: White Sangria, 75; Grilled Smoky Eggplant Salad, 87

Kingsley, Kathy: Cranberry, Cherry & Walnut Marmalade, 161; Brussels Sprouts with Chestnuts & Sage, 162
Knickerbocker, Peggy: Bold Winter Greens Salad, 185; Citrus Ginger Cake with Spiced Orange Compote, 213; Spiced Orange Compote, 214
Lovejoy, Ann: Warm Dandelion Greens, 61; New Potatoes & Peas, 64; Strawberry Fool, 231
Marchese, Mary: Wild Mushroom & Sage Pizzettas, 143
Meyers, Perla: Braised Fennel, Carrots & Pearl Onions, 166; Braised Chicken Thighs with Broccoli & Olives, 191
Morse, Kitty: Pork Roast with Walnut-Pomegranate Filling, 195; Barley & Wild Rice Pilaf with Pomegranate Seeds, 203; Pomegranate Poached Pears, 216
Ogden, Ellen Ecker: Garden-Fresh Asparagus Soup, 27; Spinach Soup with Rosemary Croutons, 28
Pierce, Charles: Wilted Winter Greens & Black-Eyed Peas, 206
Piraino, Marie: Sichuan Carrot Soup, 134
Ripert, Eric: Salmon over Warm Lentil, Apple & Walnut Salad, 155
Riccardi, Victoria Abbott: Spring Vegetable Stew, 40; Spice-Rubbed Game Hens with Rhubarb-Date Chutney, 46; Apricot-Almond Clafouti, 67; Serrano Ham with Crusty Tomato Bread, 80; Fennel & Orange Salad with Toasted Pistachios, 137; Pork Cutlets with Maple-Spiced Apples & Red Cabbage, 151; Oatmeal-Nut Crunch Apple Pie, 170; Mashed Roots with Buttermilk & Chives, 204
Romagnoli, G. Franco: Lina's Pasta & Broccoli, 200
Rule, Cheryl Sternman: Wheat Berry Salad with Red Fruit, 140; Cooked Wheat Berries, 140
Simmons, Marie: Chilled Tomato Soup with Cilantro-Yogurt Swirl, 81; Roasted Pear-Butternut Soup with Crumbled Stilton, 133; Crunchy Pear & Celery Salad, 138; Pear Risotto with Prosciutto & Fried Sage Leaves, 156; Caramelized Pear Bread Pudding, 169; Raspberry-Chocolate Chip Frozen Yogurt, 230
Stevens, Molly: Bean & Tomato Salad with Honey Vinaigrette, 86; Blueberry Tart with Walnut Crust, 120
Watson, Lucia: Triple Celery Bisque, 176
Weinstein, Bruce & Mark Scarbrough: Watercress & Sugar Snap Salad with Warm Sesame-Shallot Vinaigrette, 31; Steak & Purple-Potato Salad, 50; Grilled Shrimp Cocktail with Yellow Tomato Salsa, 79; Nectarine & Prosciutto Grilled Pizza, 104; Squash & Leek Lasagna, 190; Southwestern Stuffed Acorn Squash, 193; Spaghetti Squash & Pork Stir-Fry, 197; Braised Brisket & Roots, 198; Grapefruit Brûlée, 223
Willis, Virginia: Arugula Salad with Honey-Drizzled Peaches, 84; Pecan-Crusted Turkey Tenderloin with Grilled Peach Salsa, 95; Peach Freezer Jam, 234

Special thanks to our local Vermont farmers for their exceptional fruits and vegetables, especially: Arcadia Brook Farm, Arethusa Farm, Bloomfield Farm, Charlotte Berry Farm, Full Moon Farm, Golden Apple Orchard, Intervale Community Farm, LePage Farm, Pete's Greens, Shelburne Orchards, Stony Loam Farm, Vermont Herb & Salad Company, Windy Corner Farm

OTHER EATINGWELL BOOKS

(available at *eatingwell.com/shop*):

The Essential EatingWell Cookbook

(The Countryman Press, 2004)

ISBN: 978-0-88150-630-3 (hardcover)

ISBN: 978-0-88150-701-0 (softcover, 2005)

The EatingWell Diabetes Cookbook

(The Countryman Press, 2005)

ISBN: 978-0-88150-633-4 (hardcover)

ISBN: 978-0-88150-778-2 (softcover, 2007)

The EatingWell Healthy in a Hurry Cookbook

(The Countryman Press, 2006)

ISBN: 978-0-88150-687-7 (hardcover)

EatingWell Serves Two

(The Countryman Press, 2006)

ISBN: 978-0-88150-723-2 (hardcover)

The EatingWell Diet

(The Countryman Press, 2007)

ISBN: 978-0-88150-722-5 (hardcover)

ISBN: 978-0-88150-822-2 (softcover, 2008)

EatingWell for a Healthy Heart Cookbook

(The Countryman Press, 2008)

ISBN: 978-0-88150-724-9 (hardcover)

EatingWell Comfort Foods Made Healthy: The Classic Makeover Cookbook

(The Countryman Press, 2008)

ISBN: 978-0-88150-829-1 (hardcover)

ISBN: 978-0-88150-887-1 (softcover, 2009)